VIDEO GAME SECRETS

Unlock tons of hidden codes and cheats to help you WIN!

Introduction

Play It Your Way!
The game's never over when you have this insider's guide to popular codes, great tips, and top tricks from the video game industry! If you're looking for new ways to skip ahead, unlock new levels, uncover hidden surprises, and more, you'll find it all here. This book is packed with codes for the hottest systems and the games YOU love to play.

What Are Codes?
Codes unlock secret features hidden in games by the designers. Some codes make games easier or add new surprises. Sometimes programmers create codes to help them jump from stage to stage or to test out different parts of the games they're working on. Codes put a unique spin on your games!

> **Check Out Insider Tips!**
> Look for the Insider Tip boxes throughout this book and you'll learn even more information about how a code works and other cool game features.

Enter Codes Right the First Time!
It's tough to imagine, but even the video gaming pros make mistakes. It's easy to mess up codes by misspelling a word or by entering a capitalized letter that should be lowercase. Make sure that you enter a code exactly as it appears or there is a good chance that the code won't work.

Loosen Up Your Fast Fingers
Way back in the old days of 8-bit games, most codes required feverish button pushing and quick reflexes, but today's codes often require steady button input without hesitations. Depending on the code you choose, you might need to practice before the code works. Give it a dozen or so tries and you'll be into your game!

Look at the Pictures!
We crammed this book with helpful screenshots that often show you exactly what you need to do when entering codes. If you need more information, check out the pictures!

Are You Ready to Play?
Flip to your favorite games, choose a few codes, and start playing YOUR way!

Wii TITLES

Wii TITLES (cont.)

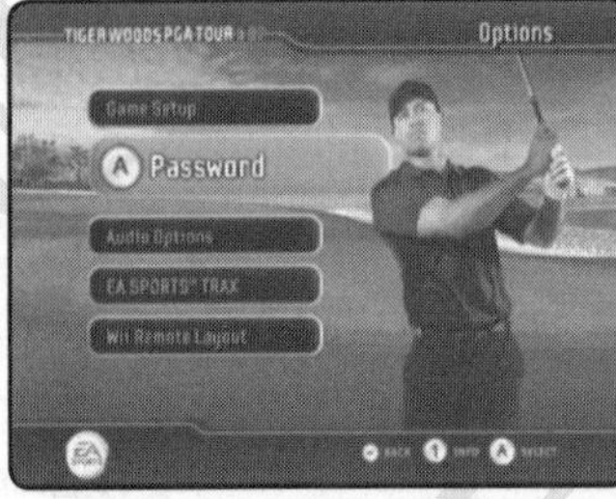

XBOX 360 TITLES

XBOX 360 TITLES (cont.)

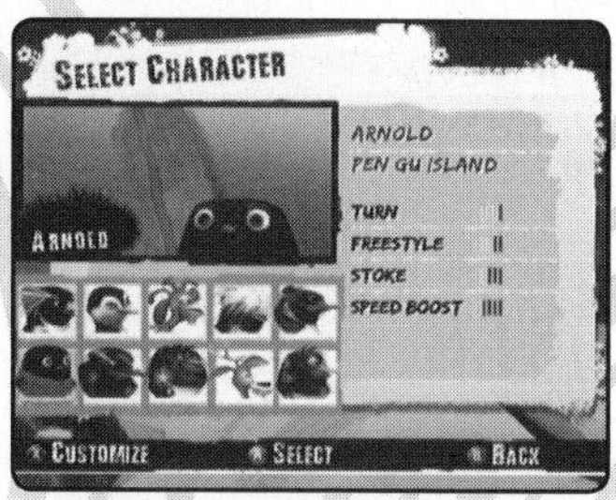

XBOX TITLES

XBOX TITLES (cont.)

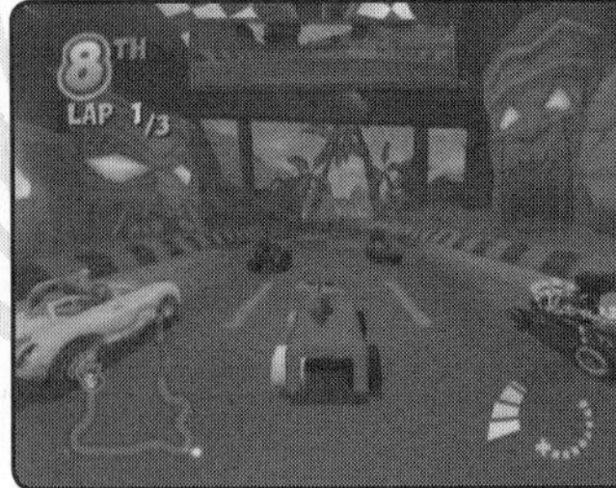

GAMECUBE TITLES

GAMECUBE TITLES (cont.)

PLAYSTATION 3 TITLES

PLAYSTATION 2 TITLES

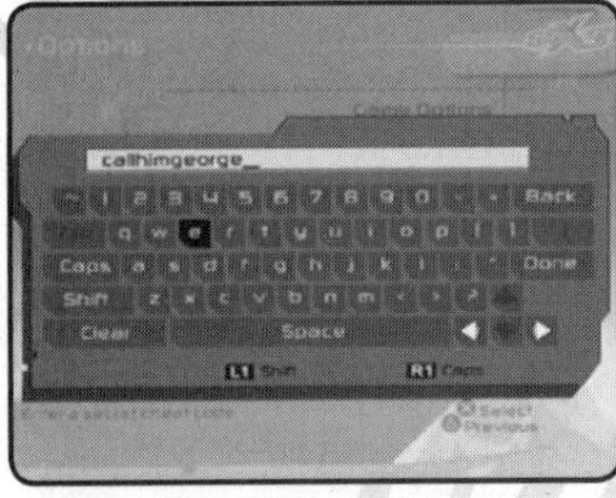

NINTENDO DS TITLES

Wii
Xbox 360
Xbox
GC
PS3
PS2
DS
GBA
PSP

NINTENDO DS TITLES (cont.)

GAME BOY ADVANCE TITLES

GAME BOY ADVANCE TITLES (cont.)

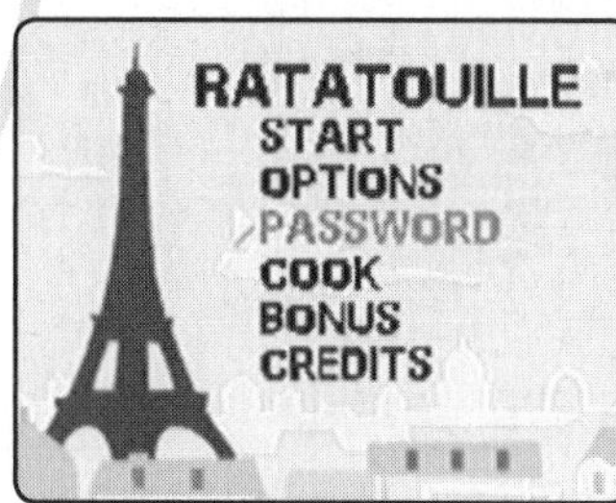

PSP TITLES

Altered Beast (Virtual Console)

Insider Tip
While many codes for Wii Virtual Console games work with both the Classic and the GameCube controller, Altered Beast has different codes for different controllers.

Unlockable Sound Test

To access the Sound Test with your Classic controller, go to the Title screen, and while pressing the directional pad diagonally Up and Right, hold Y and A and press Start. Press Up or Down on the directional pad to scroll through different songs and sound clips, and press A to play them.

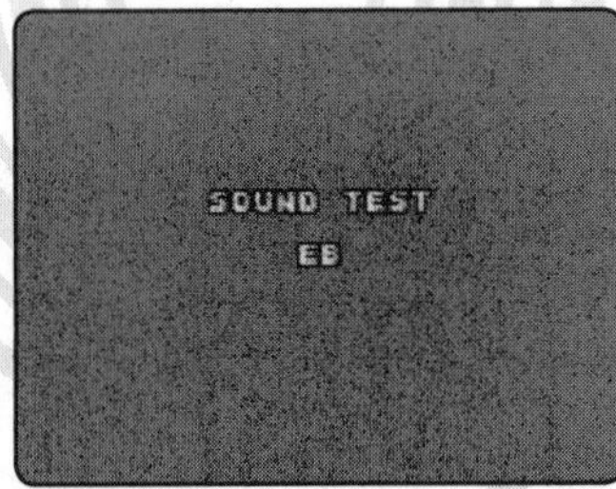

If you're using the GameCube controller, go to the Title screen, and while pressing the directional pad diagonally Up and Right, hold B and X and press Start. Press Up or Down on the directional pad to scroll through different songs and sound clips, and press X to play them.

Choose Your Beast

This code allows you to select which beast you'll become in each stage. On the Title screen, while pressing the directional pad diagonally Down and Left, hold Y, B and A if you're using the Classic controller (or hold B, A and X on the GameCube controller) and press Start. Use the directional pad to choose your animal avatars, and then press Start to return to the Title screen.

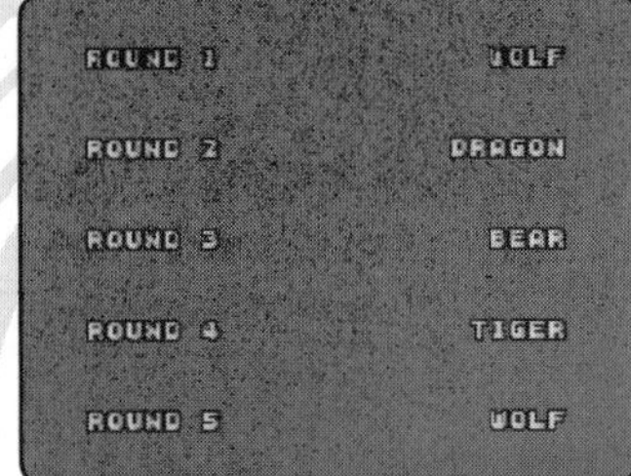

Infinite Continues

Normally, once you lose all your lives, your game will be over and you'll have to start over from the first stage. However, there is a way to sidestep this fate, if you know the secret. Once you've lost your last life, press Start to exit the Game Over screen. On the Title screen, hold Y on the Classic controller (or B on the GameCube controller) and press Start. You'll continue from the last stage you played.

Altered Beast (Virtual Console) (cont.)

Ultimate Code

This powerful code allows you to choose your starting stage, difficulty level, power level, and number of lives. On the Title screen, hold B if you're using the Classic controller (or A on the GameCube controller) and press Start. On the cheat menu, use the directional pad to adjust the game settings to your liking, then press Start to return to the Title screen. Now hold Y on the Classic controller (or B on the GameCube controller) and press Start to begin your game.

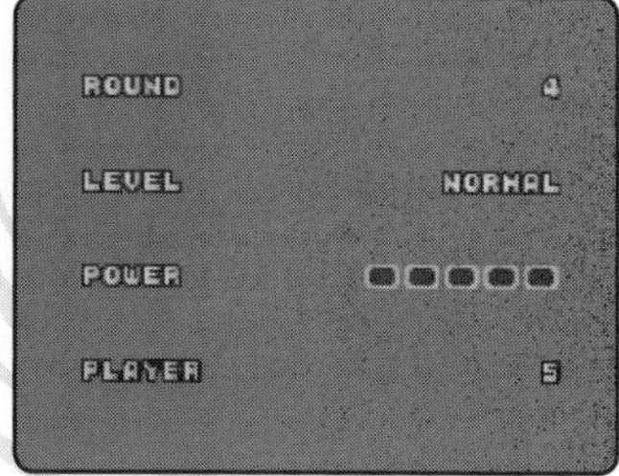

Avatar: The Last Airbender

Unlockable Extras

To gain unlimited copper or chi, or enhance your Airbender abilities, you must first create a game file (or open an existing file) before you use these codes. From the Main menu, go to the Extras menu and then to the Code Entry screen to enter the following codes:

Cheat	*Code*
Unlimited Copper	23637
Unlimited Chi	24463
Double Damage	34743
All Treasure Maps	37437
Neverending Stealth	53467
1-Hit Dishonor	54641
Unlimited Health	94677
Character Art Gallery	97831

If you enter a code correctly, you'll see a message describing the cheat you unlocked.

Wii Xbox 360 Xbox GC PS3 PS2 DS GBA PSP

Avatar: The Last Air Bender—The Burning Earth

Zip Code Cheats
Dish out double damage or check out the bonus art! From the Main Menu, select the Code Entry option and enter the following five-digit codes:

Activate double damage	90210
Activate unlimited health	65049
Activate unlimited special attacks	66206
Max-level upgrade	89121
Unlock all bonus games	99801
Unlock gallery	85061
Unlock one-hit dishonor	28260

Barnyard

Unlockable Bonuses and Antics
To unlock Bonus Items, such as concept artwork and test animations of the characters, go to the Main menu, hold C and Z on the Nunchuk and press Up, Right, Down, Left, Left, Down, Right, and Up on the Remote directional pad.

To unlock the Antics (which are actually mini-games) go to the Main menu, hold C and Z on the Nunchuk and press Up, Left, Down, Right, Right, Down, Left, and Up on the Remote directional pad.

Bonus Items include test animations for the game, like this clip of the Bucking Human Ride.

The Antics are quite clever. Try Cow Tipping for a good laugh.

Max Out Your Gopher Bucks and Knapsack Items
To rack up 9,999 Gopher Bucks, hold C and Z on the Nunchuk during normal gameplay and press Down, Down, Left, Left, Left, Left, Up, and Left on the Remote directional pad.

To award yourself all the Flower Power and Knapsack items, hold C and Z on the Nunchuk during normal gameplay and press Down, Down, Up, Right, Left, Left, Right, and Up on the Remote directional pad.

Insider Tip
Enter both of these codes during normal gameplay, not while the game is paused.

Bases Loaded (Virtual Console)

Get a Jump on Your Winning Season

Tired of being a chump in a slump? Want to skip batting practice for the next 79 games? Use these Bases Loaded passwords to give your team a winning record for the pennant race:

Western League

Hawaii	LNADJPD
Kansas	PNCBNHD
Los Angeles	PFBCNDPD
Omaha	LNDAJPD
Texas	LNCBJPD
Utah	LNBCJPD

Eastern League

Boston	LFBDJHE
D.C.	PFACNHK
New York	PFDAJHH
Miami	PFCANHK
New Jersey	LFADNHH
Philadelphia	LFDBJHE

Insider Tip:

If you're new to Bases Loaded, most old-timers consider Los Angeles to be the best team in the game, although Utah, Miami and D.C. can easily win it all after you have a little practice. Bases Loaded first appeared on the 8-bit Nintendo Entertainment System twenty years ago. It was considered the best baseball game available until SNK's Baseball Stars arrived in 1989.

Bomberman '93 (Virtual Console)

Boss Stage Passwords

To jump straight into the fiery boss battles, go to the Password screen and plug in the following passwords:

Boss Stage	*Password*
Planet Quarry A-8	H M P H C K N C
Blossom Planet B-8	H M P H B H L C
Planet Inferno C-8	L N P H G H R C
Planet Wither D-8	M N P H B K Q C
Planet Surf E-8	N N P H B K R C
Icicle Planet F-8	Q N P H B K S C
Planet Techo G-8	R N P H B K T C

Wii
Xbox 360
Xbox
GC
PS3
PS2
DS
GBA
PSP

Cars

Unlockable Turbo, Tracks, and Mini-Games

From the Main menu, go to the Options menu, and then to the Cheat Codes screen. Press 2, rather than Start, to lock in a code. If you enter a code correctly, you'll exit the Cheat Codes screen. Keep in mind that codes are not saved with your profile, and must be entered every time you turn on the game.

Cheat	*Code*
Boost at the Start of a Race	IMSPEED
Unlimited Turbo	VROOOOM
Unlock All Cars	YAYCARS
Unlock All Paint Jobs	R4MONE
Unlock Tracks and Mini-Games	MATTL66
Unlock Tracks, Mini-Games, Cars, and Paint Jobs	IF900HP
Unlock Mater's Speedy Circuit and Mater's Countdown Clean-Up	TRGTEXC
Unlock All Videos	WATCHIT
Unlock All Concept Art	CONC3PT

Insider Tip

Note that MATTL66 and IF900HP unlock all arcade tracks except Mater's Speedy Circuit (one of the Road Races) and Mater's Countdown Clean-Up (one of the Mini-Games).

Keys to Hidden Cars

Tired of taking the same cars all the way across the country? At the garage, highlight any other car except the red Italian sports car and press and hold Y, X and Down on the Right Control Stick. As you flip through the cars (this can be tricky because you need to keep holding down the buttons) you'll see a police car, school bus and an off-road vehicle! Once you find the vehicle you like, press START to drive it out of the garage.

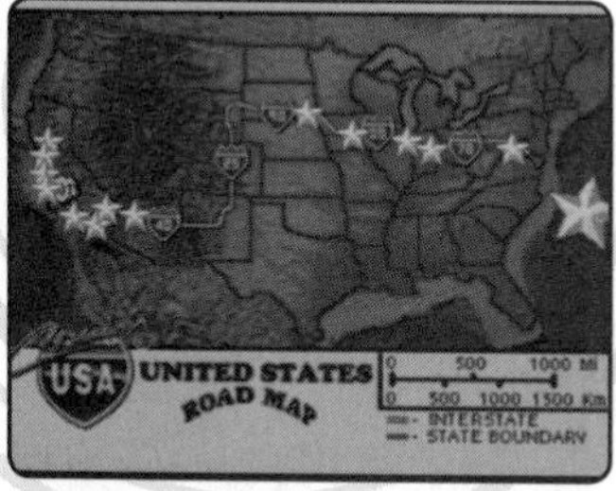

Lights and Sirens!

You can activate the lights and sirens on the police car, but it involves a bit of work. Earn a high score on the "Hot Times" scoreboard and hold your Left Control Stick left to operate the conveyor belt. Keep doing it until a programmer's head appears and he says "I love this job!" Now return to the vehicle selection screen and choose the police car. While driving, quickly tap the brake button twice to activate the lights and sirens.

Insider Tip

Turning on the police car's lights and sirens doesn't always work on the Wii Virtual Console version of Cruis'n USA. In some cases we had to start a new game file to repeat this trick (and no, none of the other racers ever bother yielding to your flashing lights).

Wii Xbox 360 Xbox GC PS3 PS2 DS GBA PSP

Devil's Crush (Virtual Console)

Pinball Passwords

Devil's Crush may sound like an action or RPG game, but it's actually a fantasy-themed pinball game. Whether you're up for a one-player challenge or a two-player match-up, these passwords will offer you lots of pinball pleasure.

Cheat	*Password*
One-Player, 27 Balls, 594,974,700 Points	ONECRUSHME
One-Player, 73 Balls, 924,217,700 Points	EFGHIJKLMB
One-Player, Unlimited Balls, No Points	PPPPPPPPPA
One-Player, Unlimited Balls, 206,633,300 Points	NAXATSOFTI
One-Player, Unlimited Balls, 734,003,200 Points	AAAAAAHAAA
One-Player, Beat the Game with One Hit	THECRUSHEL
Two-Player, Player One Has Unlimited Balls, Player Two Has 32 Balls	AAAAAAAAAAAAAAABCE

Insider Tip

When using the Two-Player game code, be sure to choose the Two-Player game mode before you input the password, or it may not work.

Disney's Chicken Little: Ace in Action

Unlockable Weapons, Shields, and L

To enter these codes, first select any mission. You'll find the Cheats menu option on the Start Mission screen. Now use the directional pad on the Remote (not the joystick on the Nunchuk) to enter a code. If you enter a code correctly, you'll see a message telling you what you've unlocked.

Cheat	*Code*
Unlock All Weapons	Right, Down, Right, Left
Unlimited Shields	Right, Down, Right, Down, Right
Unlock All Levels	Right, Up, Left, Right, Up

Donkey Kong Country (Virtual Console)

50 Extra Lives

Go to the Select a Game menu, highlight the Erase Game option, and press B, A, R, R, A, and L on your Classic controller. If you enter the code correctly, you'll hear a musical tone. Now begin a game, and you'll have 50 lives in reserve.

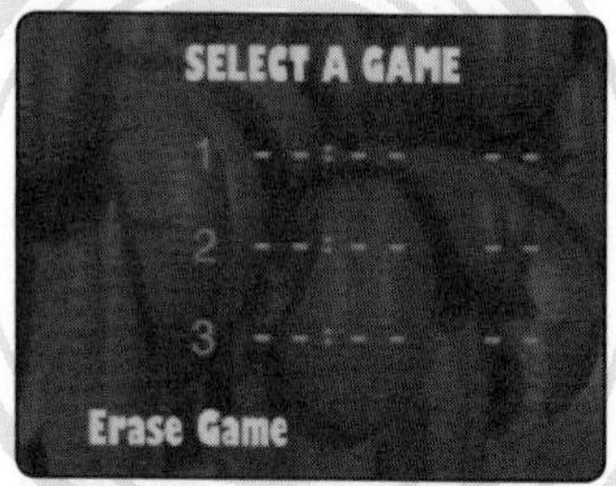

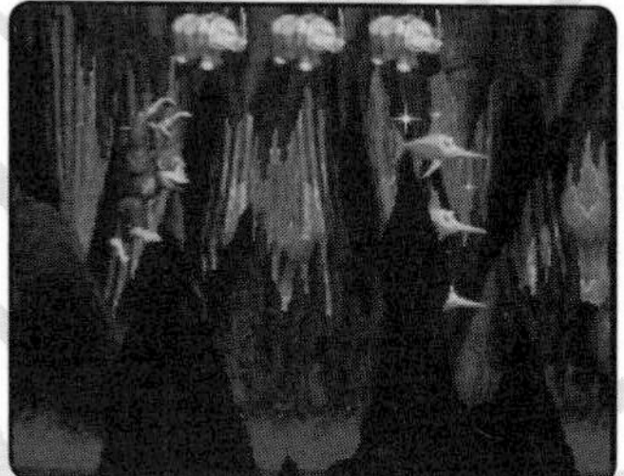

Bonus Round Rehearsal

This little trick allows you to practice the bonus rounds without risking your saved game. First begin a normal game, then press the Home button on your Remote and Reset the game back to the Title screen. Do not press any buttons until the intro movie starts to play. When the movie starts, press Down, Y, Down, Down, and Y on your Classic controller. If you enter the code correctly, you'll warp to the first bonus round. You can progress through the stages one after another or use the Remote to Reset back to the Title screen whenever you wish.

Listen to the Soundtrack

On the Select a Game menu, highlight the Erase Game option, and press Down, A, R, B, Y, Down, A, and Y on your Classic controller. Now press Select repeatedly to hear different songs from the game soundtrack.

> **Insider Tip**
> These codes only work with the Classic controller.

Donkey Kong Country 2: Diddy's Kong Quest (Virtual Console)

Music Test

From the Title screen, go to the Select Game menu, choose an empty game slot and press A. Now highlight Two Player Contest and press Down five times very quickly on the directional pad. The Music Test option will appear. Highlight Music Test and press Left or Right on the directional pad to cycle through the game soundtracks.

Cheat Mode

Once you unlock the Music Test, you can then unlock the Cheat Mode. Just highlight Music Test and press Down on the directional pad five times very quickly. Now highlight Cheat Mode and press B, A, Right, Right, A, Left, A, and X. If you enter this code correctly, you'll start every stage with both Diddy and Dixie, and all the DK Barrels in the game will be gone.

To start the game with 50 lives in reserve, highlight Cheat Mode and press Y, A, Select, A, Down, Left, A, and Down. If you enter either code correctly, you'll hear a musical tone and a monkey sound effect.

Insider Tip

To use the Music Test and Cheat Mode codes, you will have to begin a new game or use a saved game. If you are continuing a game from a Suspend Point, you will go straight to the point in the game where you left off and skip the Mode Select screen where you input the codes. If you are playing from a Suspend Point, you can Reset your game using your Remote, go back to the Title screen, and then proceed to the Mode Select screen to input the codes. Keep in mind, though, that you will lose all of your progress!

(continued)

75 Kremcoins

Gathering Kremcoins is the key to unlocking the Lost World, and this trick will bag you 75 of the golden goodies right off the bat. In a new or saved game, go to the first stage, Pirate Panic. From the starting point, walk a few steps to the right to see the door to K. Rool's cabin. Be careful not to collect the two bananas right outside the cabin door during this entire trick.

Go inside K. Rool's cabin, but do not collect the 1-Up balloon.

Exit the cabin, and go to the right until you see a bunch of bananas above some barrels. Collect the bananas and then return to K. Rool's cabin, again avoiding the two bananas outside his door.

Collect the 1-Up balloon and then exit. Go to the right and collect the same bunch of bananas you did before.

Go back to K. Rool's cabin, still avoiding the two bananas outside his door. Inside the dastardly lizard's lair you'll find a glittering icon equal to 75 Kremcoins. You can now use your golden hoard at any Klubba's Kiosk to buy access to the Lost World.

DoReMi Fantasy: Milon's DokiDoki Adventure (Virtual Console)

Mini Game and Sound Effects Passwords

Enter the passwords at the Password option screen and you can unlock these mini games:

Counting Mini Game	4074
Bird Hunting Mini Game	0220
Memory Mini Game	1104

Open New Worlds!

You can skip ahead to new DoReMi areas by entering these passwords at the Password option screen:

World 2	1940
World 3	3938
World 4	5488
World 5	0615
World 6	6072
World 7	0730

To access the DoReMi sound effects menu, enter your password as 7777.

Insider Tip
DoReMi Fantasy: Milon's DokiDoki Adventure is the 16-bit sequel to the 1988 Milon's Secret Castle for the 8-bit NES. Because it was only released in Japan for the Super Famicom in 1996, it was never translated from Japanese.

F-Zero X (Virtual Console)

Unlockable Cars, Cups, and More
This code unlocks everything in the game, from higher difficulty levels to new cups and cars, but it works with the Classic controller only. From the Start screen, go to the Select Mode screen and press Up on the directional pad, L, R, Up on the right joystick, X, Y, ZR, and Start. If you enter the code correctly, the screen will wobble and you'll hear a musical tone. You'll unlock the Master difficulty level, the Joker, and X Cup series, as well as 24 vehicles.

Gradius III (Virtual Console)

Play with Random Weapons
In Gradius III, you normally take one of the pre-selected weapon loadouts or devise your own on the Edit screen. If you're confident of your skills, however, you can have the game choose your weapons for you. At the Weapon Select screen, press Right to go to the Edit screen. Now press X, Y, X, X, Y, Y, X, and Y. Your weapons and shields will be chosen at random, and you'll just have to live (or not) with the consequences.

Play with Full Weapons
Pause your game and press Up, Up, Down, Down, L, R, L, R, B, A, and Start. Your weapons and shields will be charged to full power, but keep in mind that this code works only once per stage.

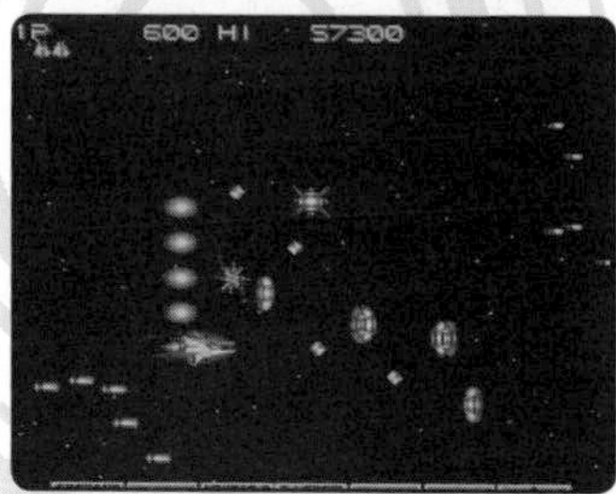

(continued)

Gradius III (Virtual Console) (cont.)

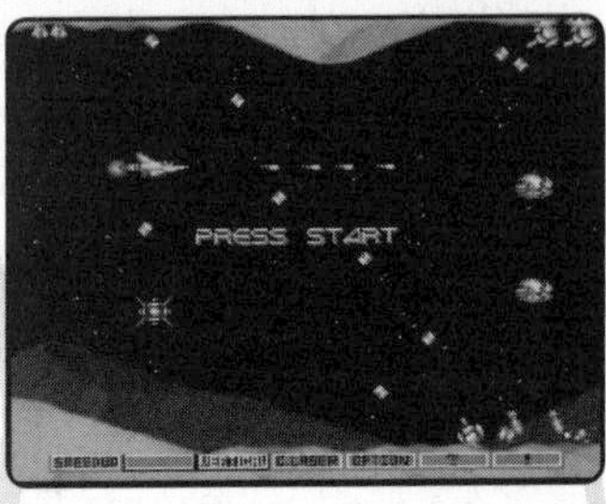

Arcade Attract Mode

The game demos or movies that play automatically before you start a game are often called "attract modes" or "attract movies" because they are meant to entice people to play. To see a special version of the attract movie, press and hold A when the Title screen appears. Continue to hold the A button (you may see the ship-launching movie and return to the Title screen again for a short time) until the gameplay movie begins. This version of the attract movie features the hidden Arcade difficulty level (see below to unlock).

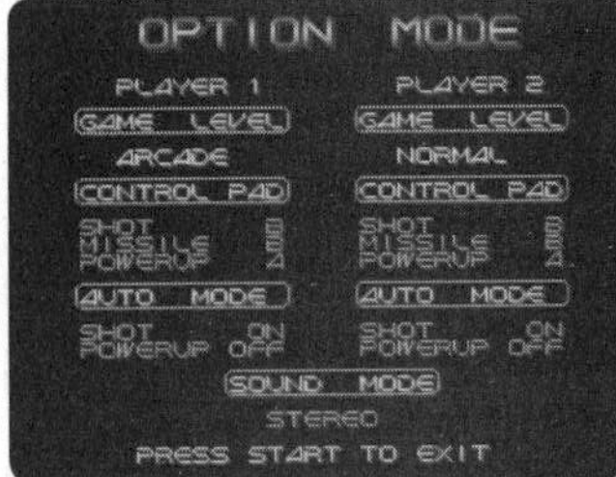

Arcade Difficulty

To unlock Arcade difficulty—a much faster, much more challenging version of the game—go to the Options screen, highlight Game Level and press the A button very quickly. If you press the button fast enough, the Game Level will change to Arcade. Now exit this screen and start your game…just don't expect to survive very long!

Extra Credits

You normally begin the game with four credits, but it's possible to push this number up to eight, if you're quick. On the Title screen, press X as quickly as you can. The number of credits will begin to go up. Start your game before the Title screen disappears, or your extra credits will disappear too.

30 Extra Ships

To begin your game with 30 ships in reserve, go to the Title screen, highlight the game mode you wish to begin, hold Left on the directional pad, and press A, A, A, and Start. If you enter the code correctly, the Title screen will flash.

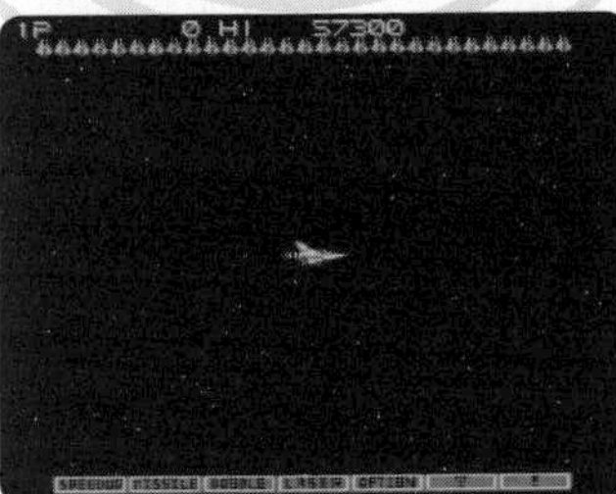

Ice Age 2: The Meltdown

Unlockable Health, Energy, and Pebbles

Unlocking these codes will require some fast fingers and a little memorization. Start a game and then pause your game. Use the directional pad on the Remote to enter the following codes:

Cheat	*Code*
Unlimited Health	Up, Right, Down, Up, Left, Down, Right, Left
Unlimited Energy	Down, Left, Right, Down, Down, Right, Left, Down
Unlimited Pebbles	Down, Down, Left, Up, Up, Right, Up, Down

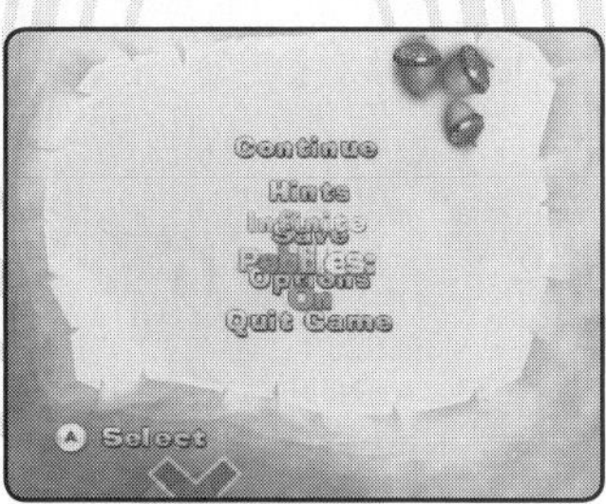

Insider Tips

Don't be surprised if you have to practice a dozen or so times before the rainbow-colored unlock message flashes on the screen. If you enter a code correctly, you'll see a message telling you what you've unlocked. If you enter a code correctly a second time, you'll actually turn the cheat off.

LEGO Star Wars: The Complete Saga

Unlock Additional Characters!

You can unlock these ships and characters at the Cantina with the following codes. If you enter a code correctly, you'll see a message confirming the code you unlocked. Then you'll need to buy it at the Character menu after you earn enough credits.

Admiral Ackbar	ACK646
Battle Droid (Commander)	KPF958
Boss Nass	HHY697
Captain Tarpals	QRN714
Count Dooku	DDD748
Disguise	BRJ437
Ewok	EWK785
Force Grapple Leap	CLZ738
General Grievous	PMN576
Greedo	ZZR636
IG-88	GIJ989
Imperial Guard	GUA850
Imperial Shuttle	HUT845
Jango Fett	KLJ897
Ki-Adi Mundi	MUN486
Luminara	LUM521
Padmé	VBJ322
R2Q5	EVILR2
Sandtrooper	CBR954
Stormtrooper	NBN431

Taun We	PRX482
TIE Fighter	DBH897
TIE Interceptor	INT729
Droid TriFighter	AAB123
Vulture Droid	BDC866
Watto	PLL967
Zam Wesell	584HJF
Zam's Airspeeder	UUU875

Madden NFL 07

Madden Gold Cards

After a strange drought of codes in Madden 06, Madden 07 comes roaring back with dozens of gameplay cheats, bonus stadiums, special teams, and more. From the Main menu, select My Madden, then Madden Cards, and then Madden Codes. To enter codes quickly, it will be easier to point your Remote away from the screen, and use the directional pad to move the cursor around.

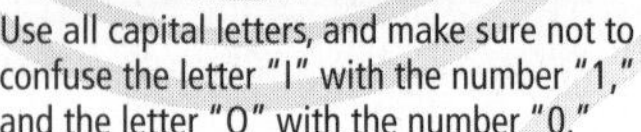
Use all capital letters, and make sure not to confuse the letter "I" with the number "1," and the letter "O" with the number "0."

If you enter a code correctly, a Madden Card will appear. Press 2 to flip the card over and see a description of the cheat or bonus.

Warning:
These codes may not work with some early copies of this game. In some cases, the cheat screen may not allow you to enter the full six characters needed for a code.

Madden Card	***Code***
Lame Duck Cheat (Opponent throws lob pass for one half)	5LAWO0
Mistake Free Cheat (You won't fumble or throw an interception for one half)	XL7SP1
QB on Target Cheat (Your QB Accuracy is 100% for one half)	WROA0R
Super Bowl XLI Stadium	RLA9R7
Super Bowl XLII Stadium	WRLUF8
Super Bowl XLIII Stadium	NIEV4A
Super Bowl XLIV Stadium	M5AB7L
'58 Colts	B57QLU
'66 Packers	1PL1FL
'68 Jets	MIE6WO
'70 Browns	CL2TOE
'72 Dolphins	NOEB7U
'74 Steelers	YOOFLA
'77 Broncos	C8UM7U
'78 Dolphins	VIU0O7
'80 Raiders	NLAPH3

Madden Card	***Code***
'81 Chargers	COAGI4
'82 Redskins	WL8BRI
'83 Raiders	H0EW7I
'84 Dolphins	M1AM1E
'85 Bears	QOETO8
'86 Giants	ZI8S2L
'88 '49ers	SP2A8H
'90 Eagles	2L4TRO
'91 Lions	J1ETRI
'92 Cowboys	W9UVI9
'93 Bills	DLA3I7
'94 '49ers	DR7EST
'98 Broncos	FIES95
'99 Rams	S9OUSW
Bears Pump Up	B1OUPH
Bengals Cheerleader	DRL2SW
Bills Cheerleader	1PLUYO
Broncos Cheerleader	3ROUJO
Browns Pump Up	T1UTOA
Buccaneers Cheerleader	S9EWRI
Cardinals Cheerleader	57IEPI

(continued)

Madden NFL 07 (cont.)

Madden Card	*Code*
Chargers Cheerleader	F7UHL8
Chiefs Cheerleader	PRI5SL
Colts Cheerleader	1R5AMI
Cowboys Cheerleader	Z2ACHL
Dolphins Cheerleader	C5AHLE
Eagles Cheerleader	PO7DRO
Falcons Cheerleader	37USPO

Madden Card	*Code*
'49ers Cheerleader	KLOCRL
Giants Pump Up	C4USPI
Jaguars Cheerleader	MIEH7E
Jets Pump Up	COLUXI
Lions Pump Up	3LABLU
Packers Pump Up	4HO7VO
Panthers Cheerleader	F2IASP

Insider Tip
Both "Pump Up the Crowd" and "Cheerleader" cards have the same effect: the crowd will cheer louder for the team named on the card.

Mega Turrican (Virtual Console)

Warp Ahead to the Final Stages!
Feel the need to blast your way to new stages in record time? Press START to pause the game, then press Right, Left, Down, Right, and B. Now press START to return to the game. If you entered the code correctly, the level will end and you'll end up at the start of the next stage. Keep entering this code until you reach the final level!

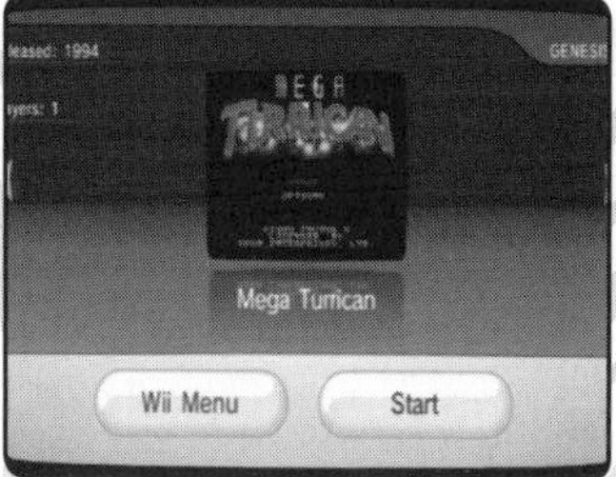

MX vs. ATV Untamed

Have It All
To unlock everything in the game for your Untamed rides, choose the cheats option on the Main Menu and enter the following:

Unlock everything	YOUGOTIT

MySims

Special Codes for Special Items
To access these items, you'll need to enter a code to access a special password menu.

While strolling around your Sims town, press the - Button to access the pause screen, then press 2, 1, Down, Up, Down, Up, Left, Left, Right, Right.

If you entered the code correctly, you'll be at a special password screen where you can enter the following codes to add these special items to your inventory:

Bunk Bed	F3nevr0
Camouflage Pants	N10ng5g
Funky Diamond Hipster Suit	Tglg0ca
Genie outfit	Gvsb3k1
Hourglass Couch	Ghtymba
Kimono Dress	I3hkdvs
Modern Couch	T7srhca
Race Car Bed	Ahvmrva
Rickshaw Bed	Itha7da
White Jacket	R705aan

Enter the pause code over and over until you have all the cool stuff listed above.

Need for Speed Carbon

Unlockable Cheats
Use the directional pad on the Remote to enter these codes on the Main menu. Be warned that you must press the pad firmly but quickly for the codes to work. If you enter a code correctly, you'll get a confirmation message.

Cheat	*Code*
Infinite Nitrous	Left, Up, Left, Down, Left, Down, Right, 1
Infinite SpeedBreaker	Down, Right, Right, Left, Right, Up, Down, 1
Infinite Crew Charge	Down, Up, Up, Right, Left, Left, Right, 1
Castrol Cash Unlocked	Down, Up, Left, Down, Right, Up, 1, B
Carbon Logo Vinyls	Right, Up, Down, Up, Down, Left, Right, 1
Special Logo Vinyls	Up, Up, Down, Down, Down, Down, Up, 1

Insider Tips
Combining Infinite Nitrous with Infinite SpeedBreaker (a kind of slow-motion mode) will make for very slow, but very easy, races! The vinyl graphics can be used to customize different cars in your garage, but they are not available for every car.

Need for Speed ProStreet

Tweak Your Ride with Extra Cheats!
If you're going to be crowned king on the street, you need to grab every advantage possible. Select the game Codes option on the Main Menu to add these cool cars, cash and tune-ups:

Add $10,000 to your spending money	cashmoney
Add another $10,000 to your spending money	reggame
Add five repair tokens	safetynet
Unlock the Castrol Syntec vinyls	castrolsyntec
Unlock the Coke Zero Golf GTI	zerozerozero
Unlock the Energizer vinyls	energizerlithium
Unlock the classic Chevelle SS	horsepower
Unlock the Audi TT	itsaboutyou
Unlock the Mitsubishi Lancer Evolution	mitsubishigofar
Unlock the Dodge Viper SRT10	worldslongestlasting
Unlock all cars for purchase	unlockallthings

Ninja Spirit (Virtual Console)

Stage Select
The Ninja Spirit instruction manual tells you to press the + button on the Title screen to bring up the Game Setup screen. Here you can select the number of players and choose which mode—Arcade or PC Engine—you wish to play. However, if you press B, A, B, B, A, B, Select, and Start instead, you'll be taken to a special cheat menu. Instead of the Sound Test option you find on the normal Setup screen, you'll see a Stage Select option. Highlight Stage Select and press A to cycle through stages 1 through 3. If you hold Select and press A, you'll scroll through stages 1 through 6. After you've set up your game to your liking, highlight Game Start and press A to begin your adventure.

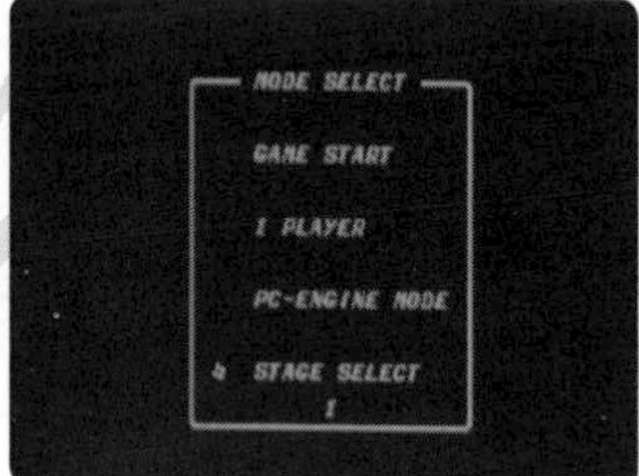

Pokémon Puzzle League (Virtual Console)

Because the First 50 Speeds Are Not Fast Enough . . .
To take your game speed beyond the 50 limit, hold the Z Button and press B, A, L, L on the title screen. If you enter the code right, you'll hear a chime. Now you can take your game speed up to 99!

Insider Tip
First introduced in 2000 for the Nintendo 64, Pokémon Puzzle League borrowed the best game play elements from Nintendo's Tetris Attack for the Super NES and added a 3-D gaming twist.

Powerball (Virtual Console)

Unlock Hidden Teams!
What your Powerball league needs are some international expansion teams! At the team selection screen, press B, B, A, B, B, A and then press Down. If you entered the code right, you should see Mexico, Germany, Canada, and France!

Game Sounds and Tunes
To unlock the Powerball Sound Test menu, choose China as your team and enter this following password:

KWGEN

Now press A to select a sound or tune, and then press B to listen to your selection!

Punch-Out!! Featuring Mr. Dream (Virtual Console)

Level Select
If you'd like to skip ahead, go to the Title screen, highlight Continue, and use the directional pad to enter the first number of the pass key. Press A to lock in the number. Repeat until the entire pass key is entered (but do NOT press A to lock in the final number, or you'll erase the pass key), then press Start.

Please note that the pass keys in the chart work with both the Classic and the GameCube controller.

Level	*Pass Key*
Major Circuit (starting with Don Flamenco)	005 737 5423
World Circuit (starting with Piston Honda)	777 807 3454
Mr. Dream	007 373 5963
Super Macho Man	940 861 8538

Insider Tip
To jump to Another World Circuit, enter the pass key 135 792 4680, but instead of pressing Start, press A, B, and Select simultaneously. Your timing has to be exact, or this pass key won't work. It can take many attempts before it finally works, so don't be discouraged after just a couple of tries. This code only works with the Classic controller.

Rampage: Total Destruction

Unlockable Extras
At the Main menu, press the + and – buttons at the same time to make the Code Entry screen appear. Now highlight each monster and press Up or Down until the correct number appears. If you enter a code correctly, you'll hear a monstrous laugh. If you're wrong, the laugh will have a metallic echo.

Cheat	*Code*
Unlock All Cities	271828
Unlock All Monsters and Cities	141421
Invincible to Attack	986960

Cheat	*Code*
Buildings Are Weak	071767
Cancel All Active Codes	000000

Shinobi III: Return of the Ninja Master (Virtual Console)

Unlimited Shurikins
From the Title screen, go to the Options menu and change the number of shurikins from 50 to zero. Now highlight S.E. (it stands for Sound Effect) and change it to Shurikin. Now highlight the number of shurikins again. After a few seconds, it will change from a zero to an infinity symbol. Once you start your game, you'll have 999 shurikins, and the number will never go down.

Invincibility
From the Title screen, go to the Options menu and highlight the Music option. Now play the following music tracks in this order: He Runs, Japonesque, Shinobi Walk, Sakura, and Getufu. If you enter the code correctly, the music will stop when you try to play the Getufu music track. Now you'll be able to withstand any attack and walk through enemies as if they weren't there.

SimCity (Virtual Console)

999 More Maps
There are an amazing 999 maps listed in this game, but even more astonishing is that there are an additional 999 hidden maps as well. To access a hidden map, first begin a game with any map. Once the game starts, immediately go to the Load.Save menu and choose the Go To Menu option. Now select the Start New City option, but do not change the map number. When the map loads, it will not be the map you selected before, but its hidden alternate.

(continued)

An Easy $999,999

At any point in the game, spend every dollar you have. Now wait for the tax screen to appear at the end of December. As soon as the screen goes dark, press and hold the L and R buttons. Turn down all the funding percentages to zero, but leave the tax rate as it is. Press the Go With Figures button to go back to the main play screen. While still holding L and R, go back to the Tax screen and change the funding percentages to 100%, and the tax rate to 20%. At this point, your Current Funds must be a negative number for this trick to work. Press the Go With Figures button to go back to the main play screen, and then release L and R. You'll now be one dollar shy of a being a millionaire, and have more than enough cash to turn your city into a thriving community.

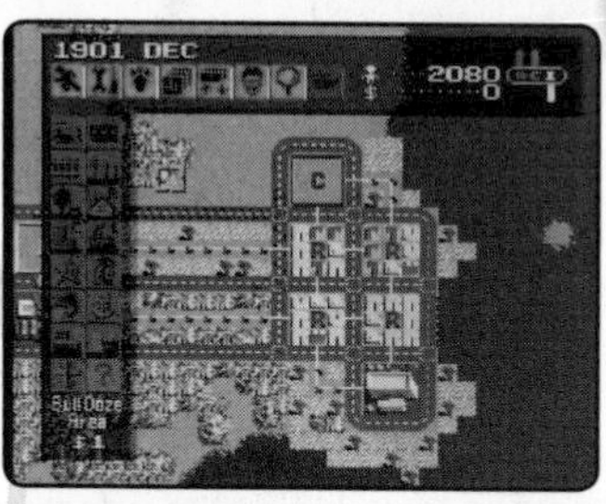

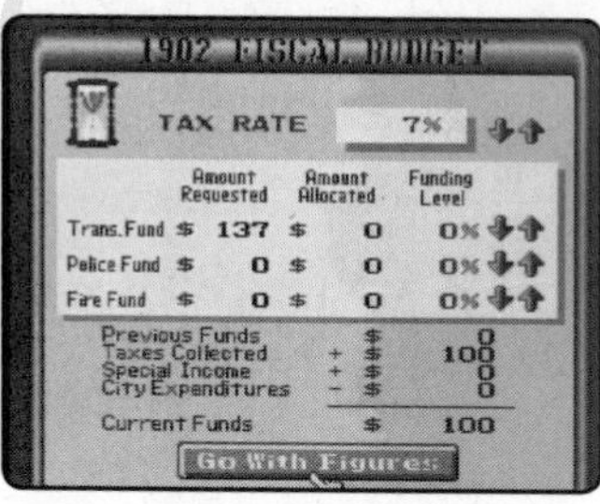

Insider Tip

If you're having trouble getting your Current Funds down into negative territory for the $999,999 trick, be sure to develop zones that you'll have to pay yearly upkeep for, such as Police and Fire Stations. The other thing to do is turn down your tax rate during the year to 1%.

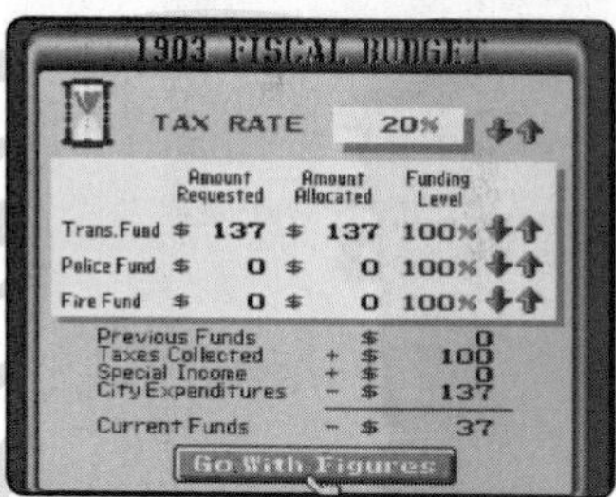

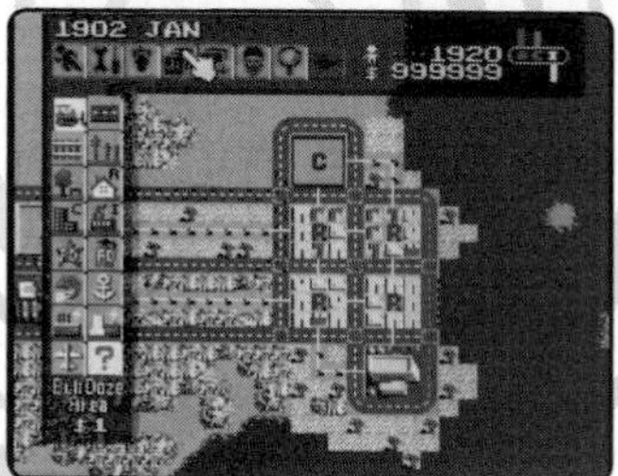

Sonic the Hedgehog 2 (Virtual Console)

Slow Motion Sonic

On the Title screen, press Down twice to highlight Options. Enter the Options menu and then the Sound Test screen. Using the directional pad to select sound files and the A button to play them, play the following sound files in this order: 19, 65, 09, and 17. If you enter the code correctly, you'll hear a chime before soundtrack 17 begins to play. Press Start to exit the Options menu and then begin a game as normal. During your game, press Start to pause, and then press B repeatedly to move one frame at a time. You'll need to unpause to jump, but you can pause again in mid-air. Your game may take a long time to complete, but this trick will make reaching a perfect ring score a lot easier.

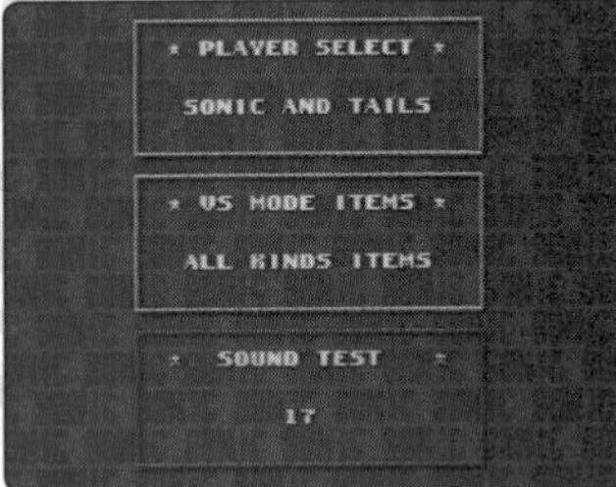

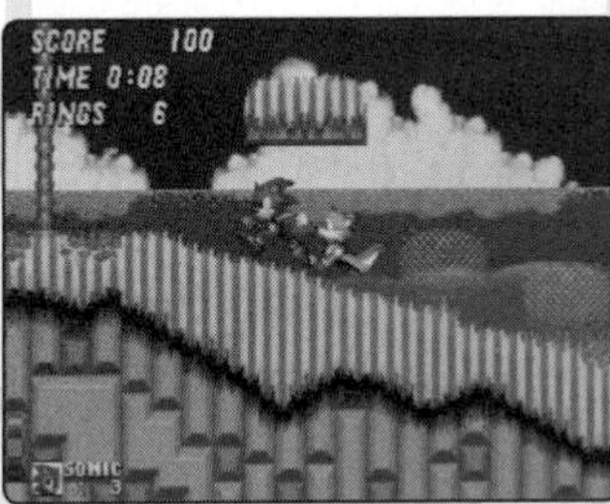

Speed Racer the Video Game

Codes for the Road

To enter these codes, you need to choose the Options menu and then the Enter Code option. Remember to hold your Wii controller horizontally before tapping out these codes, or your attempts to get ahead will hit a dead end!

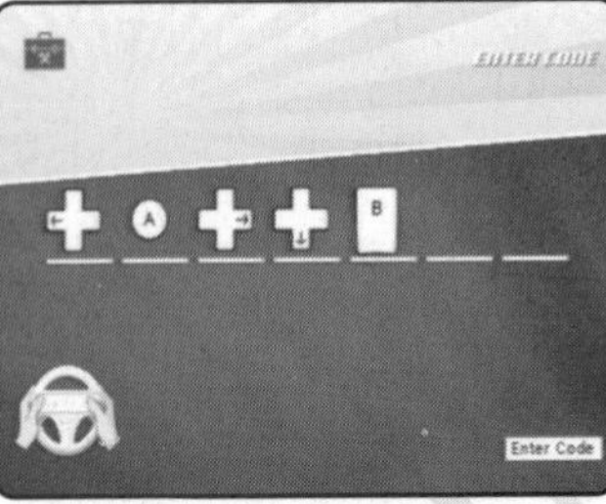

Insider Tip

Too many codes are not a good thing if you're trying to complete Speed Racer the Video Game. Deactivate the codes that you don't want by entering the code again at this menu.

(continued)

Speed Racer the Video Game (cont.)

Aggressive Opponents:	Up, Left, Down, Right, Up, Left, Down,
Granite Car:	B, Up, -, +, 1, Up, +
Helium:	-, Up, -, 2, -, Up, -
Invulnerability:	A, B, A, Up, Left, Down, Right
Monster Truck:	B, Up, -, 2, B, Up, -
Moon Gravity:	Up, +, Up, Right, -, Up, -
Overkill:	A, -, +, Down, Up, +, 1
Pacifist Opponents:	Up, Right, Down, Left, Up, Right, Down
Psychedelic:	Left, A, Right, Down, B, Up, -
Tiny Opponents:	B, A, Left, Down, -, Up, -
Unlimited Boosts:	B, A, Down, Up, B, A, Down
Unlock the last three cars:	1, 2, 1, 2, B, A, +

SpongeBob SquarePants: Creature from the Krusty Krab

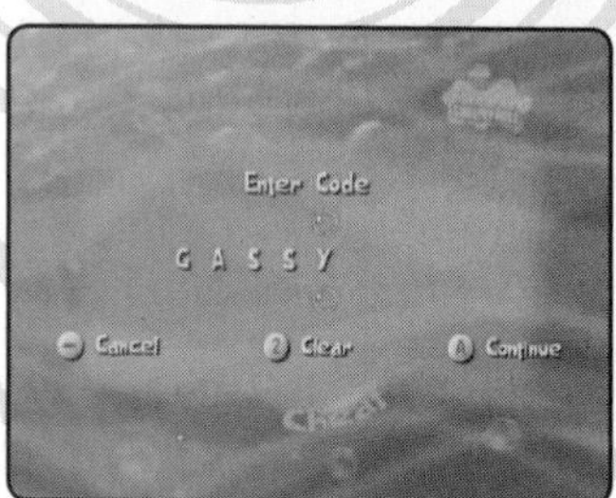

Unlockable Bonus Items

From the Main menu, go to the Extras menu, and then the Cheat Codes screen. If you enter a code correctly, you'll see a message telling you what you've unlocked.

Cheat	*Code*
30,000 Z's	ROCFISH
Infinite health in the platforming worlds	VIGOR
Infinite fuel in the flying worlds	GASSY
Unlock every world in the game	GUDGEON
Unlock the Sleepy Seed Detector	TISSUE
Unlock all Bonus Games	PORKPIE
New look for SpongeBob in Diesel Dreaming	SPONGE
New paint job for SpongeBob's hot rod in Diesel Dreaming	HOTROD
New flame effect for SpongeBob's hot rod in Diesel Dreaming	FLAMES
New look for Plankton's hovercraft	HOVER
New color for Plankton's atomic eye laser	LASER
New rocket laser for Patrick's rocket	ROCKET
Play as Pirate Patrick in Rooftop Rumble	PIRATE
New paint job for Patrick's rocket	SPACE
SpongeBob costume for Plankton	PANTS
Play as robot Plankton in Revenge of the Giant Plankton Monster	ROBOT
Tuxedo costume for Patrick	PATRICK
Plankton costume for Super-Sized Patty	INVENT
New costume for SpongeBob in It Came from Bikini Bottom	PILOT
Squeaky Duck Gun in It Came from Bikini Bottom	DUCKGUN

(continued)

SpongeBob SquarePants (cont.)

Cheat	Code
Spooky costume for SpongeBob in Alaskan Belly Trouble	KRABBY
New costume for SpongeBob in Hypnotic Highway	BRAIN
New costume for Patrick in Hypnotic Highway	BONES
New paint job for SpongeBob's hot rod in Hypnotic Highway	HYPCAR
New paint job for Patrick's rocket in Hypnotic Highway	BUNRUN
New costume for Patrick in Rocket Rodeo	SAFARI
New "Pow!" effect for Patrick in Starfish-Man to the Rescue	SPIN

Insider Tip
Most of the codes unlock bonus items, which are usually available in a particular stage only, and must be turned on or off. From the Main menu, go to the Activate Bonus Items screen. Press 1 or 2 to scroll through the stages. When you find the stage you're looking for, use the joystick or the directional pad to highlight the items you wish to use.

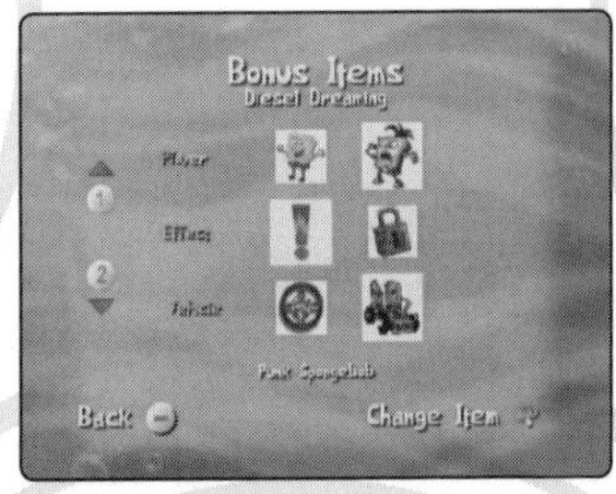

SSX Blur

Unlockable Characters, Clothes, and Tracks

Entering cheats in this game is a bit trickier than usual. From the Main menu, go to the Options menu, then to the Cheats menu. Now press A one more time to open the Cheat Entry screen. To switch between different types of letters and numbers, highlight the appropriate tab at the top of the screen and press A. Unlocked tracks are available in multiplayer games.

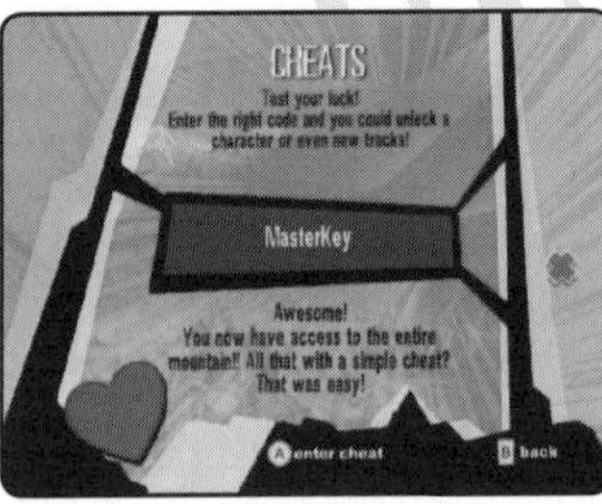

Cheat	Code
Unlock All Tracks	MasterKey
Unlock All Characters	NoHolds
Unlock All Outfits	ClothShop
Unlock Yeti Costume	WildFur

Insider Tip
The Yeti Costume is available for all characters in the Career mode, but not in the Quick Race mode.

Super Castlevania IV (Virtual Console)

Level Select

These passwords will get you to some of the trickier areas, including the big, bad Dracula himself. From the Title screen, select the Continue option, skip the Name Entry screen, and then enter any of the following passwords. The Hard Difficulty stages feature more enemies.

Level	*Password*
2-1	Blank – Blank – Blank – Blank Water – Blank – Blank – Blank Blank – Blank – Blank – Blank Water – Blank – Blank – Blank
4-1	Blank – Blank – Blank – Water Water – Water – Blank – Blank Blank – Water – Blank – Axe Blank – Blank – Blank – Blank
5-1	Blank – Blank – Blank – Blank Water – Blank – Blank – Blank Blank – Blank – Blank – Axe Water – Axe – Blank – Blank
6-1	Blank – Blank – Blank – Blank Water – Water – Blank – Blank Blank – Water – Blank – Axe Water – Axe – Blank – Blank
8-1	Blank – Blank – Blank – Blank Water – Water – Blank – Blank Blank – Water – Blank – Water Water – Water – Blank – Blank

Level	*Password*
B-1	Blank – Blank – Blank – Axe Water – Blank – Blank – Blank Blank – Blank – Blank – Heart Heart – Heart – Blank – Blank
B-4 (Dracula)	Blank – Blank – Blank – Water Water – Water – Blank – Blank Blank – Water – Blank – Blank Blank – Heart – Axe – Blank
6-1 (Hard Difficulty)	Blank – Axe – Blank – Blank Water – Water – Blank – Blank Blank – Heart – Blank – Axe Water – Axe – Blank – Blank
7-1 (Hard Difficulty)	Blank – Axe – Blank – Heart Water – Heart – Blank – Blank Blank – Blank – Blank – Water Blank – Axe – Blank – Blank
8-1 (Hard Difficulty)	Blank – Axe – Blank – Blank Water – Water – Blank – Blank Blank – Heart – Blank – Water Water – Water – Blank – Blank

Insider Tip

At the beginning of level B-4, there are invisible platforms down and to your left. If you jump down and make your way to the left side of the screen, a stream of items will rain down on you, including 99 hearts, a fully upgraded whip, and other bonuses. Be careful making your way back to the staircase, as there are two big gaps you can fall through. If you jump high and to the right, you should be safe.

Super Mario Galaxy

The Two-Controller Teamwork Trick!
Sometimes it's easier to rule the galaxy with a friend! While Super Mario Galaxy is a one-player game, you can have a friend help you out if you have a second Wii controller. Turn on the second Wii controller and you'll see another cursor. Your partner can collect Star Bits and also slow down some tricky obstacles like large rolling rocks. Depending on where you are in the game, your partner can also shoot Star Bits at some enemies!

Super R-Type (Virtual Console)

Set a Course for Your Favorite Stage!
Want to jump ahead to your favorite R-Type stage? At the "Push Start" screen, hold the R Button and press Up on the Control Pad nine times. Go ahead and begin a game and then press START to pause it. Now hold R, A, and SELECT at the same time until you see a number where the difficulty level normally appears. If you press Up or Down on the Control Pad, you can change the level number from 1 to 17. Now press START to enter the game at your new destination!

Insider Tip
Released on the 16-bit Super NES in 1991, critics dismissed Super R-Type because the game would slow down when multiple enemies appeared on the screen. In reality, the slowdown in the video game processor made the game easier to play because you had more reaction time for blasting and avoiding alien attackers.

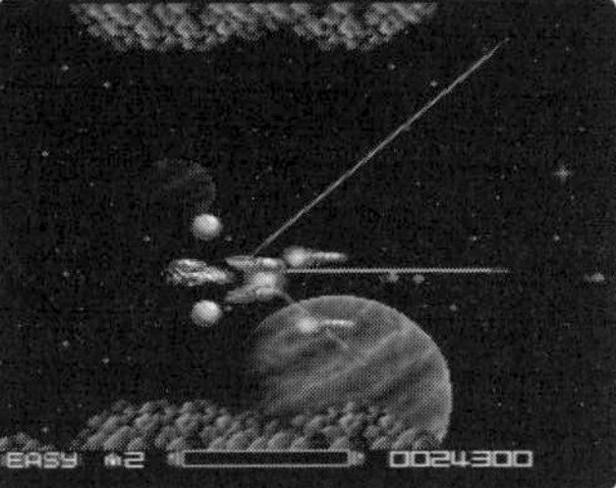

(continued)

Super R-Type (Virtual Console) (cont.)

Begin the Game with Your Favorite Weapons!
Sometimes having the right weapon at the start makes the game more enjoyable. At the title screen, press Down, R, Right, Down, Right, Right, Down, Right, Down, and Down. If you entered the code correctly, you'll hear the same musical chime that you hear when you press START to begin the game.

After you begin a new game, press START to pause and then enter R, Right, Down, Y, Down, Right, Down, Left, Right, Down, Right, and Right.

You're not done entering the code. Now you need to choose your first weapon by pressing one of these buttons:

A	Anti-Air Laser
B	Anti-Ground Laser
X	Reflecting Laser
Y	Split Laser
R	Shooting Gun Laser

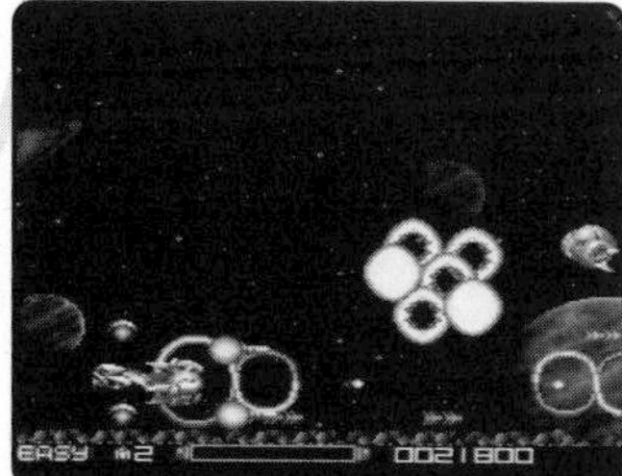

And now press one of these buttons to equip missiles or bombs:

A	Chasing Missile
X	Anti-Ground Missile

Super Star Soldier (Virtual Console)

Sound Test and Difficulty Select
If you'd like to ramp up the action to warp speed, enter one of the codes below on the Title screen to access a special Cheat menu that includes a Sound Test and a Difficulty Select option. Be sure to use the code that's appropriate to the controller you're using.

Classic controller

1. Press Left, B, Up, B, Right, B, Down, B, Left, A, Up, A, Right, A, Down, A
2. Press B and A eight times simultaneously
3. Press Select and A eight times simultaneously

GameCube controller

1. Press Left, B, Up, B, Right, B, Down, B, Left, A, Up, A, Right, A, Down, A
2. Press B and A eight times simultaneously
3. Press Z and A eight times simultaneously

Once you're on the Cheat menu, highlight Sound Test, use the directional pad to select a sound effect or musical track, and press A to play it. Now highlight Game Level and use the directional pad to select a difficulty level. Highlight Exit and press A to go back to the Title screen, then press Start to begin the game at your chosen difficulty level.

(continued)

Wii Xbox 360 Xbox GC PS3 PS2 DS GBA PSP

Super Star Soldier (Virtual Console) (cont.)

Insider Tip
Besides the standard Official Level difficulty setting, there's also the easier Poor Body setting, the tougher Go Go Enemys setting, and a super-hard setting whose name we can't read because it's in Japanese! On the Go Go Enemys setting, there are more and faster enemies, while the toughest setting also decreases the effects of weapon power-ups.

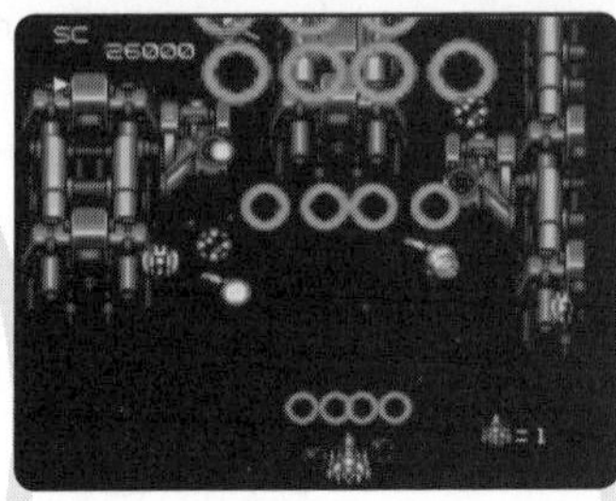

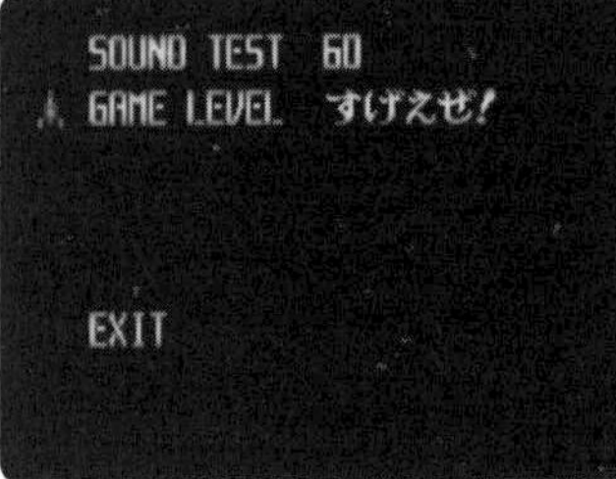

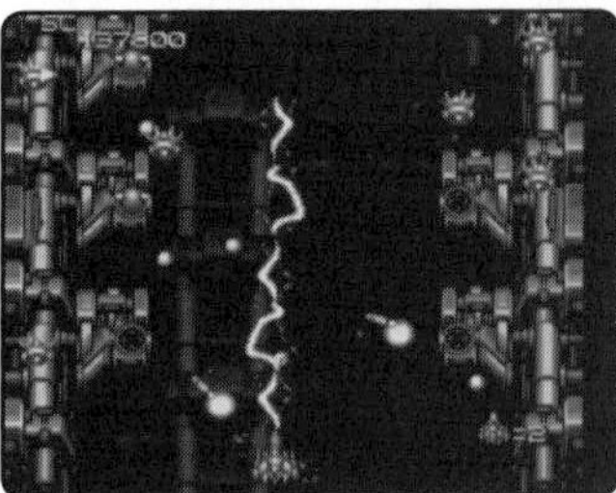

Super Turrican (Virtual Console)

Skip Ahead to New Stages!
Want to jump ahead to a tough spot and blast your way out of a jam? Press START to pause your Super Turrican game and then press Right, Left, Down, Right and A. Now press START to return to the stage. If you entered the code correctly, the stage will end and you'll move ahead to the next stage. You can keep repeating this code until you reach the last boss in the game!

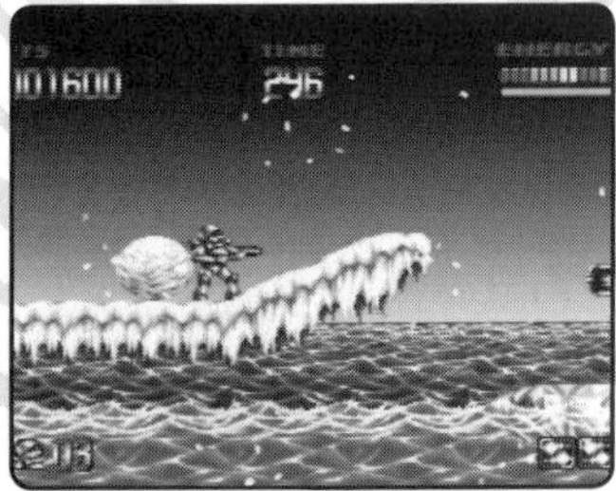

Surf's Up

Boards, Galleries and Surfer Critters
Catch a wave of *Surf's Up* secret extras! Choose "Extras" and "Cheat Codes" from the Main Menu, then enter these codes:

Unlock the Astral surfboard	ASTRAL
Unlock Tank Evans	IMTHEBEST
Unlock Tatsushi	KOBAYASHI
Unlock the Monsoon surfboard	MONSOON
Unlock all multiplayer levels	MULITPASS
Unlock all surfboards	MYPRECIOUS
Unlock all galleries	NICEPLACE
Unlock Geek	SLOWANDSTEADY
Unlock Elliot	SURPRISEGUEST
Unlock Zeke Topanga	THELEGEND
Unlock Arnold	TINYBUTSTRONG
Unlock the Tiny Shockwave surfboard	TINYSHOCKWAVE
Unlock character customization options	TOPFASHION
Unlocks the videos	WATCHAMOVIE

Thrillville: Off the Rails

In-Game Cheats
The Thrillville: Off the Rail codes are easy to input because most of the unlock codes are similar. Enter these codes while walking around in the parks:

Earn an additional $50,000
C Button, Z Button, B Button, C Button, Z Button, B Button, A Button

Add an extra 500 Thrill Points to your game
Z Button, C Button, B Button, Z Button, C Button, B Button, C Button

Unlock all mini-games
C Button, Z Button, B Button, C Button, Z Button, B Button, Right Control Pad

Unlock all missions
C Button, Z Button, B Button, C Button, Z Button, B Button, Z Button

Unlock all parks
C Button, Z Button, B Button, C Button, Z Button, B Button, C Button

Unlock all rides
C Button, Z Button, B Button, C Button, Z Button, B Button, B Button

Xbox 360
Xbox
GC
PS3
PS2
DS
GBA
PSP

Tiger Woods PGA Tour 07

Unlockable Extras

To bring your play up to par, go to the Options menu, and then to the Cheats menu. Use the on-screen keyboard to type in a code. Whether you enter a code correctly or incorrectly, you'll hear a sound. There's no way to be sure you've entered a code correctly until you start a multiplayer game or go to the pro shop. The pro shop is found in the GAMEFACE menu.

Cheat	*Code*
Unlock players (multiplayer)	GAMEFACE
Bridgestone items	SHOJIRO
Cobra items	SnakeKing
Grayfalloye items	JustShafts
MacGregor items	MACTEC
Nike items	JustDoIt
Ping items	SOLHEIM
TaylorMade items	MrAdams

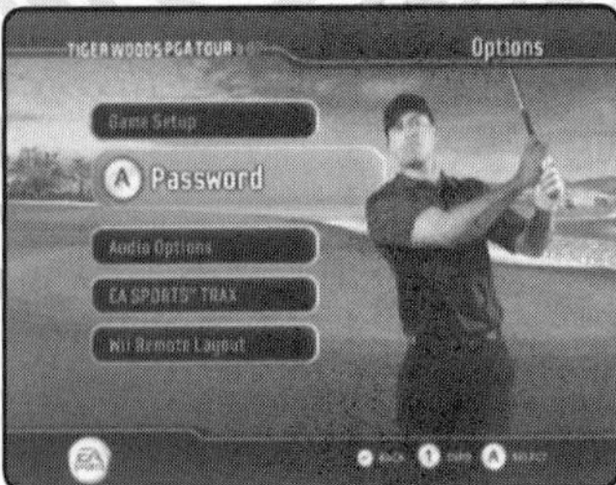

TMNT

Bump Up the Challenge

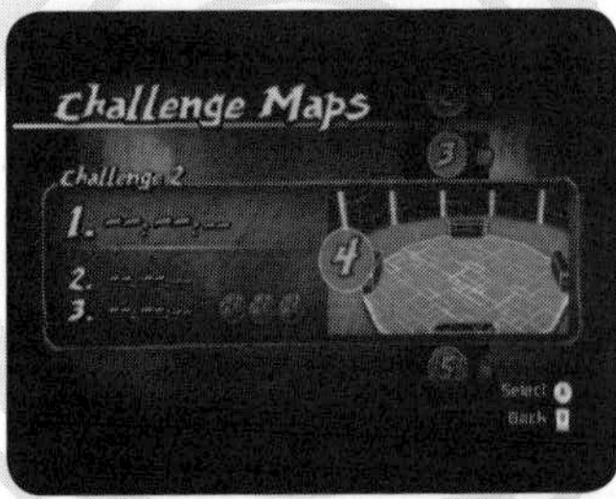

To unlock the Challenge 2 map, go to the Main menu, hold the Z button on the Nunchuk, and press A, A, A, 1, and A on the Remote. Now let go of the Z button. If you entered the code correctly, you'll see a message confirming that you've unlocked a Challenge. Go to the Extras menu and then to the Challenge Maps menu. Scroll down to find the Challenge 2 bonus stage, where you'll face a timed, four-on-one challenge against enemy ninjas.

Big Head Donatello

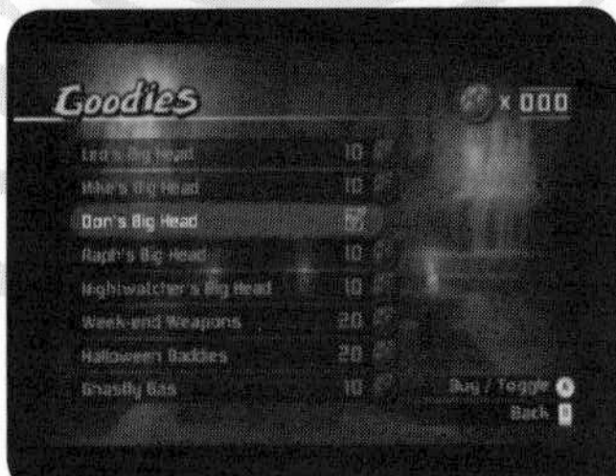

To give Donatello a huge head, go to the Main menu, hold the Z button on the Nunchuk, and press 1, A, C, and 2 on the Remote. Now let go of the Z button. If you entered the code correctly, you'll see a message confirming that you've unlocked a Goodie. Go to the Extras menu and then to the Goodies menu to enable the Don's Big Head cheat. Instead of his normal noggin, Don's head will look enormous!

Tony Hawk's Downhill Jam

Unlockable Skaters, Boards, Events, and More

This latest Tony Hawk title still puts a lot of emphasis on tricks, but also throws in a big dose of downhill thrill. On the Main menu, go to Options and then to Cheat Codes. Once you enter a code and press Done, you'll exit the Cheat Codes screen. If you enter a code correctly, the Enter Cheats option and the Toggle Cheats option will now appear. The Toggle Cheats option allows you to turn any cheat on or off, as you like.

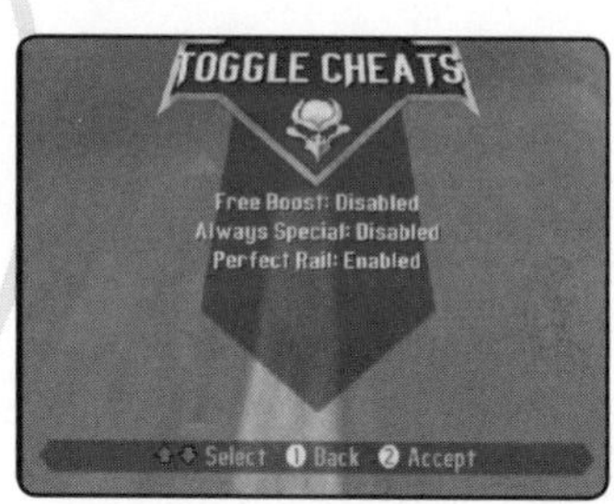

Cheat	*Code*
Unlock All Skaters	IMINTERFACING
Unlock All Boards	RAIDTHEWOODSHED
Unlock All Events	ADVENTURESOFKWANG
Unlock All Movies	FREEBOZZLER
Free Boost	OOTBAGHFOREVER
Always Special	POINTHOGGER
Perfect Rail	LIKETILTINGAPLATE
Perfect Manual	TIGHTROPEWALKER
Perfect Stats	IAMBOB
First Person Skater	FIRSTPERSONJAM
Shadow Skater	CHIMNEYSWEEP
Demon Skater	EVILCHIMNEYSWEEP
Skate as a Work of Art	FOURLIGHTS
Invisible Skater	NOWYOUSEEME
Mini Skater	DOWNTHERABBITHOLE
Giganto-Skater	IWANNABETALLTALL
Large Birds	BIRDBIRDBIRDBIRD
Especially Large Birds	BIRDBIRDBIRDBIRDBIRD
Tiny People	SHRINKTHEPEOPLE
Extreme Car Crashes	WATCHFORDOORS
Chipmunk Voices	HELLOHELIUM
Power of the Fish!	TONYFISHDOWNHILLJAM
Display Coordinates	DISPLAYCOORDINATES

Selecting the color does not affect the stars on your bowling ball, which appear once you reach Pro status.

Bowling: Pick Your Ball Color
After you select your Mii, a warning screen appears. Press and hold Up, Down, Left, or Right on the directional pad on the Remote. While still holding the directional pad, press and hold A until the game begins. The direction you press will determine your ball color.

Up = blue
Down = green
Left = red
Right = gold

Golf: Challenge Yourself with No Maps or Meters
If you're up to the challenge, try a round of golf without the map, power, and wind meters. When selecting a golf game, simply press and hold 2, point to the game or course you wish to play, then press A.

Tennis: Play on a Blue Court
For a change of pace, you can switch from the default green court to a cheerful blue court. After you select your Mii, a warning screen appears. Press and hold 2, then press A.

Yoshi's Cookie (Virtual Console)

Start Cooking at Level 99!
If starting out in Yoshi's Cookie at level 10 seems half-baked, you can really cook by unlocking difficulty levels 11 through 99!

To begin, start a 1-player game and enter the game options menu. Move the Music Type option to "Off" and set the Speed to "High." Now move the round number all the way up to 10.

Level 10 might be the ordinary limit in a typical game, but if you hold Up on the cross pad and press SELECT on your controller, you'll move up to level 11! Keep tapping SELECT until you find your favorite top chef levels!

Insider Tip
Most old-timers know that Yoshi's Cookie has appeared on the 8-bit NES, Game Boy and 16-bit Super NES, but what they might not realize is that the artists made Yoshi's head larger (to look cuter) in later versions of this game!

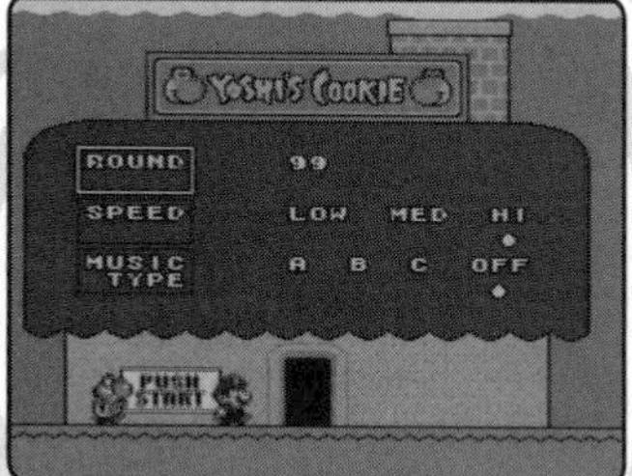

2K Sports NHL 2K8

Unlock All the New Reebok Edge NHL Hockey Jerseys!
Luckily for your tortured thumbs, 2K Sports NHL 2K8 allows you to unlock all the new Reebok Edge NHL hockey jerseys with one code. Choose features at the Main Menu, then select "Unlock 2007-2008 Uniforms" and finally choose Enter password. Pay close attention to the UPPERCASE and lowercase letters when you enter this password:

S6j83RMk01

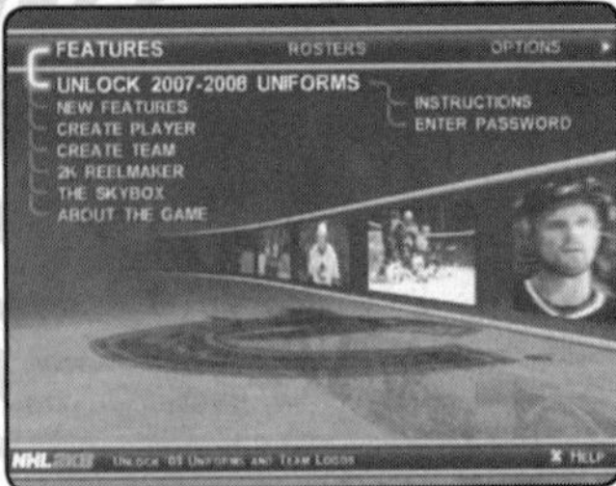

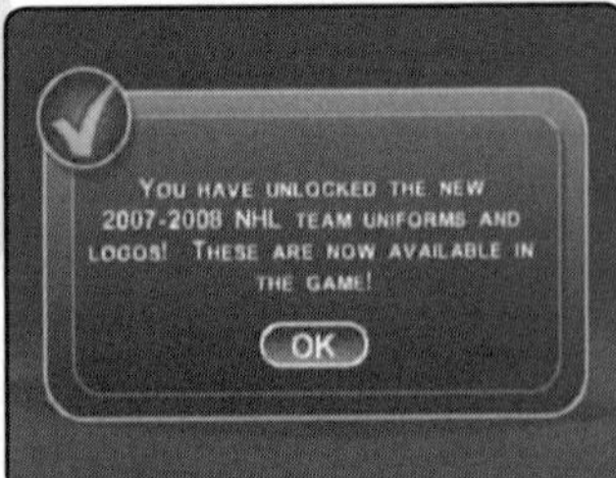

Avatar: The Last Air Bender—The Burning Earth

Zip Code Cheats
Deal out double damage with unlimited health! From the Main Menu, select the Code Entry option and enter the following five-digit codes:

Activate double damage	90210
Activate unlimited health	65049
Activate unlimited special attacks	66206
Max-level upgrade	89121
Unlock one-hit dishonor	28260

Contra

This Xbox 360 Live Arcade title uses a code originally for coin-operated machines and entering the code correctly takes a little more practice than the NES version. At the arcade game title screen quickly (and smoothly) enter the following:

Up, Up, Down, Down, Left, Right, Left, Right, B, A

This code is a bit tricky, so you'll need a little patience to tap the buttons just right. Also, you won't accumulate any Xbox 360 Gamerscore points while using this cheat!

Disney's Cars

License Plate Cheats

From the Main Menu, go to the Options menu and select the Cheat Codes option. If you enter a code correctly, you'll exit the Cheat Codes screen, but if you hear a siren, it means that you made an error entering the code. These codes are not saved with your profile, and you'll need to enter them every time you start a game.

Cheat	Code
Boost at the Start of a Race	IMSPEED
Unlimited Turbo	VROOOOM
Unlock All Cars	YAYCARS
Unlock All Paint Jobs	R4MONE
Unlock Tracks and Mini-Games	MATTL66
Unlock Tracks, Mini-Games, and Paint Jobs	IF900HP
Unlock All Videos	WATCHIT
Unlock All Concept Art	CONC3PT

Forza 2 Motorsport

Late Braking News for Beating Tough Rivals

Most of the tips in this book are all about codes, but this racing strategy is too good to ignore—especially as you advance in Forza 2 Motorsport and race cars with higher top speeds or better acceleration than your car. Computer-controlled drivers often make fewer mistakes than most gamers, so you'll need to use this trick to remain in the lead. Do it right and you could net Xbox 360 Gamerscore points for your Hard Charger accomplishment!

At the Starting Grid menu before the race, select Change Difficulty and make sure to turn on the Suggested Line to at least Braking Only. This will reveal the braking line and show yellow and red arrows at the turns. During the race, brake before the turns, but only enough to turn the arrows in the braking line from red to yellow or sometimes orange. Don't let those braking line arrows disappear or you'll be racing too slowly! With most cars in the game, you'll find that you carry more speed through the turns than the competitor cars and you'll avoid spinning out. Keep in mind that in longer races tire wear can be a factor depending on how fast you take those tricky corners!

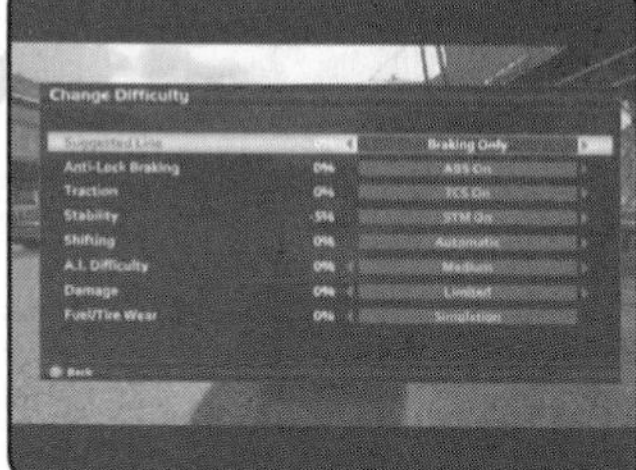

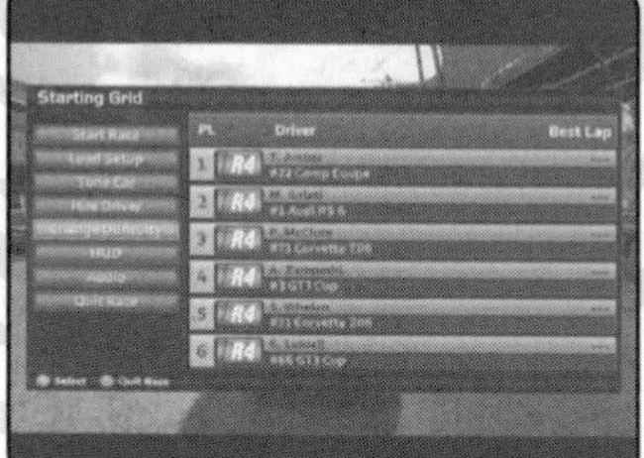

LEGO Star Wars II: The Original Trilogy

Unlockable Characters and Ships

To unlock characters and ships for use in Free Play (replay) mode, go to the bar in the Cantina, select the Enter Codes option, and type in the following codes. If you enter a code correctly, you'll see a message telling you what you've unlocked, and you can then buy it in the Characters menu, as long as you have enough credits. Remember that you must complete a stage at least once to enable Free Play for that stage, and that ships are available in certain stages only.

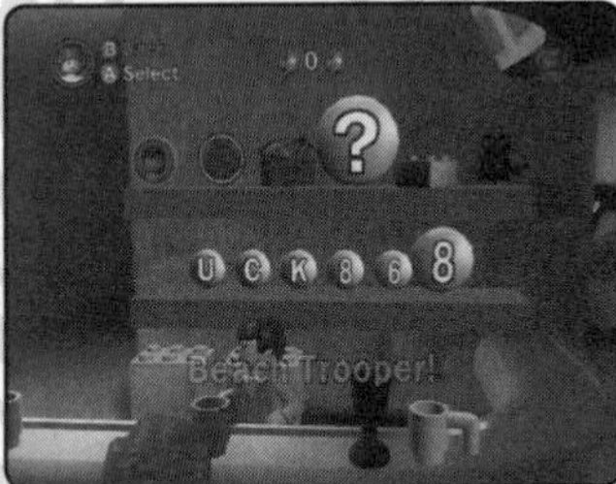

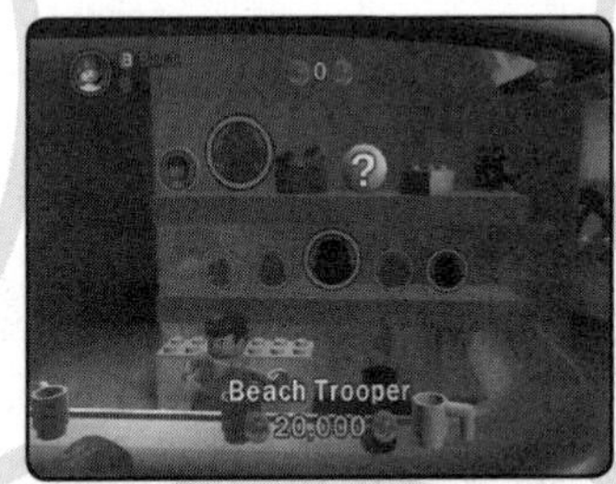

Cheat	*Code*
Beach Trooper	UCK868
Ben Kenobi's Ghost	BEN917
Bespin Guard	VHY832
Bib Fortuna	WTY721
Boba Fett	HLP221
Death Star Trooper	BNC332
Ewok	TTT289
Gamorean Guard	YZF999
Gonk Droid	NFX582
Grand Moff Tarkin	SMG219
Greedo	NAH118
Han Solo (with hood)	YWM840
IG-88	NXL973
Imperial Guard	MMM111
Imperial Officer	BBV889
Imperial Shuttle Pilot	VAP664

Cheat	*Code*
Imperial Spy	CVT125
Jawa	JAW499
Lobot	UUB319
Palace Guard	SGE549
Rebel Pilot	CYG336
Rebel Trooper (Hoth)	EKU849
Sandtrooper	YDV451
Skiff Guard	GBU888
Snowtrooper	NYU989
Stormtrooper	PTR345
The Emperor	HHY382
TIE Fighter	HDY739
TIE Fighter Pilot	NNZ316
TIE Interceptor	QYA828
Tusken Raider	PEJ821
Ugnaught	UGN694

Insider Tip

Use different characters in Free Play mode to unlock areas that were not accessible the first time you played a stage. Any credits or other bonuses you gather in a Free Play game are yours to keep.

LEGO Star Wars: The Complete Saga

Cantina Code Characters

You can unlock these ships and characters at the Cantina with the following codes. If you enter a code correctly, you'll see a message confirming the code you unlocked. Remember, you'll need to buy it at the Character menu if you have enough credits.

Admiral Ackbar	ACK646
Battle Droid (Commander)	KPF958
Boss Nass	HHY697
Captain Tarpals	QRN714
Count Dooku	DDD748
Disguise	BRJ437
Ewok	EWK785
Force Grapple Leap	CLZ738
General Grievous	PMN576
Greedo	ZZR636
IG-88	GIJ989
Imperial Guard	GUA850
Imperial Shuttle	HUT845
Jango Fett	KLJ897
Ki-Adi Mundi	MUN486
Luminara	LUM521
Padmé	VBJ322
R2Q5	EVILR2
Sandtrooper	CBR954
Stormtrooper	NBN431
Taun We	PRX482
TIE Fighter	DBH897
TIE Interceptor	INT729
Droid TriFighter	AAB123
Vulture Droid	BDC866
Watto	PLL967
Zam Wesell	584HJF
Zam's Airspeeder	UUU875

Major League Baseball 2K6

Unlockable Extras

From the Main menu, go to the My 2K menu, and then to the Enter Cheat Code screen. Once you enter a cheat correctly, you must still activate it. Go back to the My 2K menu and then to the My Cheats screen to turn cheats on and off.

Cheat	*Code*
Classic Jerseys	Lookin Good
Classic Stadiums	Home Sweet Home
Classic Teams	Ghosts of Greatness
Bouncy Ball (Balls Bounce High)	Crazy Hops
Rocket Arms (High Throwing Power for All Fielders)	Gotcha
Super Pitches (Huge Curves and Breaks)	Unhittable
Super Wall Climbs (Fielders Can Scale Any Wall)	Last Chance
Topps 2K6 All-Stars Team	Dream Team
Unlock Game Room Games	Game On
Unlock Most Gameplay Cheats	Black Sox
Unlock Most Gameplay Cheats and All Other Unlockables	Derek Jeter

(continued)

Major League Baseball 2K6 (cont.)

Insider Tip
The "Black Sox" code unlocks most of the gameplay cheats except Bouncy Ball, Rocket Arms, Super Pitches, Super Wall Climb, and the Home Run Derby: Team Challenge mode. The "Derek Jeter" code does not unlock Bouncy Ball, Rocket Arms, Super Pitches, and Super Wall Climb, but it does enable all other gameplay cheats and unlockables. Derek Jeter is the featured ballplayer in Major League Baseball 2K series, so it's only right that he has the best cheat in the game!

If you'd like to see the complete list of cheats and unlockables or visit your Game Room, go to the My 2K6, then to the My Skybox option, and then to the Skybox menu.

Major League Baseball 2K7

Big League Cheats
To give yourself a major league edge, go to the My 2K7 menu and then to the Enter Cheat Code screen. Once you enter a cheat correctly, you must still activate it. Go back to the My 2K7 menu and then to the My Cheats screen to turn cheats on and off.

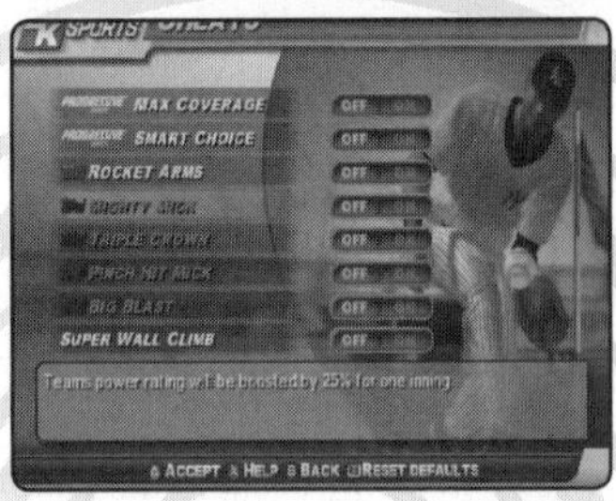

Cheat	*Code*
Unlock All Cheats Except Mighty Mick, Triple Crown, Pinch Hit Mick, and Big Blast	Derek Jeter
Mighty Mick (Team Power Rating Boost for One Inning)	mightymick
Triple Crown (Hit Abilities Boosted for Hitters 3, 4, and 5)	triplecrown
Pinch Hit Mick (Mickey Mantle Available to Pinch Hit)	phmantle
Big Blast (Hit Huge Home Runs)	m4murder
Mickey Mantle Available as a Free Agent	themick
Unlock Arcade Games	Game On

Insider Tip
Once Unlock Arcade Games is enabled, go to the My 2K7 menu, then to the My Skybox menu, and then to the Game Room to play shuffleboard, darts, or air hockey.

MX vs. ATV Untamed

Fox Gear
To unlock all the riding gear made by Fox, press the Y Button at the Main Menu to open the cheats option, then enter the following:

CRAZYLIKEA

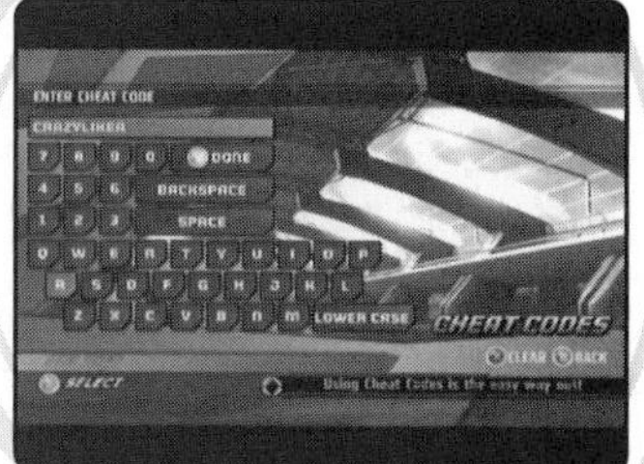

NASCAR 08

Drive Away with These Cheats
From the Main Menu at the garage, choose EA Sports Extras and then select Cheat Codes. Now enter the following codes:

Unlock All Fantasy Drivers	Race the Pack
Unlock Chase Cars	Checkered Flag
Unlock EA Sports Car	EA Sports Car
Unlock Walmart Track and Car	Walmart Everyday

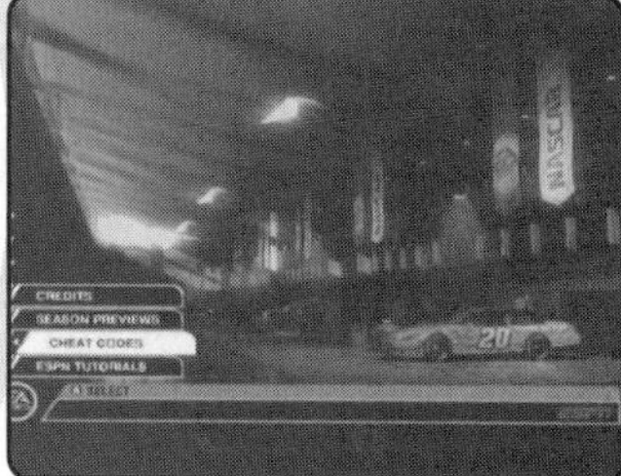

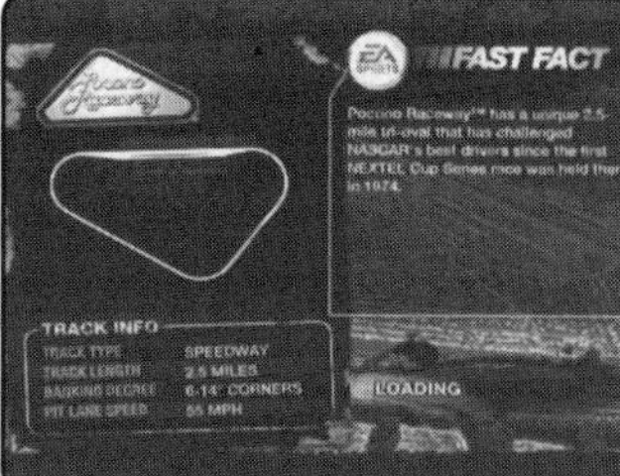

NBA 2K6

Bonus Features, Jerseys, and Shoes

From the Main menu, go to the Features menu and then the Codes screen. Enter the codes below to unlock bonus gameplay features, alternate jerseys, and special shoes. Some codes must be turned on manually. Look for them in the code list and use the directional pad to enable and disable them.

Cheat	*Code*
Play as Celebrities in Street Mode	ballers
Unlock 2K6 Team	nba2k6
Unlock 2K Sports Team	2ksports
Unlock VC Team	vcteam
2005-06 Pacers Uniform	31andonly
2006 All-Star Uniform	fanfavorites
Bulls Retro Uniform	chi retro
Cavaliers Secondary Uniform	cle 2nd
Celtics Secondary Uniform	bos 2nd
Clippers Retro Uniform	lac retro
Grizzlies Retro Uniform	mem retro
Heat Retro Uniform	mia retro
Hornets Retro Uniform	no retro
Kings Secondary Uniform	sac 2nd
Knicks Retro Uniform	ny retro
Magic Retro Uniform	orl retro
Nets Retro Uniform	nj retro
Nuggets Secondary Uniform	den 2nd
Pistons Secondary Uniform	det 2nd
Rockets Retro Uniform	hou retro
Sonics Retro Uniform	sea retro
St. Patrick's Day Uniform	gogreen
Suns Retro Uniform	phx retro
Wizards Retro Uniform	was retro
Nike Shox MTX	crazylift
Nike Up Tempo Pro	anklebreakers
Nike Zoom 20-5-5	lebronsummerkicks
Nike Zoom Kobe 1	kobe
Nike Zoom LeBron III All-Star Colorway	lb allstar
Nike Zoom LeBron III Black/Crimson	lb crimsonblack
Nike Zoom LeBron III Special Birthday	lb bday
Nike Zoom LeBron III White/Gold	lb whitegold

Vending Machine Codes

While most of the cheats are entered on the Codes screen, some are actually used at the vending machine in The Crib. From the Main menu, go to Features and then The Crib. Turn around to find the vending machine. Walk up to it and press A, then look down to find the Code option. Press A to make the Code Entry screen appear. Once unlocked, these cheats must be turned on manually. Exit The Crib and go to Features and then to the Codes screen.

Cheat	*Code*
+10 Defensive Awareness	lockdown
+10 Offensive Awareness	getaclue
Maximum Durability	noinjury
PowerBar Tattoo in Create Player Mode	pbink
Unlimited Stamina	nrgmax

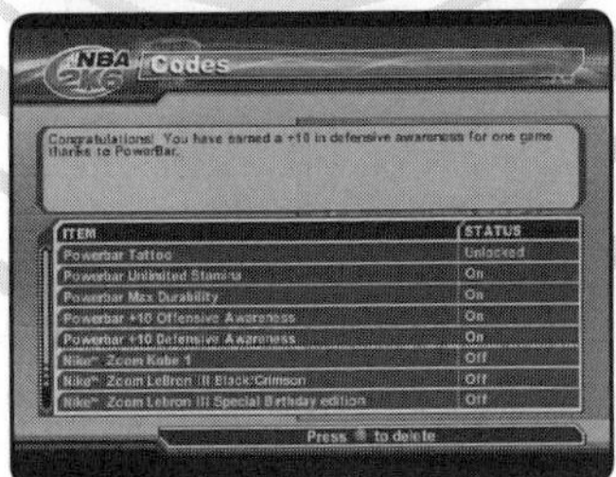

Unlockable Teams and Options
Navigating the menus in this game can be a bit confusing, so follow these detailed instructions. After you select a favorite team, you won't be taken to a traditional Main menu. Instead, you'll see a Quick Game setup screen. Press any direction on the right joystick to make the Options screen appear. Go to the Features menu and then to the Codes screen. Press A to make the keyboard appear, and then type in a code. Press A again to lock it in. To exit the code screen, press any direction on the right joystick to make the Options screen appear again. Be aware that Codes that affect playing abilities must be turned on and off manually, so scroll through the code list to find them all. To make codes permanent, you must save your Settings file.

Cheat	*Code*
NBA 2K Team	bestsim
Topps 2K Sports All-Stars	topps2ksports
International All-Stars	tns9roi
Superstars	rta1spe
2007 All-Star Uniforms	syt6cii
St. Patrick's Day Uniforms (Bulls, Celtics, Knicks)	tpk7sgn
Valentine's Day Uniforms (Hornets)	vdr5lya
Bobcats Secondary Uniform	bcb8sta

Cheat	*Code*
Nets Secondary Uniform	nrd4esj
Jazz Secondary Uniform	zjb3lau
Wizards Secondary Uniform	zw9idla
ABA Ball	payrespect
All-Star Ball	ply8mia
Unlimited Stamina	norest
Max Durability	ironman
+10 Offensive Awareness	inthezone
+10 Defensive Awareness	getstops

Insider Tip
While most of the uniform codes unlock alternate "away" jerseys, the St. Patrick's Day code unlocks alternate "home" jerseys.

NBA 2K8

Have a Ball . . . and a Couple of Secret Teams
At the Main Menu, choose cheats and enter the following codes:

Unlock the ABA Ball	payrespect
Unlock the 2K Sports All-Star Team	2ksports
Unlock the Visual Concepts Team	vcteam
Unlock the NBA Development Team	nba2k

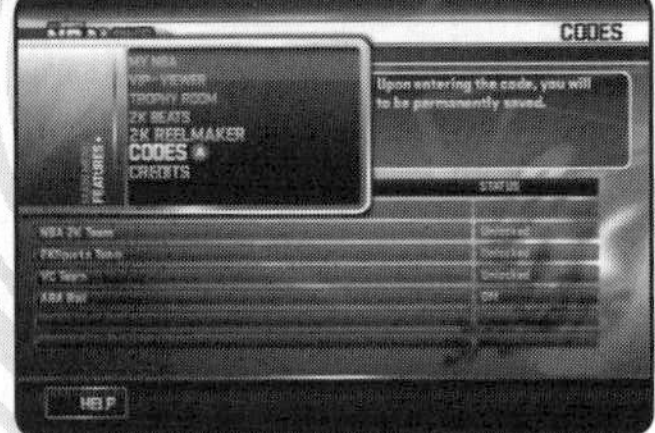

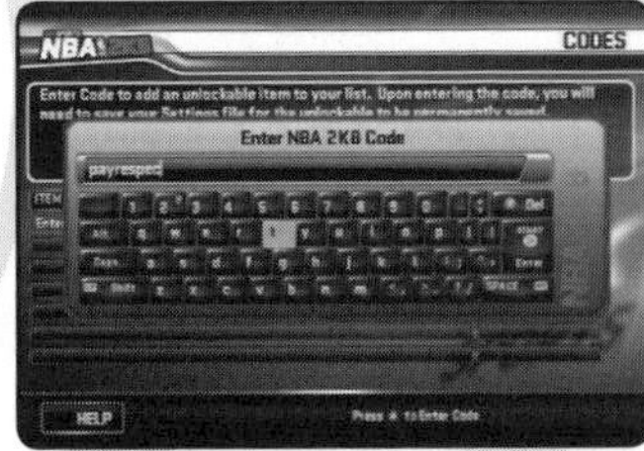

NBA Live 07

Bonus Shoes and Jerseys
You must be signed in to an NBA Live 07 profile to use and save these codes. The option to sign in appears when you turn the game on. Once you're signed in, go from the Main menu to My NBA Live 07, then to NBA Codes. Enter the codes as shown, being careful not to mix up the letter "O" with the number "0" or the letter "I" with the number "1."

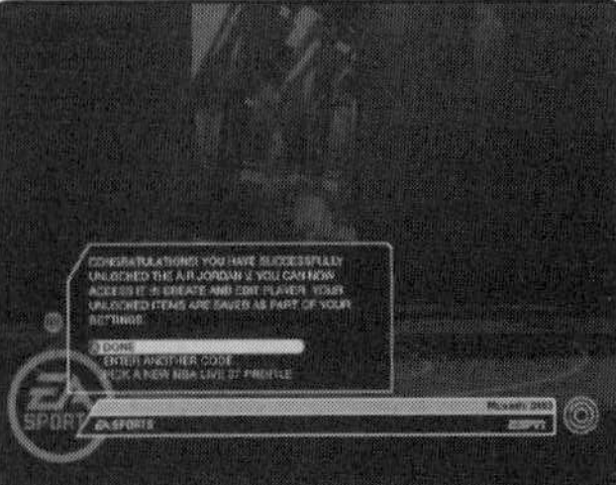

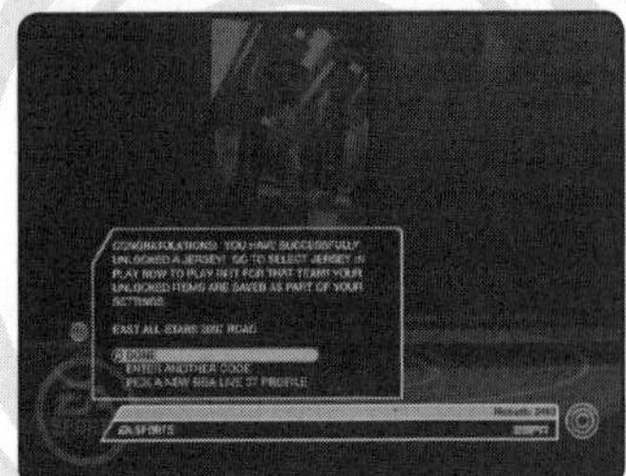

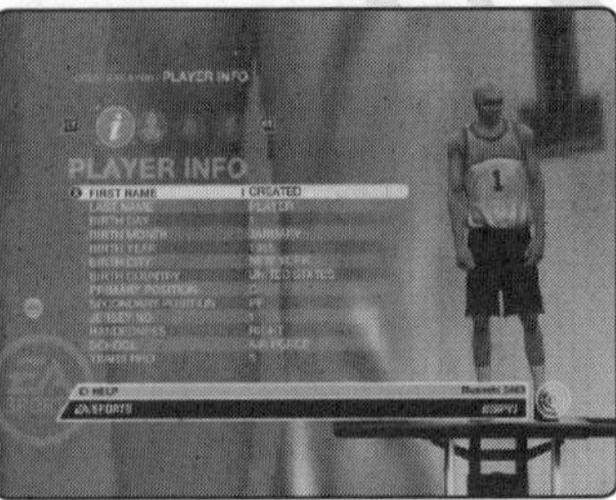

Insider Tip
Bonus shoes can be saved to a created player. To create a player, go to My NBA Live 07, then to Team Management, then to Creation Zone, and then to Create Player.

(continued)

NBA Live 07 (cont.)

Bonus Shoe	*Code*
Air Jordan V (V1)	VIR13PC451
Air Jordan V (V2)	PNBBX1EVT5
Air Jordan V (V3)	IB7G8NN91Z
C-Billups All-Star Edition	BV6877HB9N
C-Billups Vegas Edition	85NVLDMWS5
Gil Zero All-Star Edition	23DN1PPOG4
Gil Zero Mid (V1)	369V6RVU3G
Gil Zero Mid (V2)	1GSJC8JWRL
Gil Zero Vegas Edition	QQQ3JCUYQ7
Jordan Melo M3	JUL38TC485
KG Bounce All-Star Edition	HYIOUHCAAN
KG Bounce Vegas Edition	KDZ2MQL17W
Stealth All-Star Edition	FE454DFJCC
TMAC 6 All-Star Edition	MCJK843NNC
TMAC 6 Vegas Edition	84GF7EJG8V
Charlotte Bobcats Second Road Jersey	WEDX671H7S
East All-Stars 2007 Home Jersey	5654ND43N6
East All-Stars 2007 Road Jersey	WOCNW4KL7L
New Jersey Nets Second Road Jersey	D4SAA98U5H
Utah Jazz Second Road Jersey	VCBI89FK83
Washington Wizards Second Road Jersey	QV93NLKXQC
West All-Stars 2007 Home Jersey	993NSKL199
West All-Stars 2007 Road Jersey	XX93BVL20U

NBA Live 08

Will New Shoes Improve Your Game?
At the My NBA Live 08 menu, select NBA Sports Extras and then NBA Codes before entering the following:

Duncan All-Star	FE454DFJCC
Gil Zero All-Star	23DN1PPOG4

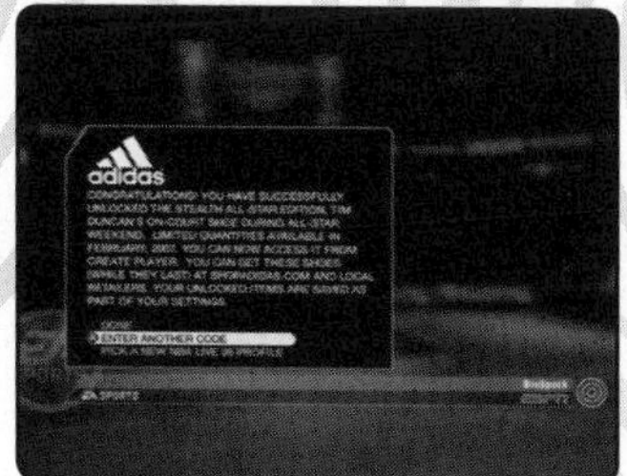

NBA Street: Homecourt

Alternate Ball

To unlock an alternate game ball, go to the Main menu, hold the left and right bumpers, and quickly press Up, Down, Left, and Right on the directional pad. If you enter the code correctly, you'll hear an explosive sound effect. It might take a couple of tries to get the moves down right, so keep trying.

Bonus Courts

Unlocking bonus courts is similar to unlocking an alternate game ball, just with a couple of different moves on the directional pad. Go to the Main menu, hold the left and right bumpers, and quickly press Up, Right, Down, and Left on the directional pad. If you enter the code correctly, you'll hear an explosive sound effect. Like the Alternate Ball code, this code may take several tries to get right. You'll now have access to more courts, such as the Brand Jordan Gym.

Many of the bonus courts are real-life locations where pros got their start, and where they continue to hone their skills.

Need for Speed ProStreet

Better Than a Free Fill-up!

Unlike previous Need for Speed games where you enter codes at the Main Menu, you must enter the Need for Speed Prostreet codes at the Career Menu. Once you start a Career mode game and have access to EA Nation online, you'll be able to select the Code entry option and add these cool cars, cash and tune-ups:

Add $10,000 to your spending money	cashmoney
Add another $10,000 to your spending money	reggame
Add five repair tokens	safetynet
Unlock the Castrol Syntec vinyls	castrolsyntec
Unlock the Coke Zero Golf GTI	zerozerozero
Unlock the Energizer vinyls	energizerlithium
Unlock the classic Chevelle SS	horsepower
Unlock the Audi TT	itsaboutyou
Unlock the Dodge Viper SRT10	worldslongestlasting

Note: All of the above codes work with the free Energizer Lithium Extender Pack downloaded from Xbox Marketplace!

NHL 2K6

Unlock It All
To get ahead of the game in one shot, create a profile named Turco813. This profile will be awarded all unlockables and trophies, as well as credited with completing all user challenges.

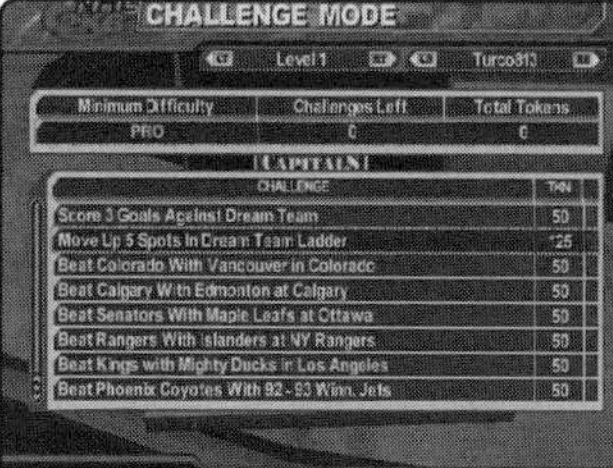

NHL 08

Hit the Ice with New Reebok Gear
On the Main Menu choose My NHL 08 and then the RBK EDGE menu before entering the following:

Reebok Gear	h3oyxpwksf8ibcgt

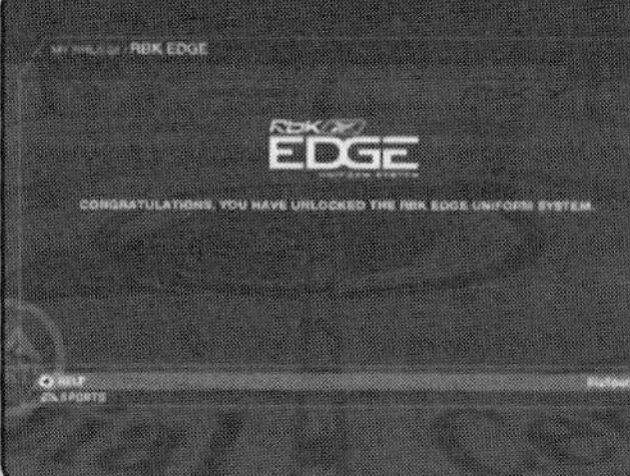

Ratatouille

Secret Unlockables
At the Menu, choose Extras and then Gusteau's Shop. At Gusteau's Shop, choose the Secrets option. At this menu you'll see a list of codes that you can buy with Gusteau points, but if you press right on the D-Pad you'll scroll through a number of blank spots for additional codes! At the Menu, choose Cheats, and then enter the following codes:

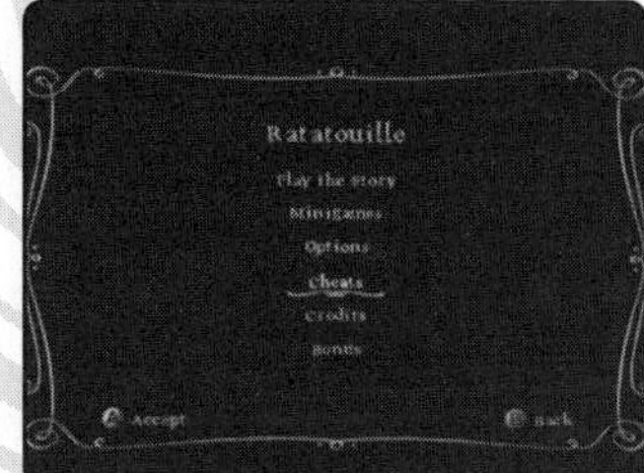

Cheat	*Code*
Pick up the pace	SPEEDY
Unlock minigames	MATTELME

Wii
Xbox 360
Xbox
GC
PS3
PS2
DS
GBA
PSP

Rockstar Games presents Table Tennis

Unlockable Options

Using the directional pad, enter the following codes quickly but firmly at the Main menu. If you enter a code correctly, you'll hear a few musical tones. The Unlock All code enables all bonus players and venues in Exhibition Mode as well as the All-Star Circuit in Tournament Mode.

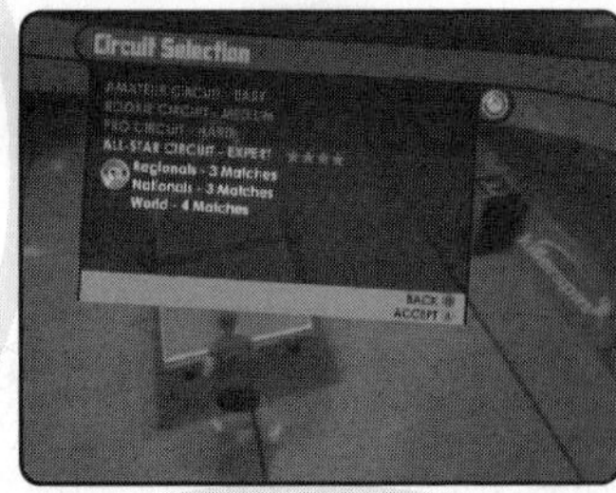

Cheat	*Code*
Big Ball	Left, Right, Left, Right, Up, Up, Up, X
Big Spindicator	Up, Down, X, X, Y, Y
Players Are Silhouettes	Up, Down, Y, Y, Left Bumper, Left Trigger, Right Trigger, Right Bumper
Players Are Big Paddles	Up, Left, Up, Right, Up, Down, Up, Up, X, X
Big Crowd Sound Effects	Up, Up, Up, Right Bumper, Right Trigger, Right Bumper, Right Trigger
Small Crowd Sound Effects	Down, Down, Down, Left Bumper, Left Trigger, Left Bumper, Left Trigger
Pong Sound Effects	Up, Up, Down, Down, Left, Right, Left, Right, Left Bumper, Right Bumper
Sweaty Characters (in Character Viewer)	Right Trigger, Up, Down, Left Trigger, Left, Right, Y, X, X, Y
Unlock All	Up, Right, Down, Left, Left Bumper, Right, Up, Left, Down, Right Bumper

Insider Tip

If you're wondering what the Spindicator is, it's the glowing animation around the ping pong ball that shows the direction in which it's spinning. The Big Spindicator code just makes it larger and easier to see. To use this code, you must first download an update for this game from Xbox Live. You can download this update using the Silver Membership, which is available for free.

Shrek the Third

10,000 Extra Far Far Coins
If you need a little more purchase power, go to the Gift Shop and enter this code on your controller direction pad: Up, Up, Down, Up, Right, Left

Insider Tip
This code requires a little practice and pacing—it's not the speed of the code, but how smoothly you press each direction on the pad.

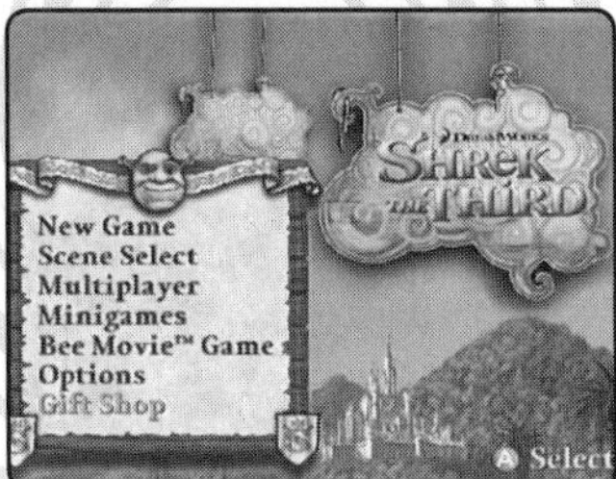

Spider-Man Friend or Foe

Add a Sidekick or Three
Beating up bad guys seems easier when you have a sidekick and extra Tech Tokens. You'll need to enter these codes on the direction pad while on Nick Fury's flying Helicarrier.

Add 5,000 Tech Tokens to inventory	Up, Up, Down, Down, Left, Right
Unlock Green Goblin sidekick	Left, Down, Right, Right, Down, Left
Unlock Sandman sidekick	Right, Right, Right, Up, Down, Left
Venom sidekick	Left, Left, Right, Up, Down, Down

These codes are tough to enter on the Xbox 360 version of Spider-Man Friend or Foe. If you have trouble, pause the game by pressing START and then un-pause the game and enter the code again. When you correctly enter a code, you'll hear the same electronic sound as when you pause the game.

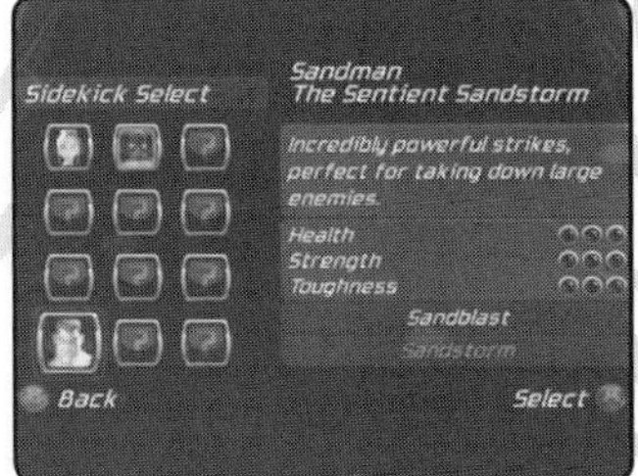

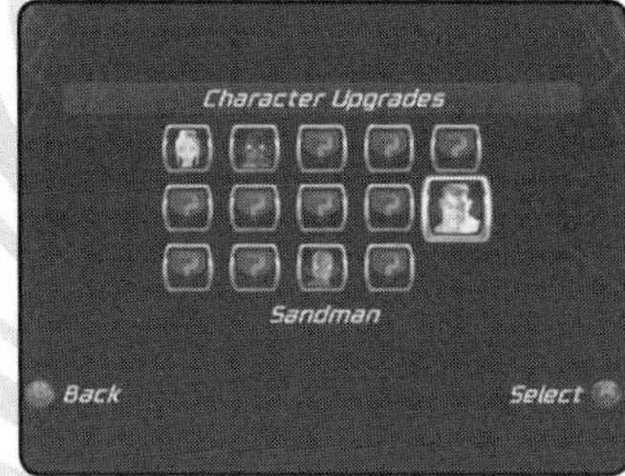

Star Trek: Legacy

Unlock the U.S.S. Legacy

To unlock this hidden Sovereign-class starship, just make sure you have enough credits by the final mission to buy four of these ultimate battleships. Once you begin the mission, your fourth and final ship will be named the U.S.S. Legacy.

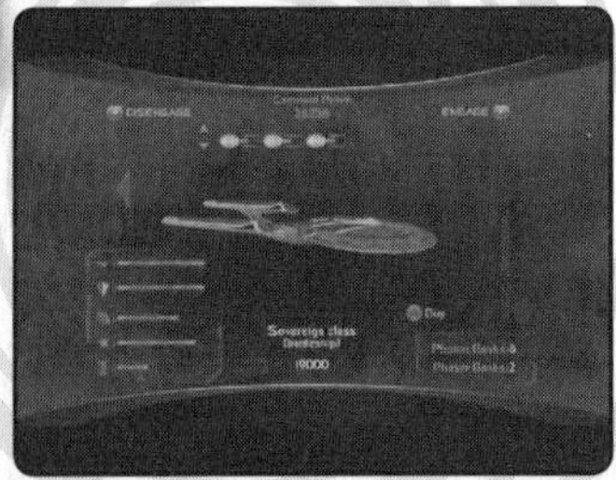

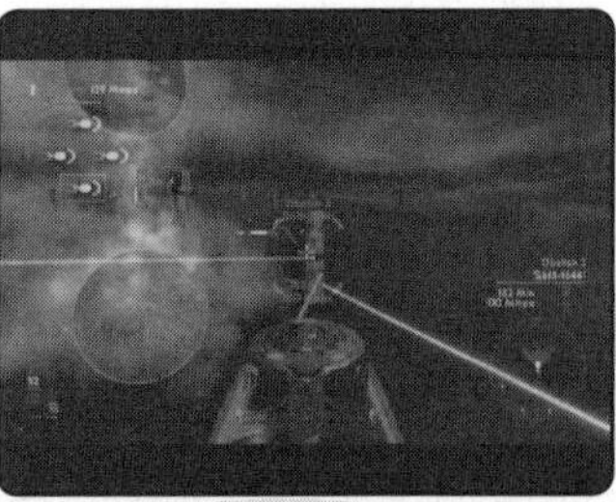

Insider Tip

The key to having lots of credits by the final mission is, of course, not to spend so much during the course of the game. Do not buy ships unless absolutely necessary, and don't trade in ships if they are still performing well. In fact, to win the Antique Collector Achievement, you must begin a Next Generation-era mission with an Enterprise-era ship. On the flip side, you must complete the final mission with just a single ship at your command to win the Autonomous Operator Achievement.

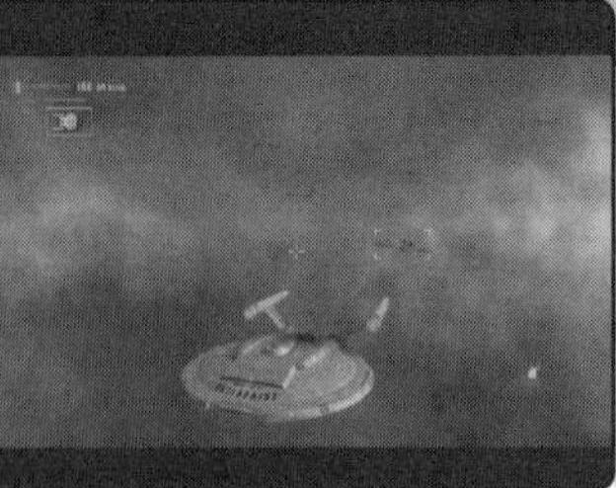

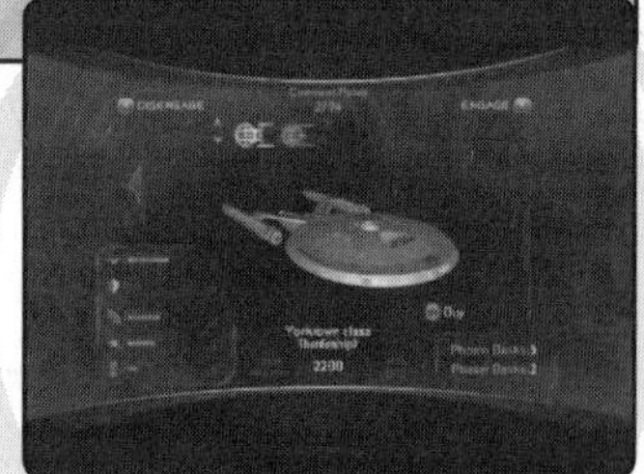

Extra Story Videos

The Star Trek: Legacy storyline is deep and can be difficult to follow in the short cutscenes offered during the game. As you complete each chapter, go to the Extras menu to find a new video expanding on the storyline of that chapter. You'll learn additional information about Starfleet history, the origin of the Borg, and more.

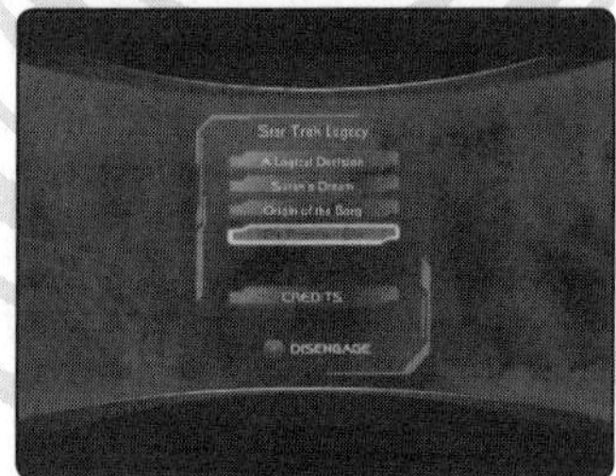

Surf's Up

Sometimes catching the perfect wave isn't as important as riding the right board. Here are a few codes that will add extra surfboard choices. Enter these codes after you select "Extras" and "Cheat Codes" from the Main Menu:

Effect	Code
Unlock the Astral surfboard	ASTRAL
Unlock Tank Evans	IMTHEBEST
Unlock Tatsushi Kobayashi	KOBAYASHI
Unlock the Monsoon surfboard	MONSOON
Unlock all multiplayer levels	MULITPASS
Unlock all surfboards	MYPRECIOUS
Unlock all galleries	NICEPLACE
Unlock Geek	SLOWANDSTEADY
Unlock Elliot	SURPRISEGUEST
Unlock Zeke Topanga	THELEGEND
Unlock Arnold	TINYBUTSTRONG
Unlock the Tiny Shockwave surfboard	TINYSHOCKWAVE
Unlock character customization options	TOPFASHION
Unlock the videos	WATCHAMOVIE

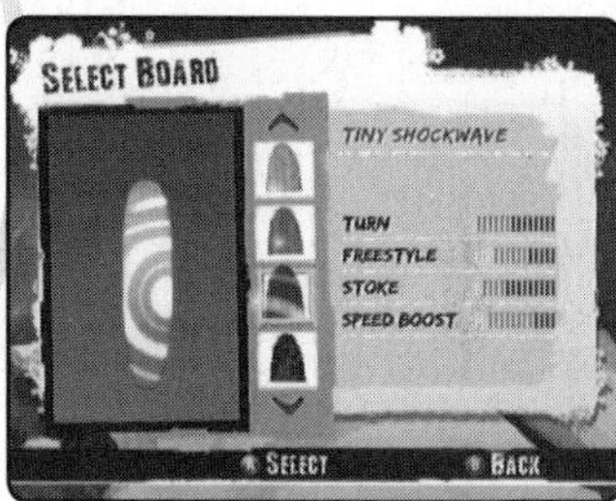

Thrillville: Off the Rails

In-Game Cheats

The Thrillville: Off the Rail codes are easy to input because most of the unlock codes are similar. Enter these codes while walking around in the parks:

Effect	Code
Earn an additional $50,000	X Button, B Button, Y Button, X Button, B Button, Y Button, A Button
Add an extra 500 Thrill Points to your game	B Button, X Button, Y Button, B Button, X Button, Y Button, X Button
Unlock all mini-games	X Button, B Button, Y Button, X Button, B Button, Y Button, Right D-Pad
Unlock all missions	X Button, B Button, Y Button, X Button, B Button, Y Button, B Button
Unlock all parks	X Button, B Button, Y Button, X Button, B Button, Y Button, X Button
Unlock all rides	X Button, B Button, Y Button, X Button, B Button, Y Button, Y Button

Tiger Woods PGA Tour 06

Unlockable Bonus Golfers and Equipment
Go to the Options menu and then the Password screen to enter the codes below. To change your character's equipment, go to the Game Face menu, load your profile, and then select the Pro Shop.

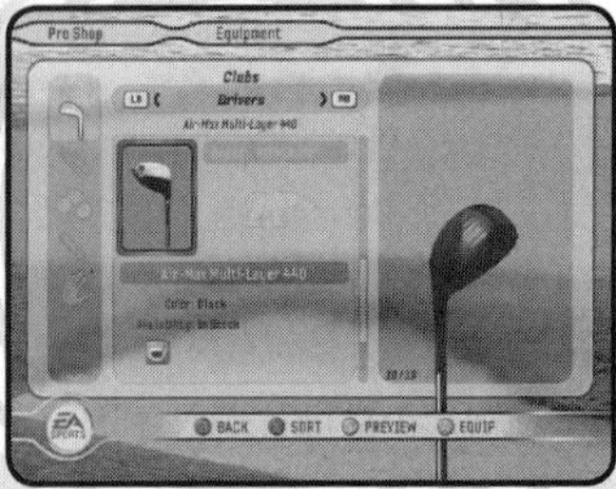

Cheat	*Password*
Unlock Vijay Singh only	VICTORY
Unlock all golfers	ITSINTHEGAME
Unlock all courses	EYECANDY
Unlock all clubs	CLUBS11
Unlock Jack Nicklaus branded items	GOLDENBEAR
Unlock EA Sports Gold Collection ball	GOLFISFUN

Insider Tip
Considering Jack Nicklaus' record for PGA victories, you should seriously consider using his signature clubs. In addition, Vijay Singh is among the top-ranked in the PGA, and a good choice for taking on Tiger on almost any course.

Tiger Woods PGA Tour 08

The Grand Slam of Golf Game Codes
From the Main Menu select EA Sports Extras, then Passwords and enter the following:

Add infinite funds to your golf account	CREAM
Unlock all Golfers	ALLSTARS
Unlock Manchester United star Wayne Rooney	PLAYFIFA08

TMNT

A Few Extra Goodies
You'll need to complete the 16 levels in TMNT to find most of the good stuff, but there are a couple of easy cheats to get you started.

Press and hold the LB Button at the Main menu, then enter one of these codes:

Cheat	*Code*
Unlock Don's Big Head Goodie	B, Y, A, X
Unlock Challenge Map 2 Arena	A, A, B, A

Virtua Tennis 3

Unlockable Court
To unlock the cruise ship court, go to the Main menu and quickly press Up, Up, Down, Down, Left, Right, Left, and Right on the directional pad. If you enter the code correctly, you'll hear a chime.

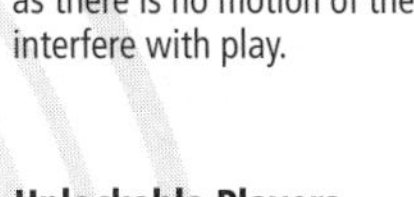

Luckily, the cruise ship seems to be docked, as there is no motion of the ocean to interfere with play.

Unlockable Players
To unlock old-time players King and Duke, go to the Main menu and quickly press Up, Up, Down, Down, Left, Right, Left Bumper, and Right Bumper. If you enter the code correctly, you'll hear a chime.

Old-fashioned though they are, King and Duke can stand up to any of the modern champions…and then some.

Unlockable Gear
This code will unlock all the gear in any World Tour career. On the Main menu, quickly press Left, Right, B, Left, Right, B, Up, and Down. As usual, you'll hear a chime if you enter the code correctly.

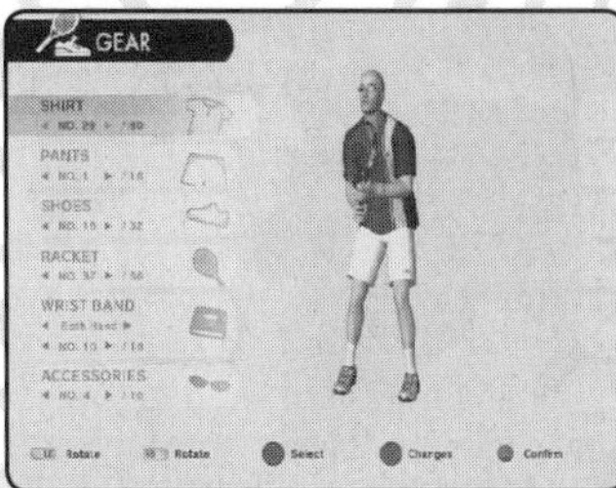

Amped 2

Unlockable Tricks, Skills, and More

To use the Cheats below, you must first create a boarder for Career mode. Once that's done, go to the Options menu and then to the Cheats screen. Enter the codes exactly as they appear, with uppercase and lowercase letters, and no spaces. If you enter a code correctly, the code will disappear. If you make a mistake, the text will remain on the screen and you'll hear a tone.

Cheat	*Code*
Runs Are Icy	AllIce
All Levels Unlocked (Free Ride Mode)	AllLevels
All Hidden Boarders Unlocked (Free Ride Mode)	AllMyPeeps
Won't Ever Crash	DontCrash
Move Faster	FastMove
Low Gravity (Big Jumps)	LowGravity
Your Character Has Max Skills	MaxSkills
Cancels Active Cheats	NoCheats
No Collisions with Other Boarders	NoCollisions
Unlock Reward Videos (Career Mode)	ShowRewards
Spin Faster	SuperSpin
All Tricks Unlocked	TrickedOut

Insider Tip

Using cheats disables game saves in Career mode and prevents you from playing any Multiplayer games. Use the "NoCheats" code to cancel all active cheats—well, almost all of them. "NoCheats" actually does not disable "AllMyPeeps." The bonus boarders will still be available in Free Ride mode.

AND 1 Streetball

Unlockable Extras

From the Main menu, go to Options and then to Cheat Codes. Enter any of the codes below and press A to lock them in. Unlocked characters are available in Pickup Games, and the bonus cash applies to the Tour mode, but the rest of the codes affect all game modes. Repeat a code to disable it.

Cheat	*Code*
$1,000,000	Y, B, X, X, B, Y, A, Y
All IBall Moves Enabled	A, B, B, A, X, Y, A, X
No Timing Penalty for IBall Moves	B, Y, X, X, Y, B, A, X
All Breakdowns Enabled	A, A, Y, X, X, B, Y, B
Shot Text Enabled	B, X, Y, Y, X, X, Y, B
All Messages Enabled	B, X, Y, X, B, A, X, B

(continued)

AND 1 Streetball (cont.)

Cheat	Code
Easy Shots	X, A, Y, X, A, Y, B, B
Always on Fire	X, B, A, B, X, A, X, Y
DJ Green Lantern Unlocked	Y, Y, B, A, X, A, B, Y
Flash Unlocked	B, A, A, Y, A, B, B, X
Shane Unlocked	X, A, B, A, B, Y, B, A
Skip To My Lou Unlocked	Y, A, Y, X, B, A, Y, X
All Characters Unlocked	B, X, X, Y, B, X, A, A
Videos Unlocked	X, A, X, B, Y, X, A, A
Side Games Unlocked	Y, X, B, A, A, Y, Y, X
Global (All Cheats) Unlocked	B, B, A, A, X, Y, X, Y

Cars

Unlockable Turbo, Tracks, and Mini-Games

Choose the Options menu and then select Cheat Codes and spell out these names on the license plates. If you mess up on a code, you'll hear a siren. Give it another try! If you enter a code correctly, you'll exit the Cheat Codes screen. Keep in mind that codes are not saved with your profile, and must be entered every time you turn on the game.

Cheat	Code
Boost at the Start of a Race	IMSPEED
Unlimited Turbo	VROOOOM
Unlock All Cars	YAYCARS
Unlock All Paint Jobs	R4MONE
Unlock Tracks and Mini-Games	MATTL66
Unlock Tracks, Mini-Games, and Paint Jobs	IF900HP
Unlock Mater's Speedy Circuit and Mater's Countdown Clean-Up	TRGTEXC
Unlock All Videos	WATCHIT
Unlock All Concept Art	CONC3PT

Insider Tip

Note that MATTL66 and IF900HP unlock all arcade tracks except Mater's Speedy Circuit (one of the Road Races) and Mater's Countdown Clean-Up (one of the Mini-Games).

Crash Tag Team Racing

Unlock a Faster Car, One-Hit Knockouts, and More

Enter the following codes on the Title screen. If you enter a code correctly, you'll hear a musical tone.

Cheat	*Code*
Faster Car	Hold L and R and press B, B, Y, Y
Crash's Car Made Out of Toy Blocks	Hold L and R and press B, B, Y, X
Disable HUD	Hold L and R and press A, X, Y, B
One-Hit Knockouts	Hold L and R and press A, B, B, A
Alternate Version of Crash	Hold L and R and press X, B, X, B
People in the Park Areas Have Chicken Heads	Hold L and R and press A, B, B, X

Insider Tips

The Faster Car code will give your vehicle extra speed, no matter your current race or game settings. The Disable HUD code eliminates the lap counter, track map, and other displays normally shown during races. The One-Hit Knockouts code is the most useful for winning races, turning your opponents' cars into flaming torches with a single touch. The Alternate Version of Crash code is just for fun, making Crash look as he does in the Japanese version of the game. The Chicken Heads code is great for a laugh!

The Incredibles: Rise of the Underminer

Unlockable Extras

To enter these codes as you're playing, pause the game, press X to go to the Menu, and then go to the Secrets screen. To lock in a code, you must highlight the checkmark, and press A (just pressing Start won't work).

Cheat	*Code*
1,000 Experience Points for Mr. Incredible	MRIPROF
1,000 Experience Points for Frozone	FROZPROF
Max Out Mr. Incredible's Stats	MRIMASTER
Max Out Frozone's Stats	FROZMASTER
Unlock Gallery Art	SHOWME
Unlock All Levels	EVELOCKSMITH
Big Heads	EGOPROBLEM
Increase Difficulty	THISISTOOEASY
Decrease Difficulty	THISISTOOHARD
Watch the Credits	ROLLCALL

Insider Tip

The Increase and Decrease Difficulty codes change the amount of damage dealt, damage received, health recovery rate, and experience points earned.

LEGO Star Wars II: The Original Trilogy

Unlockable Characters and Ships

To unlock characters and ships for use in Free Play (replay) mode, go to the bar in the Cantina, select the Enter Codes option, and type in the following codes. If you enter a code correctly, you'll see a message telling you what you've unlocked and you can then buy it in the Characters menu, as long as you have enough credits. Remember that you must complete a stage at least once to enable Free Play for that stage, and that ships are available in certain stages only.

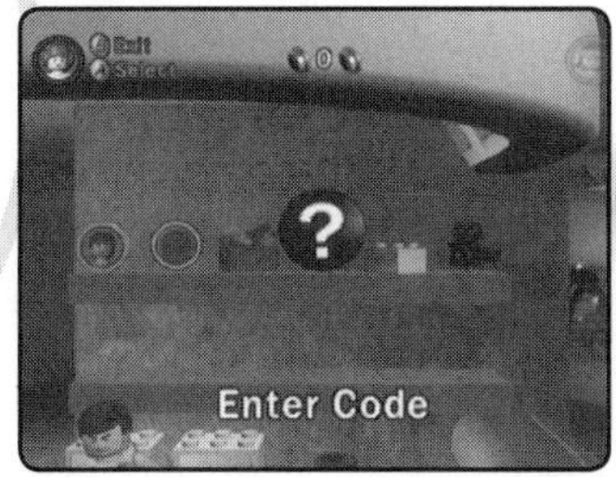

Cheat	*Code*
Beach Trooper	UCK868
Ben Kenobi's Ghost	BEN917
Bespin Guard	VHY832
Bib Fortuna	WTY721
Boba Fett	HLP221
Death Star Trooper	BNC332
Ewok	TTT289
Gamorrean Guard	YZF999
Gonk Droid	NFX582
Grand Moff Tarkin	SMG219
Greedo	NAH118
Han Solo (with hood)	YWM840
IG-88	NXL973
Imperial Guard	MMM111
Imperial Officer	BBV889
Imperial Shuttle Pilot	VAP664

Cheat	*Code*
Imperial Spy	CVT125
Jawa	JAW499
Lobot	UUB319
Palace Guard	SGE549
Rebel Pilot	CYG336
Rebel Trooper from Hoth	EKU849
Sandtrooper	YDV451
Skiff Guard	GBU888
Snowtrooper	NYU989
Stormtrooper	PTR345
The Emperor	HHY382
TIE Fighter	HDY739
TIE Fighter Pilot	NNZ316
TIE Interceptor	QYA828
Tusken Raider	PEJ821
Ugnaught	UGN694

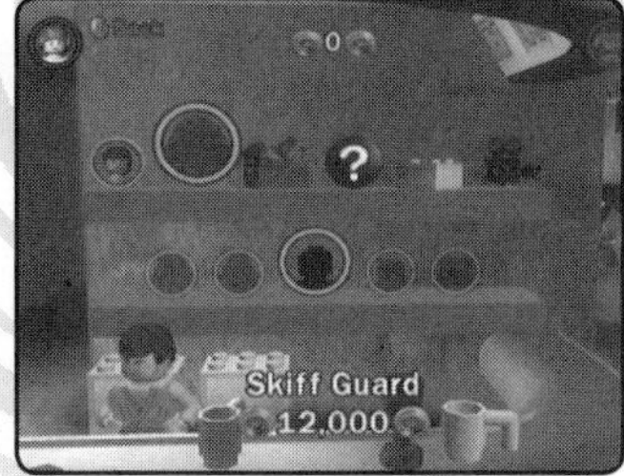

NASCAR 06: Total Team Control

Change Your Name, Change Your Game

Whether you need extra cash or a new level of prestige, it's all about editing your name in NASCAR 06: Total Team Control for Xbox. After you start a driver file and save it in Fight to the Top mode, go to the Main Menu and select the My NASCAR menu. Here you'll see an option to Edit Driver. Select this option and then enter one of these first and last names:

Add $10 million to your budget	Walmart Money
Max out fan level	Super Star
Max out prestige level	MeMyself AndI
Max out team prestige level	All ForOne
Unlock all Chase Plates in Fight to the Top Mode	Gimme Gimme
Unlock Dale Earnhardt Sr.	The Intimidator
Unlock Wal-Mart cars	Walmart Exclusive

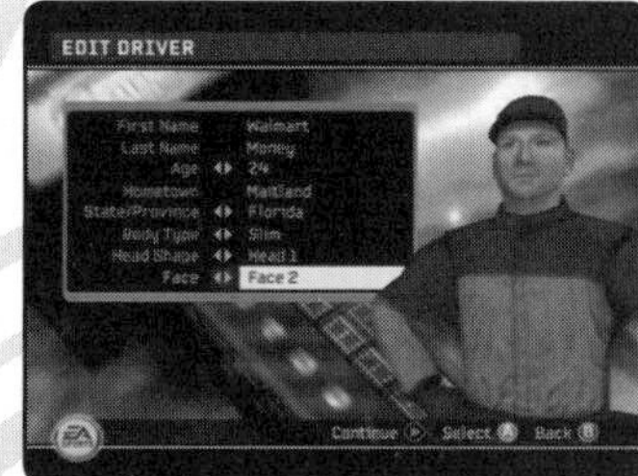

NASCAR 07

Unlockable Bonuses

From the Fight to the Top Main menu, go to My NASCAR and then to Edit Driver. Now rename your driver using the first and last names shown below to unlock various bonuses, including hidden Chase Plates.

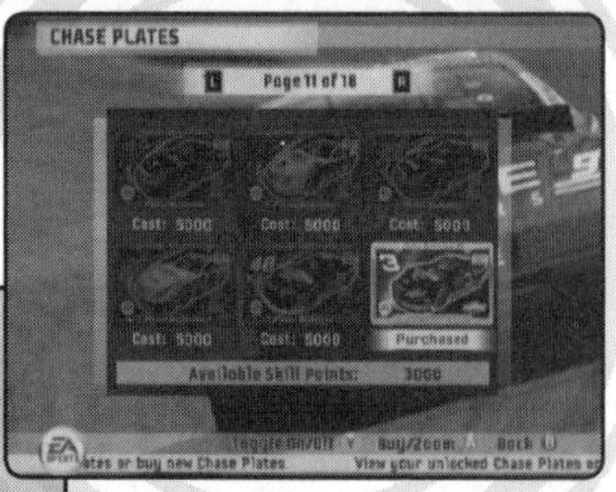

> **Insider Tip**
> The Chase Plates are in an unexpected place in the menu. Go to My NASCAR, then to Skill Points, and then to Chase Plates. Once you unlock the Dale Earnhardt Platinum Chase Plate, he'll be available as a driver in the Season mode.

Bonus	*First Name*	*Last Name*
100% Team Prestige	MoMoney	BlingBling
10,000,000 Fans	AllBow	ToMe
$10,000,000 in the Bank	GiveMe	More
2,000,000 Prestige Points	Outta	MyWay
Dale Earnhardt Platinum Chase Plate	TheMan	InBlack
All Old Spice Chase Plates	KeepCool	SmellGreat
All Chase Plates Except Wal-Mart Plates	ItsAll	ForMe
Wal-Mart No Collision Mode Chase Plate	Walmart	NoCollision
All Other Wal-Mart Chase Plates	Walmart	EveryDay

Pick Up Cheats

From the Main menu, go to the Play It menu, then to Pick Up Game, then select a difficulty level. Now you have the option to enter a name or not. Once you lock in a name, or skip the name entry altogether, you can enter any of the codes below. If you enter a code correctly, you'll hear the "chirp" of a car alarm being set. If not, you'll hear a quiet buzzer sound instead and will need to try again.

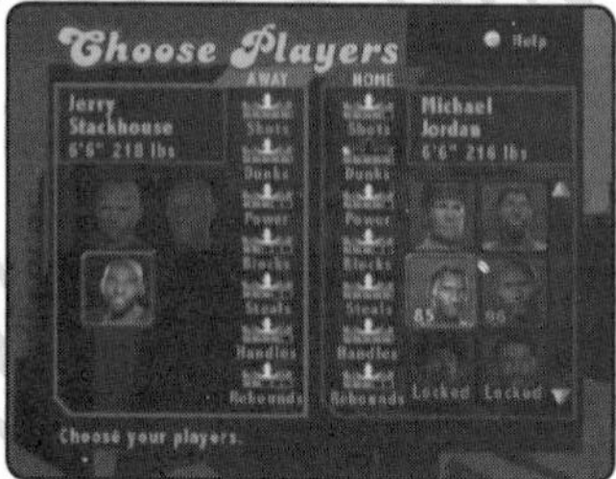

Cheat	*Code*
All Courts	Hold L and press X, Y, Y, X
Ball Trails Always On	Hold L and press Y, Y, Y, X
Exploding Rims	Hold L and press B, B, B, Y
Players Are Small	Hold L and press Y, Y, B, X
Players Have Big Heads	Hold L and press B, X, X, B
No HUD	Hold L and press X, B, B, B
'85 Michael Jordan	Hold L and press B, Y, B, B
More Old School Team Players	Hold L and press B, Y, Y, X
St. Lunatics Team	Hold L and press B, Y, X, Y
Unlimited Turbo	Hold L and press X, X, Y, Y
Easy 2 Pointers	Hold L and press Y, B, X, Y
Hard 2 Pointers	Hold L and press Y, X, B, Y
WNBA Ball	Hold L and press B, Y, Y, B
NBA or ABA Alternate Ball	Hold L and press B, X, B, X
All Jerseys	Hold L and press B, Y, X, X

Insider Tips

The All Jerseys code actually unlocks uniforms for players that you create. From the Main menu, go to My Team, and then to Create a Baller. The '85 Michael Jordan appears on the Old School team roster, but you must use his specific code to unlock him; the More Old School Team Players code does not enable '85 MJ.

NCAA Football 07

Unlockable Pennants

From the Main menu, go to My NCAA, and then to Pennant Collection. Enter the codes below to unlock numbered pennants that represent gameplay cheats, special All-Time teams, and Mascot teams. Unlocked All-Time teams and Mascot teams are available in Play Now mode.

Pennant	***Code***
#16 Baylor (Positional Ratings Boost for this Team)	Sic Em
#63 Illinois (Positional Ratings Boost for this Team)	Oskee Wow
#160 Texas Tech (Positional Ratings Boost for this Team)	Fight
#200 First and Fifteen (Opponent Needs 15 Yards for First Down)	Thanks
#201 Blink (Ref Spots Ball Short for Opponent)	For
#202 Boing (Increase Chance of Opponent Dropping Passes)	Registering
#204 Butter Fingers (Increase Chance of Opponent Fumbles)	With EA
#205 Crossed the Line (You Can Throw Past Line of Scrimmage)	Tiburon
#206 Cuffed (No Fumbles or Interceptions for Your Team)	EA Sports
#207 Extra Credit (Points for Interception or Sack)	Touchdown
#208 Helium (Improves Your Players' Catching Ability)	In The Zone
#209 Hurricane (Improves Your Team's Pass Rush)	Turnover
#210 Instant Replay (You Have Five Downs)	Impact
#211 Jumbalaya (Gives You Points if Your Player is Injured)	Heisman
#212 Molasses (Increases Opponent Fatigue Factor)	Game Time
#213 Nike Free (Improves Ability to Break Tackle)	Break Free
#214 Nike Magnigrip (Increase Your Chance of Intercepting)	Hand Picked
#215 Nike Pro (Improve QB's Passing Accuracy)	No Sweat
#216 Nike Speed TD (Improve Chances of Catching Deep Pass)	Light Speed
#219 QB Dud (Opponent's Passes Are High and Wobbly)	Elite 11
#221 Steel Toe (Increase Kicker's Range)	Gridiron
#222 Stiffed (Doubles Opponent Penalty Yardage)	NCAA
#223 Super Dive (Increase Your Team's Dive Ability)	Upset
#224 Take Your Time (Unlimited Timeouts)	Football
#225 Thread & Needle (Narrows the Uprights for Opponent)	06
#226 Tough As Nails (Your QB is Tough to Sack)	Offense
#227 Trip (Increase Your QB's Chance of Jamming at the Line)	Defense
#228 What a Hit (Increase Chance of Opponent Injury)	Blitz
#229 Kicker Hex (Wind in Your Favor on Field Goals)	Sideline

(continued)

Pennant	*Code*
#273 2004 All-American Team	Fumble
#274 All-Alabama Team	Roll Tide
#276 All-Arkansas Team	Woopigsooie
#277 All-Auburn Team	War Eagle
#278 All-Clemson Team	Death Valley
#279 All-Colorado Team	Glory
#280 All-Florida Team	Great To Be
#281 All-FSU Team	Uprising
#282 All-Georgia Team	Hunker Down
#283 All-Iowa Team	On Iowa
#284 All-Kansas State Team	Victory
#285 All-LSU Team	Geaux Tigers
#286 All-Miami Team	Raising Cane
#287 All-Michigan Team	Go Blue
#288 All-Mississippi State Team	Hail State
#289 All-Nebraska Team	Go Big Red
#290 All-North Carolina Team	Rah Rah
#291 All-Notre Dame Team	Golden Domer
#292 All-Ohio State Team	Killer Nuts
#293 All-Oklahoma Team	Boomer
#294 All-Oklahoma State Team	Go Pokes
#295 All-Oregon Team	Quack Attack
#296 All-Penn State Team	We Are
#297 All-Pittsburgh Team	Lets Go Pitt
#298 All-Purdue Team	Boiler Up
#299 All-Syracuse Team	Orange Crush
#300 All-Tennessee Team	Big Orange
#301 All-Texas Team	Hook Em
#302 All-Texas A&M Team	Gig Em
#303 All-UCLA Team	Mighty
#304 All-USC Team	Fight On
#305 All-Virginia Team	Wahoos
#306 All-Virginia Tech Team	Tech Triumph
#307 All-Washington Team	Bow Down
#308 All-Wisconsin Team	U Rah Rah
#311 Arkansas Mascot Team	Bear Down
#329 Georgia Tech Mascot Team	Ramblin wreck
#333 ISU Mascot Team	Red and Gold
#335 KU Mascot Team	Rock Chalk
#341 Minnesota Mascot Team	Rah Rah Rah
#344 Mizzou Mascot Team	Mizzou Rah
#346 MSU Mascot Team	Go Green
#349 NCSU Mascot Team	Go Pack
#352 NU Mascot Team	Go Cats
#360 S. Carolina Mascot Team	Go Carolina
#371 UK Mascot Team	On On UK
#382 Wake Forest Mascot Team	Go Deacs Go
#385 WSU Mascot Team	All Hail
#386 WVU Mascot Team	Hail WV

NFL Street 2

Unlockable Extras

When you first boot the game, you'll be at the Game Modes screen. Press B to go to the Main menu, select Options, and then Cheats and Codes. Type in a code, highlight OK, and press A (just pressing Start won't confirm the code). To enable a cheat, highlight it in the cheat list and press A. The Fumble Mode code, which affects both teams, is hilarious. See how long it takes you to complete just one play!

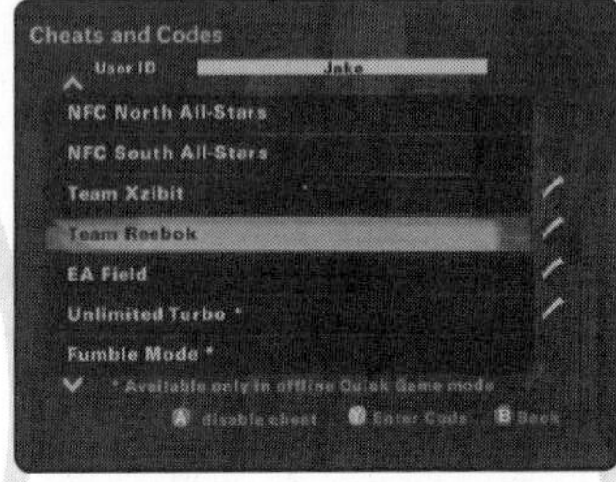

Cheat	*Code*
AFC North All Stars	NAOFRCTH
AFC South All Stars	SAOFUCTH
AFC East All Stars	EAASFSCT
AFC West All Stars	WAEFSCT
NFC North All-Stars	NNAS66784
NFC South All Stars	SNOFUCTH
NFC East All Stars	NNOFRCTH
NFC West All Stars	ENASFSCT
Team Reebok	Reebok
Team Xzibit	TeamXzibit
EA Field	EAField

Offline Quick Game Mode Codes

Cheat	*Code*
Unlimited Turbo	Nozboost
Fumble Mode	GreasedPig
No Fumble Mode	GlueHands
No First Downs	NoChains
10x Gamebreaker bonus	XxGBCraZ
Gargantuan Players	BIGSmash
Players Have Max Catching Stat	MagnetHands

Pinball Hall of Fame

Unlockable Options, Modes, and Cheats

Pinball Hall of Fame features an arcade's worth of legendary tables, including Genie, Black Hole and Tee'd Off, but there are even more classic games to unlock, as well as a host of cheats that can turn anyone into a pinball wizard. From the Main menu, go to the Enter Code screen and type in the following codes. If you enter a code correctly, you'll see a message describing what you've unlocked.

Cheat	*Code*
Unlock the Infinite Last Ball Option	INF
Unlock the Custom Balls Option	BLZ
Unlock the Tilt On/Off Option	NDG
Unlock the Tournament Mode	TMA
Unlock Gottlieb Factory Tour	DGC
Unlock the Play-Boy Machine	PKR
Unlock Payout Mode	LAS
Unlock the Love Meter Machine	LUV
Unlock the Xolten Machine	XTN

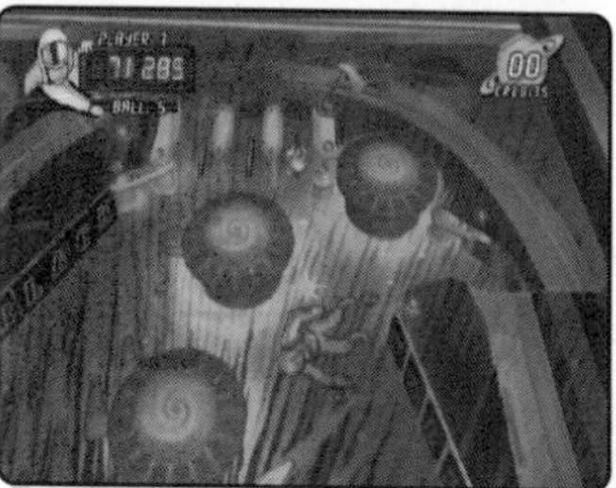

The Play-Boy machine is not actually a pinball table, but is more like a Japanese game called pachinko. The object is to guide the ball into different holes that are each worth a certain amount of points.

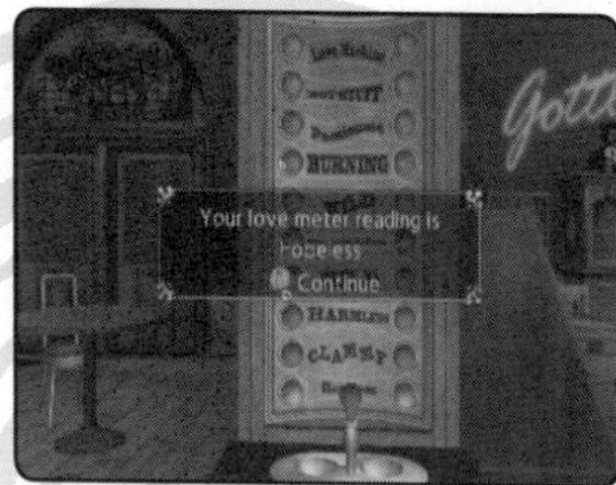

The fortune-telling Xolten machine and the Love Meter machine ("Are You Hot Stuff or Hopeless?") are both electronic versions of classic carnival games.

Insider Tip

Once you enable the Infinite Last Ball, Custom Balls, and Tilt On/Off cheats, go to the Options screen to turn them on and off.

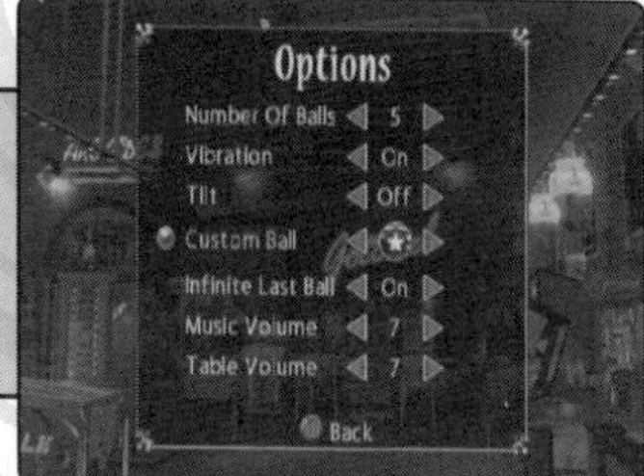

Rallisport Challenge 2

Unlockable Cars and Tracks

The following codes unlock all the bonus cars and tracks in Time Attack, Single Race, and Multiplayer modes. From the Main menu, go to the Options menu, and then to the Credits screen. While the credits play, use the directional pad to enter the codes below. Enter the codes quickly but firmly. If you enter them correctly, you'll hear a very faint musical tone. Even if you enable all the codes, there are still dozens more cars, skins (paint jobs), and events to unlock in Career mode.

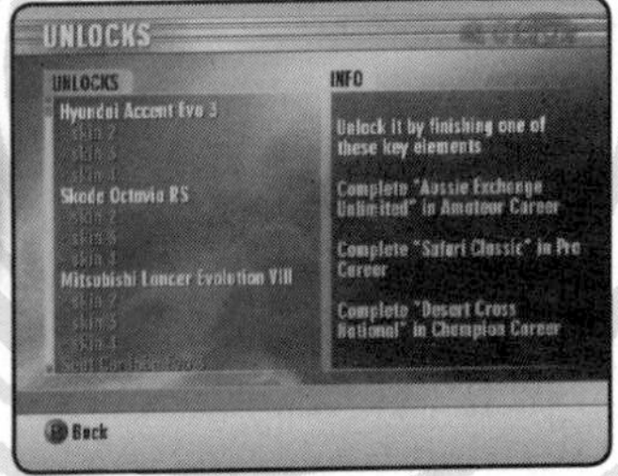

Cheat	*Code*
Cars and Tracks Set 1	Down, Left, Down, Right, Up, Up
Cars and Tracks Set 2	Left, Left, Down, Down, Right, Right
Cars and Tracks Set 3	Down, Down, Left, Left, Up, Down
Cars and Tracks Set 4	Right, Down, Right, Down, Left, Up
Cars and Tracks Set 5	Left, Left, Right, Right, Down, Left
Cars and Tracks Set 6	Right, Up, Up, Up, Down, Left
Cars and Tracks Set 7	Left, Left, Left, Up, Up, Right
Cars and Tracks Set 8	Right, Up, Left, Up, Down, Right
Cars and Tracks Set 9	Down, Up, Down, Left, Left, Down
Cars and Tracks Set 10	Up, Up, Down, Down, Left, Right

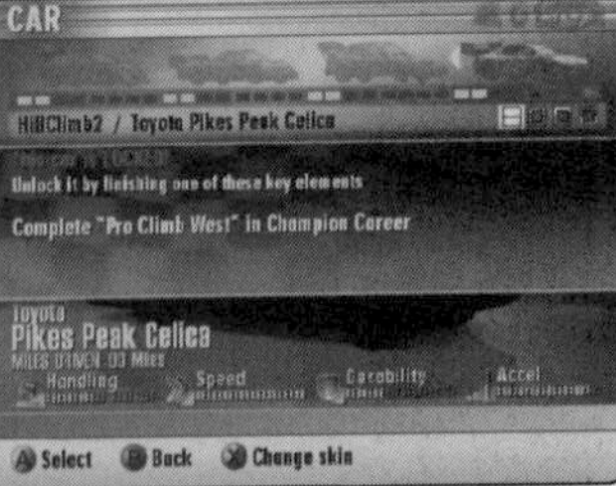

Insider Tip

If you exit the Main menu and go back to the Select Profile screen or the Start screen, your codes will be disabled, and you'll have to enter them again. The cars and events you've unlocked through normal play, however, will remain unlocked.

Shark Tale

Change Pearls Into Coins
After you save your furniture in the eviction stage, you can enter this code and convert the pearls to coins. Press the BACK button (Left Arrow button) to pause the game and then hold the Left Trigger Button as you enter the following code: X, A, X, X, X, A, X, X

Now let go of the Left Trigger button and you'll see a message that confirms that you entered the cheat correctly.

Flying Fish and Other Foes
You can enter this code after you save your furniture in the eviction stage. Press the BACK button (Left Arrow button) to pause the game and then hold the Left Trigger button as you enter the following code: X, X, X, X, A, X, X, X, X

If you touch a fish or other obstacle on the street, they'll fly off the screen. You'll still take damage from certain foes, though, so be careful!

Insider Tip
You can also disable these codes by pressing the BACK button a second time during the game and entering the same code again.

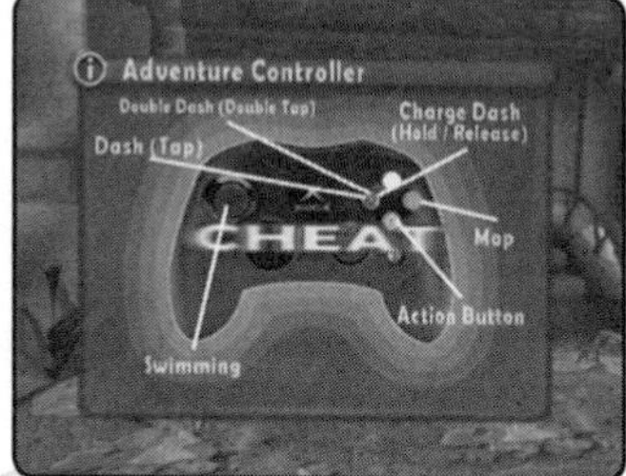

Sonic Heroes

Give Your Character a Metallic Skin
When setting up a two-player game, after you select your stage, have one player hold the A and Y buttons until the stage begins. Player One's team will be covered in a metallic skin for the duration of the stage. It doesn't matter which player performs the code, Player One's team will always be the one affected.

Insider Tip
If both players perform the code, it won't work.

SpongeBob SquarePants: Lights, Camera, PANTS!

Unlock Silver Story Mode Auditions

This code doesn't unlock the Silver Story Challenge in Story Mode play, but it does allow you to play all the Silver Story auditions in Single Audition mode. First go to the Bonuses menu, then the Rewards menu, and then to the Codes screen. Enter 486739 as your code. Now immediately go to the Single Audition menu to find all the Silver Story auditions, like Surf Resc-Goo, Inflatable Pants, and Rope Burn. If you go to any other menu, the code will be disabled and you'll have to enter it again.

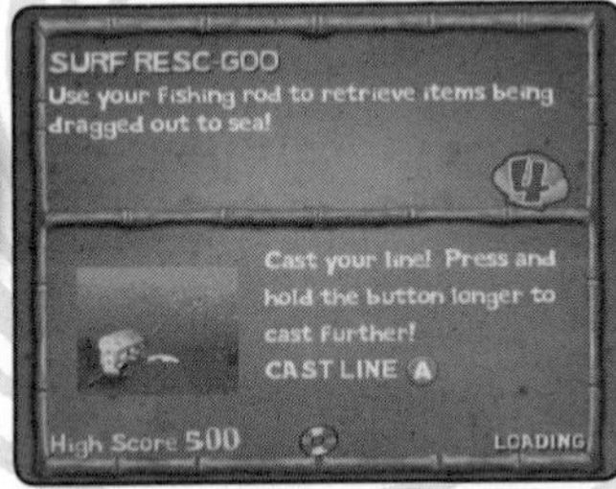

All Action Figures

You must normally complete Story Mode challenges to unlock the action figures, but if you enter 977548 on the Code screen, you'll be able to gaze upon the likes of Bubble Bass, Man Ray, and the The Big Gold SpongeBob himself.

Unlock Hook, Line & Cheddar Audition

One audition that is not included in the Silver Story code is Hook, Line & Cheddar. First go to the Bonuses menu, then the Rewards menu, and then to the Codes screen. Enter 893634 as your code. Now immediately go to the Single Audition menu to play this audition. If you go to any other menu, the code will be disabled and you'll have to enter it again.

Unleash the Hidden Riders

Enter the following codes at the Enter Cheats feature on the Options menu (press the Y Button to access Options) to unlock new riders.

Cheat	Code
Brodi	zenmaster
Bunny San	wheresyourtail
Canhuck	greatwhitenorth
Churchill	tankengine
Cudmore	milkemdaisy
Eddie	worm
Gutless	boneyardreject
Hiro	slicksuit
Jurgen	brokenleg
Luther	bronco
Marty	back2future
NW Legend	callhimgeorge
Snowballs	betyouveneverseen
Stretch	windmilldunk
Svelte Luther	notsosvelte
Unknown Rider	finallymadeitin

If you enter a code incorrectly, you'll hear a flat "buzz" sound instead of the higher tone that you hear when you choose a game function.

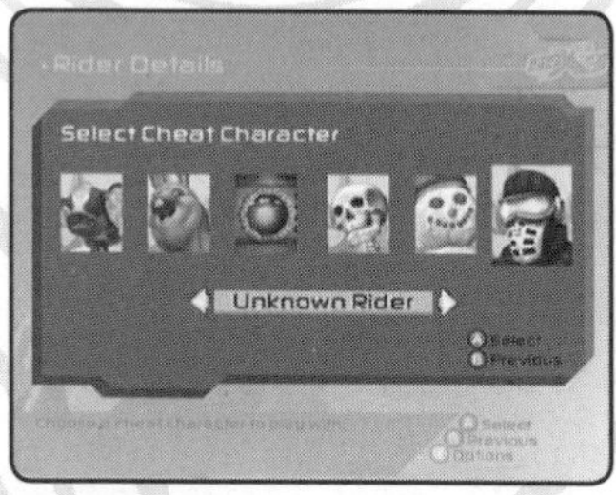

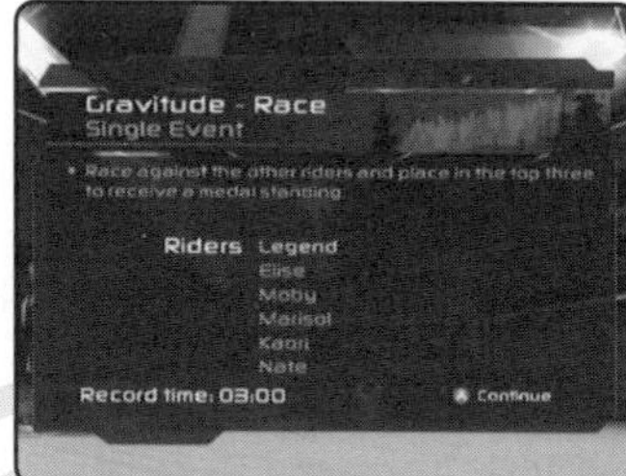

A Hidden Stash of Backcountry Gear

Enter the following codes at the Enter Cheats feature in the Options menu and you can find all kinds of cool stuff.

Cheat	Code
Access All Peaks	biggerthank7
All Game Art	naturalconcept
All Music Tracks	djsuperstar
All Peak 1 Gear	shoppingspree
All Posters	postnobills
All Snowboards	graphicdelight
All Toys	nogluerequired
All Trading Cards	gotitgotitneedit
All Videos	myeyesaredim

Teenage Mutant Ninja Turtles

Power-Up Passwords

To enable the cheats below, start off at the Main menu, then go to the Options menu, and then to the Password screen. If you enter a password correctly, you'll see a confirmation message.

Cheat	*Password*
Enable Splinter in Story Mode	LLMSR
Donatello Alternate Costume	SRSMM
Donatello Defense Increase	LLSMR
Leonardo Alternate Costume	RMMLL
Leonardo Defense Increase	MLLSR
Michelangelo Alternate Costume	DLDSM
Michelangelo Defense Increase	MRLLD
Raphael Alternate Costume	LMSDD
Raphael Defense Increase	LSMDR
Playmates Toys Database	LSDRM
Unlimited Shuriken for Leonardo	MSSRD
Unlimited Explosive Shuriken for Michelangelo	MRRSL

To begin a game with a Turtle in an alternate costume, enter the code, highlight the appropriate Turtle on the Character Select screen, hold L or R, and press Start.

When a Defense Increase code is enabled, the trailing ends of that Turtle's mask become shorter.

Insider Tip

If you exit your game, any active Defense Increase codes are disabled. You must enter them again before you reload your game.

If you set your Xbox system date to December 25th or October 31st, your Turtle will wear a holiday mask.

Unlock All Attractions

To unlock all attractions, press X, B, Y, X, B, Y, and Y during normal gameplay. Now you'll be able to build any carnival rides, coasters, race tracks, games, or stalls you wish…but you'll still have to pick and choose wisely!

Cash Cow Code

Here's a way to rake in the dough without breaking a sweat. Stand off to the side of the crowd (accidentally starting a conversation will block any code), and press X, B, Y, X, B, Y, and A.

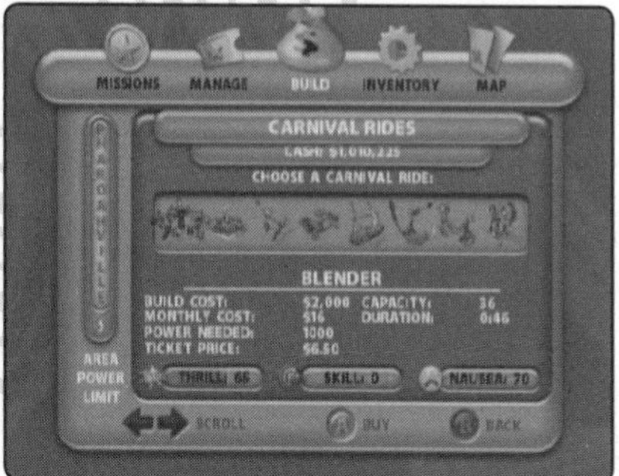

Repeat the Cash Cow Code as many times as you like. You can start any park with as much money as you want.

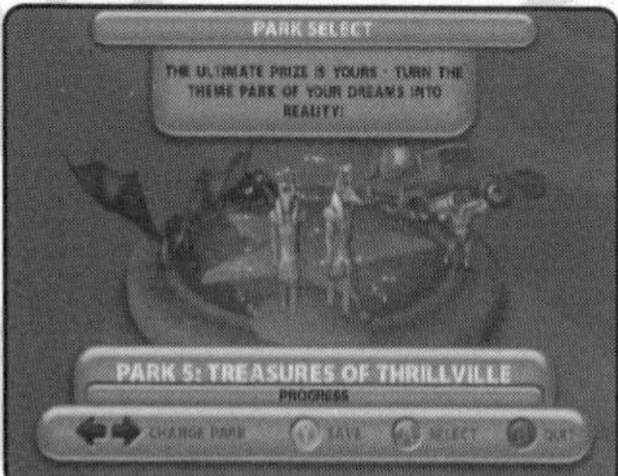

Unlock All Parks

If you'd like to skip ahead to any of the more advanced parks, press X, B, Y, X, B, Y, and X during normal gameplay. Now pause your game and go to the Park Select option.

Be sure to save your game before you proceed to the Park Select menu, or you'll lose all progress since your last save.

> **Insider Tip**
> Enter all Thrillville codes while you're walking around your park. You don't have to enter them quickly, but you have to enter them firmly.

Ty the Tasmanian Tiger 2: Bush Rescue

Unlockable Boomerangs
Normally you begin your Australian bush adventure with just a plain ol' wooden boomerang. During your game, press Start, Start, Y, Start, Start, Y, B, X, B, X to unlock the first eight boomerangs, including the standard boomerang, the Megarang, the Frostyrang, the Zappyrang, the Flamerang, the Smasharang, the Lasharang, and the Infrarang.

As if that arsenal wasn't impressive enough, you can press Start, Start, Y, Start, Start, Y, X, B, X, Y to unlock the next ten boomerangs, including the Multirang, the Omegarang, the Freezerang, the Deadlyrang, the Thunderang, the Lavarang, the Kaboomerang, the Warperang, the X-rang, and the Doomerang.

In either case, if you enter the code correctly, you'll hear a guitar strum. To select a boomerang, hold the Y button and use the left joystick to highlight the boomerang of your choice.

Unlockable Bunyip Keys
To save you the trouble of recovering the four Bunyip Keys, press Start, Start, Y, Start, Start, Y, X, B, X, A anytime during normal gameplay (while you're just walking around, not while the game is paused). If you enter the code correctly, you'll hear a guitar strum. Now check your inventory to see the Bunyip Key slots filled in.

(continued)

Ty the Tasmanian Tiger 2: Bush Rescue (cont.)

Point Out All Objects
If you press Start, Start, Y, Start, Start, Y, Up, Down, Left, Right during your game, all collectible objects will now be marked with a red glow and a red line stretching up toward the sky. It looks strange, but it comes in handy when you're looking for some of the treasures scattered around the outback.

Extra Opals
You'll never be strapped for cash if you press Start, Start, Y, Start, Start, Y, B, A, B, A during your game. In fact, every time you repeat this code, you'll be awarded 100,000 opals.

Ty the Tasmanian Tiger 3: Night of the Quinkan

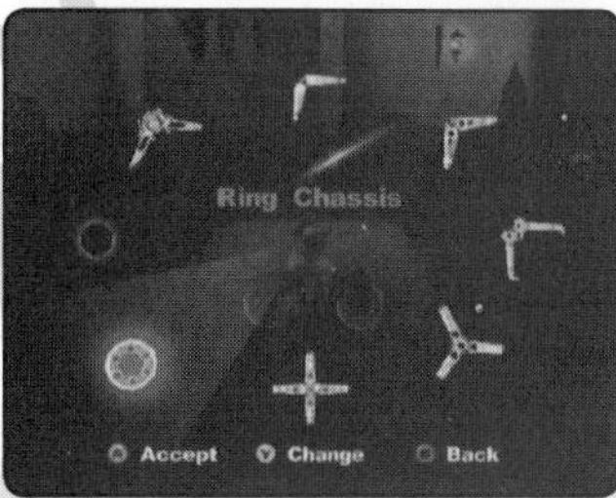

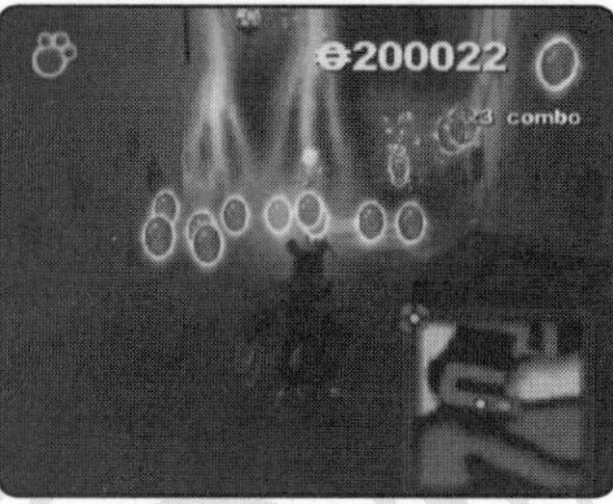

Unlockable Boomerangs
Ty returns Down Under with a new type of boomerang weapon that packs more punch than ever. During your game, press Start, Start, Y, Start, Start, Y, B, X, B, X to unlock the following eight boomerangs: Mono Chassis, Duo Chassis, Lash Chassis, Mega Chassis, Smash Chassis, Ring Chassis, Shadow Chassis, and Doom Chassis.

Extra Opals
For an instant payday, press Start, Start, Y, Start, Start, Y, B, A, B, A during your game. If you enter the code correctly, you'll be awarded 100,000 opals.

Insider Tip
If you push the number of opals too high, you might cause problems with the opal counter or other parts of the game. Best to use repeatable codes like this one only a few times, just in case.

Bratz: Forever Diamondz

Extra Blingz, Gift Sets, and More

Before you'll be able to scoop up some free blingz, you'll have to make it through the tutorial tasks and then return to the Bratz office. Once there, access the Cheat Computer to enter the following codes. If you enter a code correctly, you'll see a confirmation message.

Cheat	*Code*
1000 Blingz and Some Bonus Items	SIZZLN
2000 Blingz	FLAUNT
Gift Set A	STYLIN
Gift Set B	SKATIN
Gift Set C	JEWELZ
Gift Set E	DIMNDZ
Pet Treats	TREATZ

Insider Tip
These codes can only be used once, so don't get greedy!

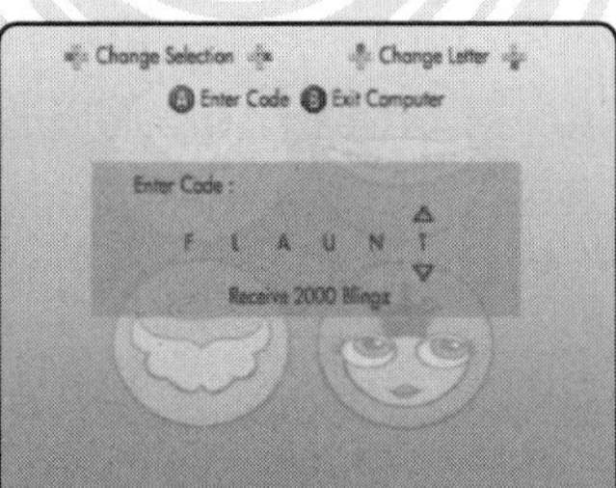

Bust-A-Move 3000

Unlock Another World of Puzzle Fun

To unlock hidden puzzle zones, press Y, Left, Right, Y on the Title screen. If you enter the code correctly, you'll hear a musical tone, and an icon labeled "Another World" will appear in the upper right corner of the screen. Now you'll have additional zones in Puzzle mode to challenge your mind and your thumbs. If you exit or lose a game, you'll be sent back to the Title screen, where you'll have to enter the code again.

Unlock Secret Characters

To unlock the hidden characters Fungila and Katze, press Y, Right, Left, Y on the Title screen. If you enter the code correctly, you'll hear a musical tone, and an icon labeled "Secret Characters" will appear in the upper left corner of the screen. Fungila and Katze will be available in all play modes, including Multiplayer. Unlike the "Another World" code, if you exit or lose a game, you won't lose access to Fungila and Katze.

(continued)

Bust-A-Move 3000 (cont.)

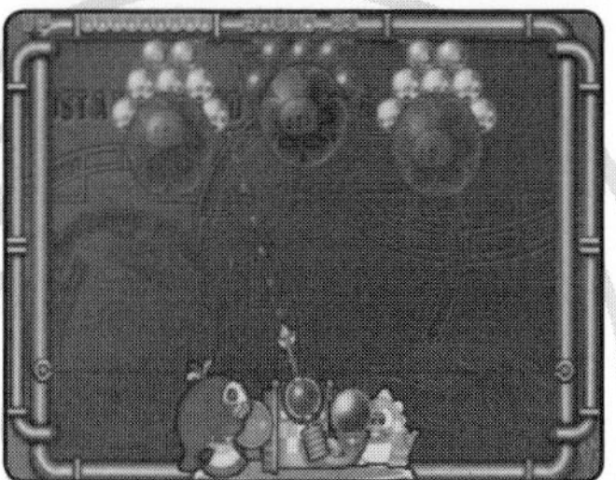

Insider Tip
You can use both the "Another World" and "Secret Characters" codes at the same time!

Codename: Kids Next Door: Operation V.I.D.E.O.G.A.M.E.

Invisibility Mode
To unlock Invisibility Mode, you must first create or load a saved game. Next, from the Main menu, go to the Top Secret screen, highlight the Invisibility option and press Y. Instead of entering numbers or letters, you must use the directional pad to select pictures of the Kids Next Door characters. In case you don't know their names, follow this handy guide, entering the codes from left to right:

Square 1: Do not change the picture
Square 2: Press Down four times
Square 3: Do not change the picture
Square 4: Press Down four times
Square 5: Press Down three times
Square 6: Press Down twice

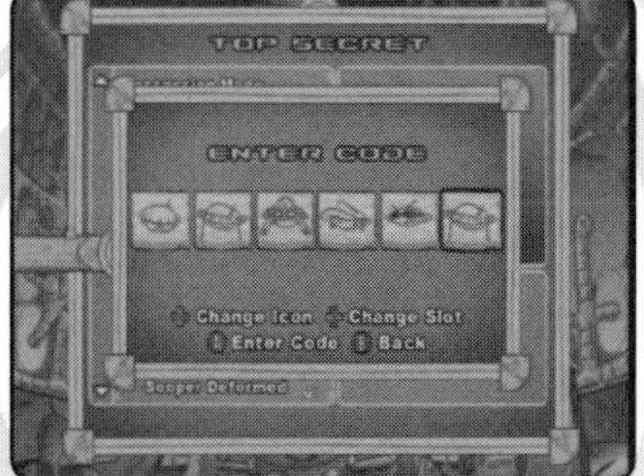

Invincibility Mode
To unlock Invincibility mode, go to the Top Secret screen, highlight the Invincibility option, and press Y. Now highlight each picture and enter the following code, from left to right:

Square 1: Press Down three times
Square 2: Press Down twice
Square 3: Press Down once
Square 4: Press Down four times
Square 5: Do not change the picture
Square 6: Press Down twice

Disney's Extreme Skate Adventure

Unlockable Tricks and Toons

From the Main menu, go to the Options menu and then to the Cheat Codes screen. Type in a code, highlight Done and press A. If you enter a code correctly, you'll hear a musical tone.

Cheat	*Code*
Unlock all skaters	entourage
Unlock all levels	ambassador
Unlock all Create-a-Skater items	trendytrickster
Unlock Lion King video	savannah
Unlock Tarzan video	nugget
Unlock Toy Story video	marin

To access the Create-a-Skater items, begin a game, select one of the kid characters (not a cartoon character), and then go to the Create-a-Skater menu.

Using Create-a-Skater, you can customize your character's clothing and deck, and even put on some face paint.

FIFA Street

Unlockable Clothing and Eyewear

Go to the Main menu and enter the following code:
Hold L and Y then press Right, Right, Left, Up, Up, Up, Down, and then Left.

Now when you go to the Create Player menu you can select Kit and choose from all the stuff that was previously locked up.

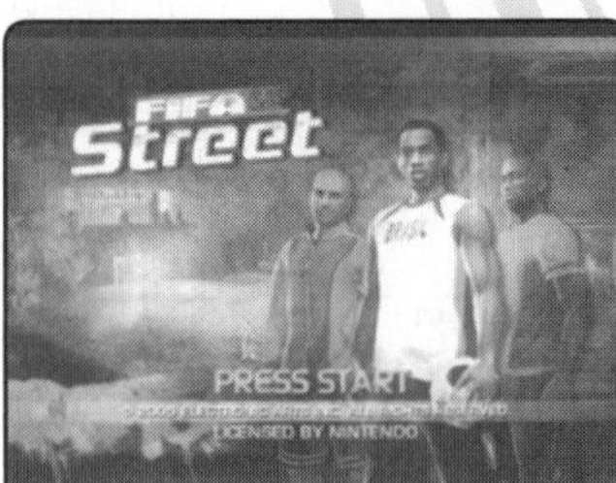

F-Zero GX

Unlock Extra Music: Mute City
From the Main menu, go to Customize, then to the F-Zero Shop screen. Using the directional pad, press X, X, X, Y, X, X, X, Y, Z, Z, Left, Right, Left, Right, Left, Right. If you enter the code correctly, you'll hear a musical tone. Now enter the Items screen to find the Sounds of Mute City soundtrack on sale for 99 tickets. You can switch to this soundtrack on any Mute City course.

Unlock Extra Music: Big Blue
If the Big Blue tracks are more your speed, follow the same instructions above, but enter Z, Left, Right, Left, Z, Y, X, Z, Left, Right, Left, Right, Z, X, Z, X, Z as your code instead. This will put the Sounds of Big Blue soundtrack on sale for 99 tickets. As you'd expect, these tunes are available on any Big Blue area course.

Harvest Moon: Another Wonderful Life

A Bumper Crop of Bonuses
Do you feel lucky? That's good, because you can never be sure what you're going to get with this secret code! Begin or load a game and then plug an extra controller into the third port on your GameCube. If you don't have an extra controller, temporarily remove the controller in your first port and put it in the third port. While the game is running, press the Z Button on the third controller and you should get a bunch of random tools and other items that you can sell or keep.

Insider Tip
If you don't like the items that you earned, you can enter this trick again for different stuff. This will also work on the Wii, but the extra controller must be in the third port!

Harvest Moon: Magical Melody

Giving the Right Gifts Makes Friendship and Marriage Easy!
Knowing the right gifts for the right people can get you ahead fast in Harvest Moon: Magical Melody. Listed below are the most favorite and some favorite items prized by villagers, bachelors and bachelorettes in the game:

Ann	Corn, Good Eggs
Alex	Herbs, Fertilized Turnips, Vegetable Juice
Basil	Herbs, Herb Tea, Tomato Juice, Fertilized Strawberries
Blue	Cheese, Eggs, Eggplants
Bob	Boiled Eggs, Eggplants, Special Eggs
Carl	Herb Tea, Special Milk
Dan	Sodas, Strawberries, Very Berry Jam
Dia	Blueberries and Blueberry Jam, Moondrop Flowers, Strawberries
Doug	Corn, Fertilized Carrots, Fertilized Green Peppers
Duke	Boiled Eggs, Grapes, Grape Sodas, Special Eggs
Ellen	Cocoa, Special Eggs, Fertilized Breadfruits
Eve	Apples, Fertilized Strawberries, Strawberries, Wine
Gina	Blueberries, Eggs of all types, Shiny Wool
Gourmet	Truffles and Truffle Sautes
Gwen	Blueberries, Fertilized Carrots, Shiny Wool, Very Berry Jam
Hank	Apple Sodas, Fertilized Turnips, Grape Sodas
Henry	Apples, Fertilized Carrots, Grapes
Jamie	Blueberry Jam, Special Milk, Strawberry Jam, Very Berry Jam
Joe	Corn, most fish, Special Eggs
Katie	Diamond Rings, Special Eggs, Very Berries, Yams
Kurt	Herb Tea, Gold, Wood
Liz	Eggplants, Purple Balms, Yams
Louis	Moonstones, Special Eggs
Lyla	Fertilized Pumpkins, Pink Balm, Pink Cat flowers, Pumpkin Puddings
Maria	Stewed Potatoes, Stewed Yams, Tomato Soup
Martha	Cocoa, Fertilized Breadfruits, Yarn
Mayor	Ores, most foods, both cooked and uncooked
Meryl	Boiled Eggs, Fertilized Tomatoes, Puddings, Special Eggs
Michael	Copper Ores, Fertilized Onions, Fertilized Potatoes, Special Milk
Nami	Fertilized Tomatoes, Special Cheese, Tomato Juice
Nina	Pink Balm, Orange Juice, Strawberries
Ray	Boiled Eggs, Fertilized Onions, Moonstones, most fish, Special Eggs
Ronald	Grapes and Sodas
Saibara	Good Clays, Pickled Turnips, Sashimi
Tai	Fertilized Eggplant, Fertilized Spinach, Special Milk, Rare Ores
Terry	Fertilized Cabbage, Fish, Good Eggs, Mushrooms
Theodore	Fertilized Potatoes, Stewed Potatoes, Stewed Yams
Tim	Boiled Eggs, Chestnuts, Copper Ores, Special Eggs
Woody	Boiled Eggs, Pickled Turnips

LEGO Star Wars

Unlockable Extras

Go up to the counter in Dexter's Diner and use the Enter Code screen to type in these passwords. Some passwords unlock cheats that can be used during any game mode, while others unlock characters that can be purchased in Dexter's Diner and used in Free Play (replay) mode. To turn gameplay cheats on and off, pause your game and go to the Extras menu.

Some gameplay cheats, such as Moustaches and Silly Blasters, are just for fun…

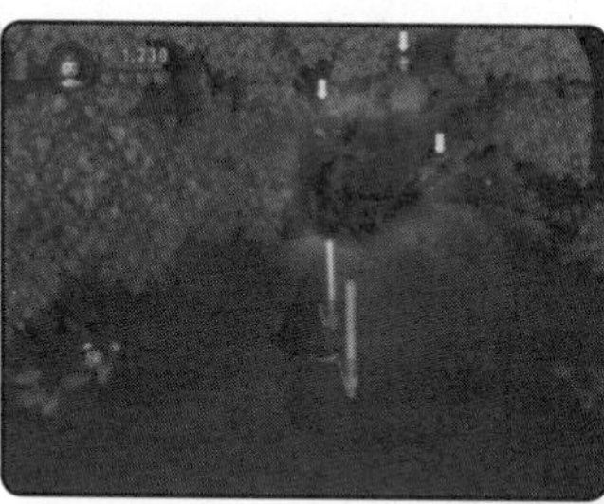

…while others, such as the Minikit Detector that points out hidden Minikits, are very useful.

Cheat	*Code*
Big Blasters	IG72X4
Brushes	SHRUB1
Classic Blasters	L449HD
Invincibility	4PR28U
Minikit Detector	LD116B
Moustaches	RP924W
Purple	YD77GC
Silhouettes	MS999Q
Silly Blasters	NR37W1
Tea Cups	PUCEAT
Battle Droid	987UYR
Battle Droid (Commander)	EN11K5
Battle Droid (Geonosis)	LK42U6
Battle Droid (Security)	KF999A
Boba Fett	LA811Y
Clone	F8B4L6
Clone (Episode III)	ER33JN
Clone (Episode III Pilot)	BHU72T
Clone (Episode III Swamp)	N3T6P8
Clone (Episode III Walker)	RS6E25
Count Dooku	14PGMN
Darth Maul	H35TUX
Darth Sidious	A32CAM
Disguised Clone	VR832U
Droideka	DH382U
General Grievous	SF321Y
Genosian	19D7NB

Cheat	*Code*
Grievous's Bodyguard	ZTY392
Gonk Droid	U63B2A
Jango Fett	PL47NH
Ki-Adi Mundi	DP55MV
Kit Fisto	CBR954
Luminara	A725X4
Mace Windu (Episode III)	MS952L
Padme	92UJ7D
PK Droid	R840JU
Princess Leia	BEQ82H
Rebel Trooper	L54YUK
Royal Guard	PP43JX
Shaak Ti	EUW862
Super Battle Droid	XZNR21

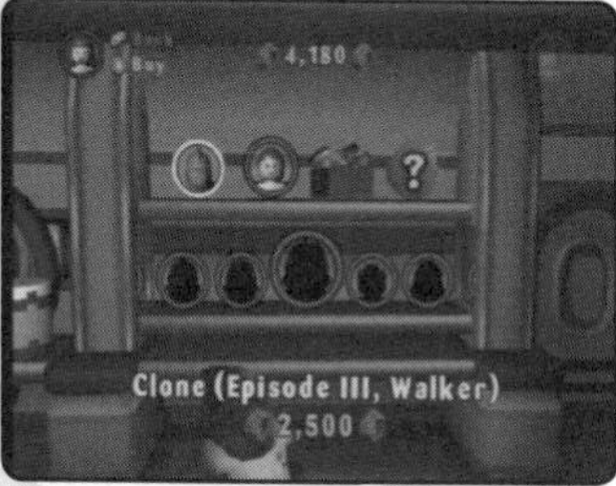

Wii Xbox 360 Xbox GC PS3 PS2 DS GBA PSP

Looney Tunes: Back in Action

ACME Bonus Items

The Main menu of Looney Tunes: Back in Action is unlike most; instead of pressing a button to go to the Options menu, you have to walk to the right to switch screens. Once there, you can access the Cheat Codes screen.

Cheat	*Code*
Unlock All Areas	PASSPORT
$500 Bonus	AMUNKEY
Invincibility	TOUGHAGE
Cannon Ball Costume	CANNON
Danger Duck Costume	DANGERD
Duck Danger Level	OUTTAKE
Fast and Furry-ous Bonus Challenges	FURRYOUS

Cheat	*Code*
Hen Grenades	HENSAWAY
ACME Shrink Ray	WEENY
Slappy Fish	SLAPPY
Free Costume Doors	SUITSYOU
Reveals Gossamer Doors in Warner Bros. Studios	GOBBLE

Be warned that the Invincibility code won't save you from some kinds of environmental hazards, such as walking out into traffic.

When using the Passport cheat to access all levels, the Checkpoints will not work, and no progress will be saved.

To access the Calling Duck Danger level in Warner Bros. Studios, first enter the code, begin a game, make at least one checkpoint save, exit, and then reload the save file.

Once you enter the Fast and Furry-ous Bonus Challenge code, the challenges stages appear at the end of each world.

Insider Tip

Some codes will disable other codes, even if they don't affect the same type of thing. For example, the Hen Grenades code disables the Danger Duck Costume code, and any special weapon code will disable any previous special weapon code.

Madden NFL 2005

Madden Card Codes

At the Main menu, select My Madden and then choose Madden Cards and go to the Madden Codes section on the menu. Now carefully enter the following codes (everything should be UPPERCASE), and there are no zeros—just letter Os!

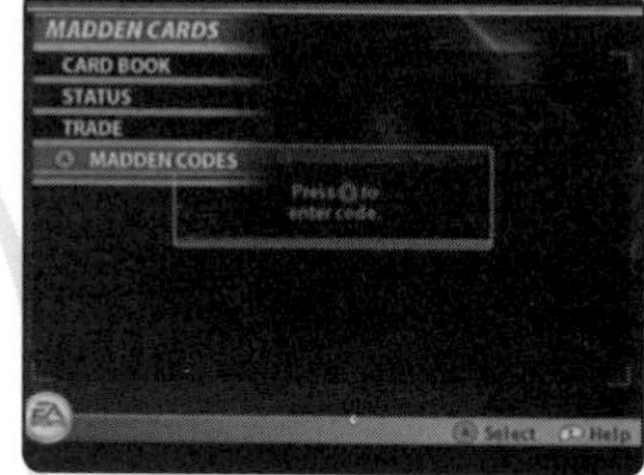

Cheat	*Code*
You rival gets three downs, not four	Z28X8K
You get five downs	P66C4L
Unlocks the Aloha Bowl stadium	G67F5X
Increases your chances for a defensive interception by 75%	J33IBF
Unlimited passing range	B61A8M
Unlimited field goal kicking range	I76X3T
You earn four award points per interception, nine points per sack	M89S8G
Your opponent must move the ball 15 yards for a first down	V65J8P
You just need five yards for a first down	O72E9B
Increase your opponent's fumble chances by 75%	R14B8Z
Increase your chance to break a tackle by 75%	L96J7P
Your opponent's QB throws lob passes	D57R5S
You can't fumble or throw an interception	X78P9Z
Your QB can't be sacked	Y59R8R
Increase the dive distance on your team by 75%	D59K3Y
Narrow the uprights for your opponent	V34L6D
Your opponent will fumble if he jukes during the half	L48G1E

Super Bowl Dreams and Legendary Teams

At the Main menu, select My Madden and then choose Madden Cards and go to the Madden Codes section on the menu. Now carefully enter the following codes (everything should be UPPERCASE), and there are no zeros—just letter Os! If you enter an incorrect code, go back and check it against the following codes:

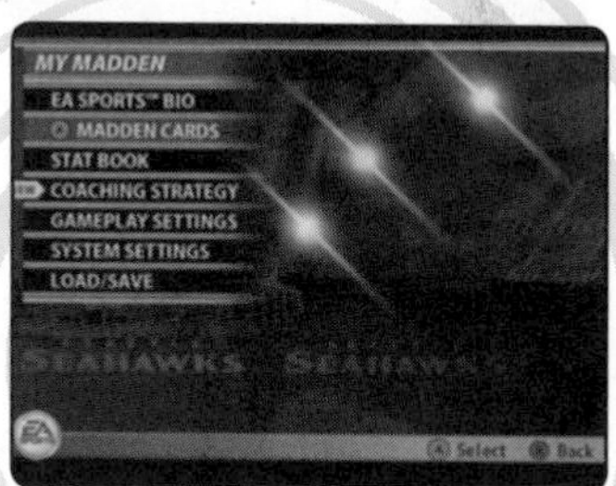

Cheat	*Code*
Unlock Super Bowl XXXIX Stadium (Jacksonville)	D58F1B
Unlock Super Bowl XL Stadium (Detroit)	O85P6I
Unlock Super Bowl XLI Stadium (Miami)	P48Z4D
Unlock Super Bowl XLII Stadium (Phoenix)	T67R1O
Unlock the 1958 Colts team	P74X8J
Unlock the 1966 Packers team	G49P7W
Unlock the 1968 Jets team	C24W2A
Unlock the 1970 Browns team	G12N1I

(continued)

Madden NFL 2005 (cont.)

Cheat	Code
Unlock the 1972 Dolphins team	R79W6W
Unlock the 1974 Steelers team	R12D9B
Unlock the 1976 Raiders team	P96Q8M
Unlock the 1978 Dolphins team	G97U5X
Unlock the 1980 Raiders team	K71K4E
Unlock the 1981 Chargers team	Y27N9A
Unlock the 1982 Redskins team	F56D6V
Unlock the 1983 Raiders team	D23T8S

Cheat	Code
Unlock the 1984 Dolphins team	X23Z8H
Unlock the 1985 Bears team	F92M8M
Unlock the 1986 Giants team	K44F2Y
Unlock the 1988 '49ers team	F77R8H
Unlock the 1990 Eagles team	G95F2Q
Unlock the 1991 Lions team	I89F4I
Unlock the 1992 Cowboys team	I44A1O
Unlock the 1993 Bills team	Y66K3O
Unlock the 1977 Broncos team	O18T2A

Madden NFL 07

Madden Card Codes

At the Main menu, select My Madden and then choose Madden Cards and go to the Madden Codes section on the menu. Now carefully enter the following codes (everything should be UPPERCASE), and mind your zeros and letter Os!

Cheat	Code
You won't make a mistake—no interceptions or fumbles	XL7SP1
Your QB is on target and he'll enjoy 100% accuracy!	WROA0R
Lame Duck Card—the other team will lob passes for a half!	5LAWO0

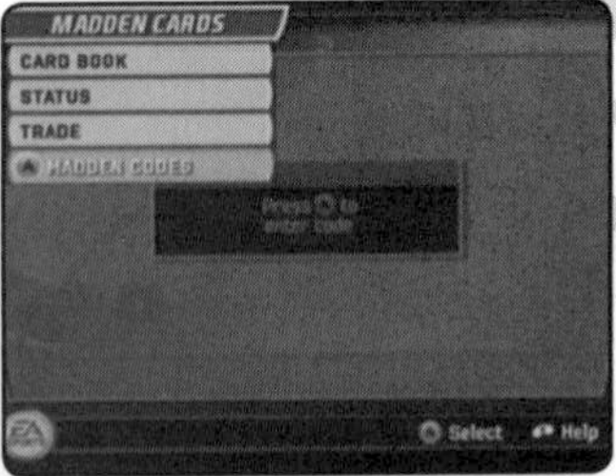

Mario Power Tennis

Unlock Event Games Mode
To unlock the multiplayer Event Games mode, hold the Z Button at the Mario Power Tennis title screen and then press Start.

Insider Tip
Try pressing A or B as your rival hits the ball and your character should tease them a bit.

Mega Man Anniversary Collection

Mega Passwords
To use these passwords, first go to the Main menu of the appropriate game and then go to the Password screen. Now place glowing spheres in the appropriate spaces in the grid to form the password. Some games use two colors of spheres, while others use only one.

Mega Man 2 Passwords

Cheat	*Password*
All Energy Tanks	A5, B1, B3, C4, D2, D3, E1, E4, E5
All Energy Tanks, Four Bosses Defeated	A5, B2, C4, C5, D3, D4, D5, E4, E5
All Energy Tanks, at Dr. Wily's Castle	A5, B2, B4, C1, C3, C5, D4, D5, E2

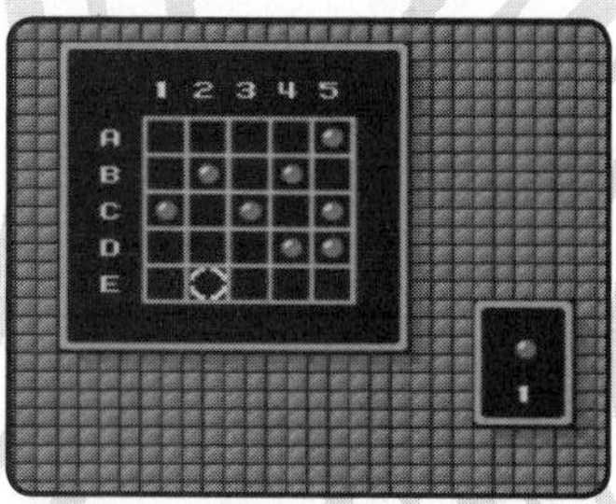

Highlight a space and press A to place a sphere. Highlight a sphere and press B to remove it from the grid.

Mega Man 3 Passwords

Cheat	*Password*
All Energy Tanks, Beginning of the Game	Red or Blue: A6
All Energy Tanks, First 8 Bosses Defeated	Red: A6 - Blue: A3, B5, D3, F4
All Tanks, at Dr. Wily's Castle	Red: A6, E1 - Blue: A1, A3, B2, B5, D3, F4

(continued)

Mega Man Anniversary Collection (cont.)

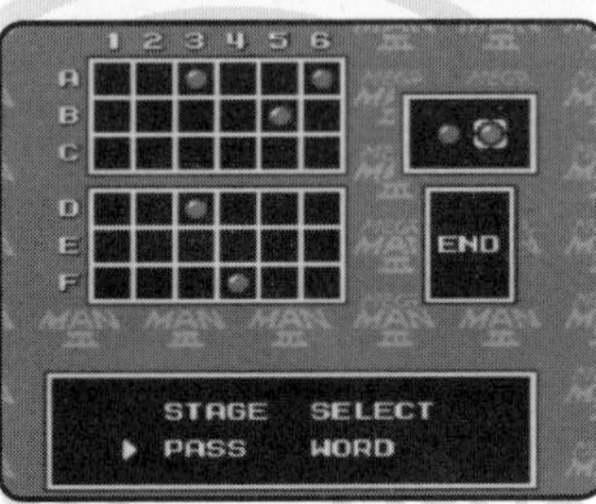

Highlight a color and press A. Now highlight a space in the grid and press A to place or remove a sphere. Press B to exit the grid.

Mega Man 4 passwords

Cheat	*Password*
No Tanks, Both Adaptors, Beginning of the Game	A2, A3, A5, B2, D1, F3
No Tanks, Both Adaptors, Pharaoh Man Defeated	A2, A5, B3, B4, D1, F3
No Tanks, No Adaptors, Dr. Cossack's Citadel	A1, A4, B5, E2, E3, E4
No Tanks, All Weapons, Dr. Cossack's Citadel	A1, A4, B5, E2, F1, F3

Mega Man 5 Passwords

Cheat	*Password*
Beat Power, Beginning of the Game	Blue: C1, D4, F6 - Red: B1, D3, F5
Beat Power, All Weapons, Proto Man's Castle	Blue: F1, B4, D6 - Red: C1, D4, F6

Mega Man 6 Passwords

Cheat	*Password*
Energy Balancer, Beginning of the Game	E5, A1, E1, A5, C3
All Weapons, Mr. X's Castle	E5, D2, B4, D6, F4

Mega Man 7 Passwords

Cheat	*Password*
All Items, Beginning of Dr. Wily's Castle	7853 5842 2245 7515
All Items, Final Level of Dr. Wily's Castle	1415 5585 7823 6251

Mega Man 7 replaces the sphere grid with a number grid. Use the L and R buttons to select each number.

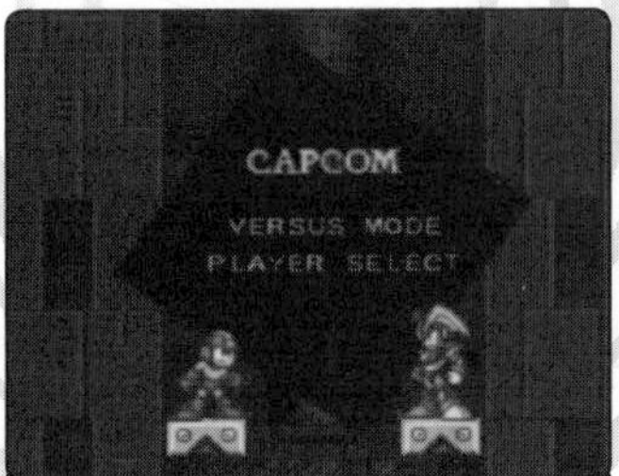

Insider Tip

In Mega Man 7, go to the Password entry screen, type in the Final Level of Dr. Wily's Castle password, hold X and Y, and press Start to access the hidden Versus mode. Two players can go head-to-head as either Mega Man or his robotic ally, Zero.

Unlockable Extras

Be warned—using the Password option can be a little confusing at first. On the overall Main menu, load Mega Man X1, X2, or X3. Now highlight the Password or Continue option and press A to go to the Load screen. Here you can load a saved game from a memory card, but there's no place to input a password. To go to the actual Password screen, press B, highlight Yes, then press A.

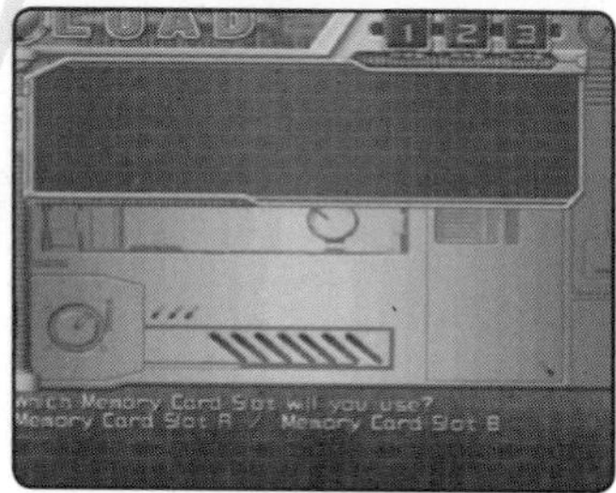

Mega Man X1 Passwords

Cheat	*Password*
All Hearts and Sub-Tanks obtained	3748 8612 5524
All Hearts, Sub-Tanks, and armor upgrades obtained	3475 5668 2581
All items obtained, all bosses defeated once	3676 4667 5148

Mega Man X2 Passwords

Cheat	*Password*
All Hearts and Sub-Tanks obtained	8121 3336 6351 5226
All Hearts, Sub-Tanks, and armor upgrades obtained	7146 3387 6246 1246
All items except Zero's parts, first Maverick stage	8277 8153 6728 7652
All items including Zero's parts, first Maverick stage	1462 3327 6488 3246

Mega Man X3 Password

Cheat	*Password*
All items except the Golden Armor, first Doppler stage	7357 7533 6462 7835

> **Insider Tip**
> The Mega Man X3 password includes all items except the Golden Armor, which can't be saved. It must be re-acquired every time you play.

(continued)

Mega Man X Collection (cont.)

Mega Man X4: Ultimate Armor and Black Zero

To obtain the Ultimate Armor for Mega Man X, highlight him on the Character Select screen, press X twice, and then Left six times. Immediately press and hold L and Z, then press Start. Continue holding L and Z until the stage begins. You'll recognize the Ultimate Armor by its blue and purple color scheme. To unlock the black-armored version of Zero, highlight him on the Character Select screen, hold R, and press Right six times. Release the R button, press and hold the X button, and press Start. Continue holding R until the stage begins. Not only does Black Zero have stylish dark armor, he also wields a powerful energy sword instead of his standard blaster.

Mega Man X5: Ultimate Armor and Black Zero

On the Character Select screen, highlight Mega Man X and press Up twice and Down nine times to unlock his Ultimate Armor. Highlight Zero and press Down twice and Up nine times to unlock his Black Zero persona.

Mega Man X6: Ultimate Armor and Black Zero

On the Mega Man X6 Main menu, highlight Game Start and press Left, Left, Left, and Right to unlock Mega Man X's Ultimate Armor, and press L, L, L, and R to unlock Black Zero. If you enter each code correctly, you'll hear a musical tone.

Carry a Big Bat
In Dynasty Mode, go to the Roster menu and select Create/Edit Player. Now create the following characters and use these names:

Keegan Paterson
Jacob Paterson
Isaiah Paterson

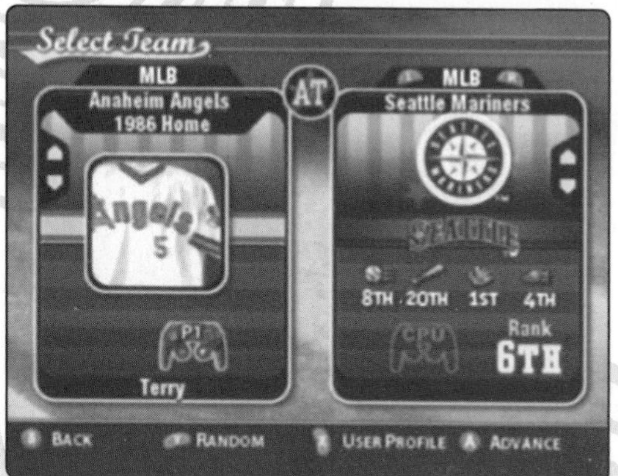

Unlock the 1986 Angels
Want to get an old 1986 Angels home jersey? Create a new profile name and change the default name from PROF1 to MVP. Want the away jersey? You'll have to earn some points and unlock that one yourself!

Looking for a Real Challenge?
In Dynasty Mode, go to the Roster menu and select Create/Edit Player. Create a new player with this name:

Erik Kiss

Consider yourself an expert MVP gamer if you can get Mr. Kiss on base with a hit.

Unlock Everything

This single code gives you access to all the locked classic stadiums, retro uniforms and hidden players in the game. To access it, go to the Manage Rosters menu and select Create/Edit Players. Now create a character with this name:

Katie Roy

St. Patrick's Day in Boston

Go to the Manage Rosters menu and select Create/Edit Players. Now create a ball player with this name:

Neverlose Sight

Now your players can select the green Boston Red Sox St. Patrick's Day uniform prior to your game!

A Tiny Player with Massive Power

Add a little spark to your Dynasty and Owner mode lineups by going to Manage Rosters and selecting Create/Edit Players. When you enter the player's name, choose the following:

Sean Paterson

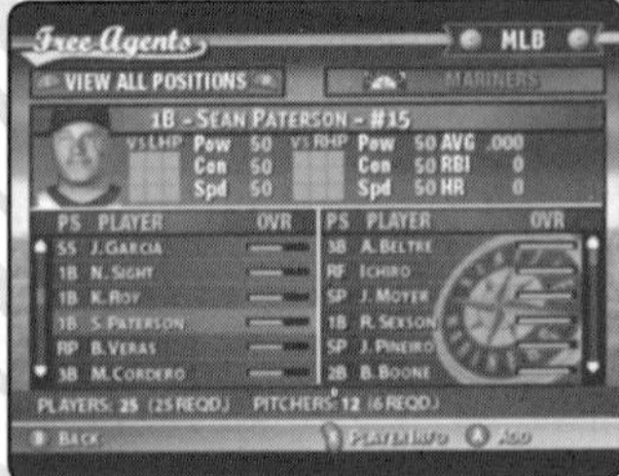

You'll find that Sean is smaller than most major leaguers, but he can hit a long way. If you're looking for more players, go ahead and enter the other Paterson names that were used in MVP Baseball 2004.

Thunder Plate Unlockables

To use the cheats below, you must edit your driver's name in a Fight to the Top mode game. However, it takes some doing to get to that point. The first time you boot the game, Fight to the Top mode begins automatically, pitting you against pro driver Ryan Newman in a one-lap road race. If you lose the race, replay it until you win. You'll now be allowed to create a driver and save a Fight to the Top game file. From the Fight to the Top Main menu, go to My NASCAR and then to Edit Driver. Edit your driver's first and last names as shown below.

Cheat	*First Name*	*Last Name*
10,000,000 Fans	MakeMe	Famous
$10,000,000 Bonus	Walmart	NASCAR
2,000,000 Prestige Points	You	TheMan
Auto Zone Drivers/Cars	GetIn	TheZone
Dale Earnhardt Sr.	The	Intimidator
Lakeshore Drive Events	Walmart	Exclusive
Dodge Drivers/Cars	Race	Dodge
Dodge Track Events	Dodge	Stadium
Mr. Clean Drivers/Cars	Mr.Clean	Racing
Mr. Clean Sponsorship (Pit Crew)	Clean	Crew
Levi Strauss Drivers/Cars	Levi	Strauss153
Old Spice Drivers/Cars	OldSpice	Motorsports
Old Spice Speedway Events	OldSpice	Venue
All Thunder Plates	Open	Sesame

Note that unlocked driver names are not shown on the Thunder Plates themselves...

...but when you're scrolling through the available drivers in the various race modes, you can find them by car number.

Wii Xbox 360 Xbox GC PS3 PS2 DS GBA PSP

Need for Speed Carbon

Performance Tune-up

You don't need speed to unlock these infinite bonuses and logo vinyls, but you do need smooth and even button pushing on the direction pad. Enter these codes on the Main menu:

Cheat	*Code*
Unlocks Castrol Cash	Down, Up, Left, Down, Right, Up, X, B
Infinite Nitrous Upgrade	Left, Up, Left, Down, Left, Down, Right, X
Infinite Speedbreaker Upgrade	Down, Right, Right, Left, Right, Up, Down, X
Unlocks NFS Carbon Logo Vinyls	Right, Up, Down, Up, Down, Left, Right, X
Unlocks NFS Carbon Special Vinyls	Up, Up, Down, Down, Down, Down, Up, X

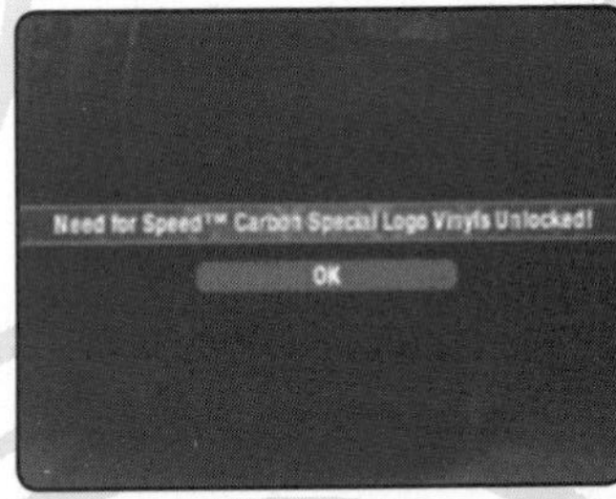

Insider Tip

Entering some codes requires patience, but if you have continued problems, try entering a menu like My Cars and then returning to the main menu to try entering these codes again.

Need for Speed Underground

Unlock All Tracks

Enter these codes at the Main menu:

Cheat	*Code*
Open all Circuit mode tracks	Down, R, R, R, X, X, X, Z
Open all Sprint mode tracks	Up, X, X, X, R Down, Down, Down
Open all Drag mode tracks	Right, Z, Left, R, Z, L, Y, X
Open all Drift mode tracks	Left, Left, Left, Left, Right, X, R, Y

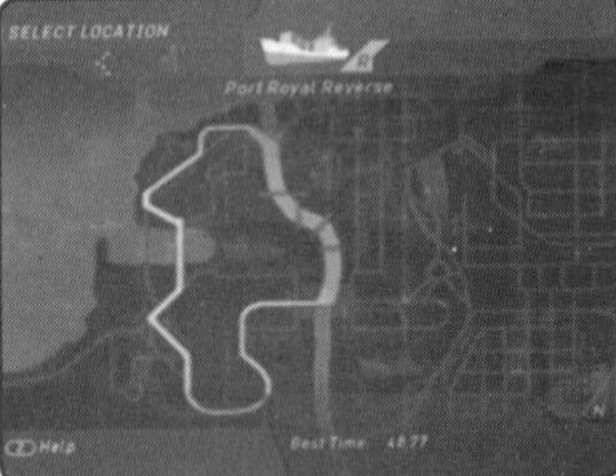

Insider Tip

You'll have to check the game mode tracks to verify that the code worked. Also, don't sweat it if you press the Z button and the Help menu appears —just keep clicking away at the code and you'll get it right.

Need for Speed Underground 2

Unlockable Sponsor Cars
Enter these codes at the Press Start title screen:

Cheat	*Code*
Lincoln Navigator	Up, Right, Up, Up, Down, Right, Down, Right
Hummer H2	Up, Left, Up, Up, Down, Left, Down, Left
Mitsubishi Eclipse	Up, Down, Right, Up, Left, Down, Right, Right
Lexus	Up, Down, Left, Up, Left, Up, Right, Left

Be sure to enter these codes on the direction pad, not with the control stick. If you enter the code correctly, you'll hear a chime that sounds just like the tone you hear when you choose a game menu selection.

Insider Tip
Unlock more than one car and you can race against a friend in Split Screen mode!

Over the Hedge

Unlockable Extras
These quick and simple codes can do everything from increasing the amount of health you get from power-ups to unlocking bonus content. To enter any code, pause your game, hold the L and R buttons, enter the code, and then release L and R.

Cheat	*Code*
All Levels	Y, X, Y, X, X, B
All Mini-Games	Y, X, Y, Y, B, B
All Melee Moves	Y, X, Y, B, B, X
Extra Melee Damage	Y, X, Y, X, Y, B

Cheat	*Code*
More Health from Power-Ups	Y, X, Y, X, B, Y
Powered-Up Projectiles	Y, X, Y, X, B, X
Unlock Bonus Comic #14	Y, X, B, B, X, Y
Unlock Bonus Comic #15	Y, Y, B, X, B, X

Health power-ups normally give you one unit of health. After using the More Health from Power-Ups code, they'll give you two.

The Powered-Up Projectiles code will give your ranged attacks just a little bit more power than usual.

Insider Tip
You can enter more than one code while on the pause screen. Use combined codes like the Extra Melee Damage cheat and Melee Moves unlock cheat to make the game easier without taking away all of the challenges.

Wii
Xbox 360
Xbox
GC
PS3
PS2
DS
GBA
PSP

Pac-Man World 3

Unlockable Level Selection Option
To unlock this helpful option, quickly but firmly press Left, Right, Left, Right, B, and Up on the Main menu.

Even if you use Level Selection, you can save and continue through the game as normal.

Insider Tip
Use the directional pad, not the joystick, to enter the code. All 15 levels will be enabled.

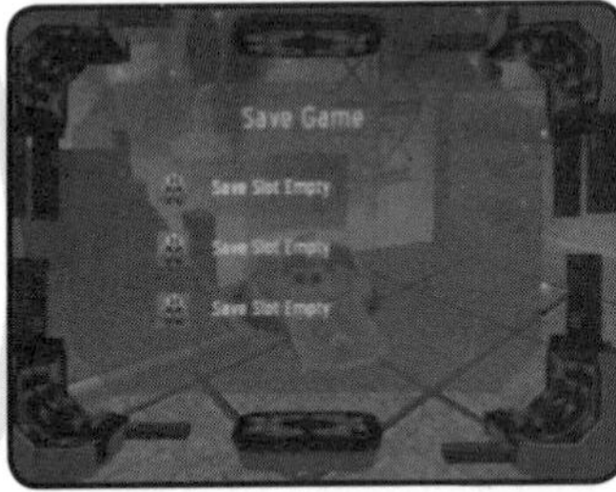

Ratatouille

A Smorgasbord of Secrets
At the Menu, choose Extras and then Gusteau's Shop. At Gusteau's Shop, choose the Secrets option. At this menu you'll see a list of codes that you can buy with Gusteau points, but if you press right on the cross pad you'll scroll through twenty blank spots for additional codes! Select a code number and then press the A Button to enter the corresponding cheat codes:

Cheat	*Code*
Code 1 unlocks Very Easy game play mode	Pieceocake
Code 2 protects Remy from impact and enemy damage	Myhero
Code 3 plays the Asobo logo	Asobo
Code 4 protects Remy from all damage except from falls and water	Shielded
Code 5 makes Remy undetected by foes	Spyagent
Code 6 gives Remy gas when he jumps	Ilikeonions
Code 7 replaces tail swipe with a head butt!	Hardfeelings
Code 8 unlocks multiplayer mode	Slumberparty
Code 9 unlocks all concept art	Gusteauart
Code 10 unlocks the four championship modes	Gusteauship
Code 11 unlocks all mini games in all modes	Mattelme

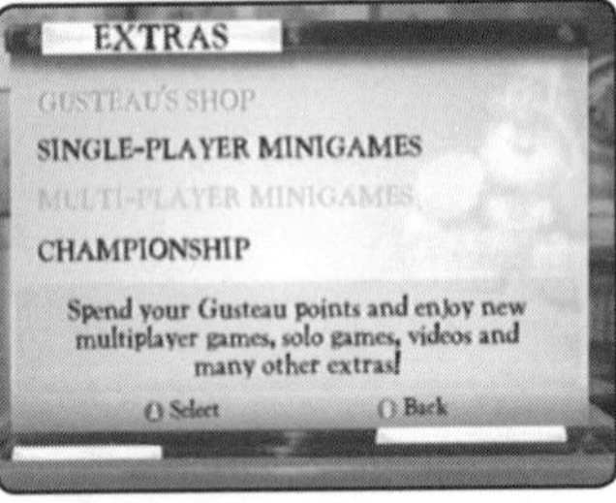

(continued)

Ratatouille (cont.)

Cheat	*Code*
Code 12 unlocks all videos	Gusteauvid
Code 13 unlocks all bonus art work	Gusteaures
Code 14 unlocks all Dream Worlds in Gusteau's Shop	Gusteaudream
Code 15 unlocks all slides in Gusteau's Shop	Gusteauslide
Code 16 unlocks all single player mini games	Gusteaulevel
Code 17 unlocks all Gusteau Shop items	Gusteaucombo
Code 18 awards 5,000 Gusteau points	Gusteaupot
Code 19 awards 10,000 Gusteau points	Gusteaujack
Code 20 awards 50,000 Gusteau points	Gusteauomni

Insider Tip
It's important to capitalize the first letter in these codes and then keep everything else lowercase. After entering a code, you'll need to highlight the code that you want to use and press the A Button to activate it.

SpongeBob SquarePants: Creature from Krusty Krab

You can enter these cheats at the cheat menu, but keep in mind that some codes will only work on specific levels! After you successfully enter a code, you should see a message that hints at where the code will work!

Cheat	Code
A thin Patrick	BONES
SpongeBob's thoughts revealed	BRAIN
A purple Patrick rocket	BUNRUN
Change SpongeBob's gun	DUCKGUN
Unlimited time limit on driving levels	EMCSQR
Modify SpongeBob's ride	FLAMES
Unlimited fuel in the flying levels	GASSY
Unlock all levels	GUDGEON
Unlock alternate car	HOTROD
Collect all Sleepy Seeds	SCOOTLES
Unlock another ship	SPACE
Modify Patrick's look when attacking	SPIN
Punk SpongeBob for Diesel Dreaming level	SPONGE
Activate Sleepy Seed Detector	TISSUE
Add infinite health in some stages	VIGOR
Modify Hovercars	HOVER
Modify SpongeBob's car	HYPCAR
A makeover for Plankton	INVENT
A thin SpongeBob	KRABBY
New laser colors	LASER
A smaller SpongeBob	PANTS

(continued)

SpongeBob SquarePants (cont.)

A makeover for Patrick	PATRICK
A new outfit for SpongeBob	PILOT
Unlock all bonus games	PORKPIE
Change Plankton's appearance	ROBOT
Add 30,000 coins	ROCFISH
Modify the rockets	ROCKET
Patrick in a safari suit	SAFARI

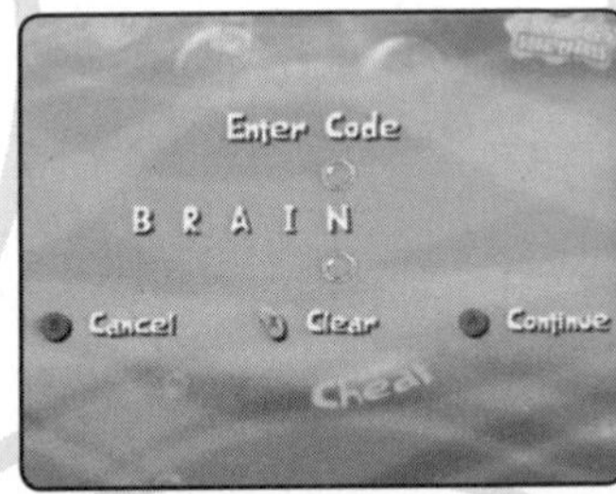

SSX On Tour

Unlockable Clothes, Cash, and Characters

In a strange but fun twist, EA and Nintendo decided to plunk down Mario, Luigi, and Princess Peach into what is otherwise a straightforward snowboard/ski racer title. Once you get past the idea of Princess Peach going head-to-head with Mitch Koobski, you can use these cheats to get ahead in both Tour and Quick Play modes. From the Main menu, go to the Extras menu and then to the Cheats menu. All cheats should be typed in using all capital letters. The All Attributes and All Tricks codes award you everything available, without you having to purchase them in the Gear Shop. The Videos found in the Extras menu are separate from the Movies, which are found on the Rewards menu in The Tour mode.

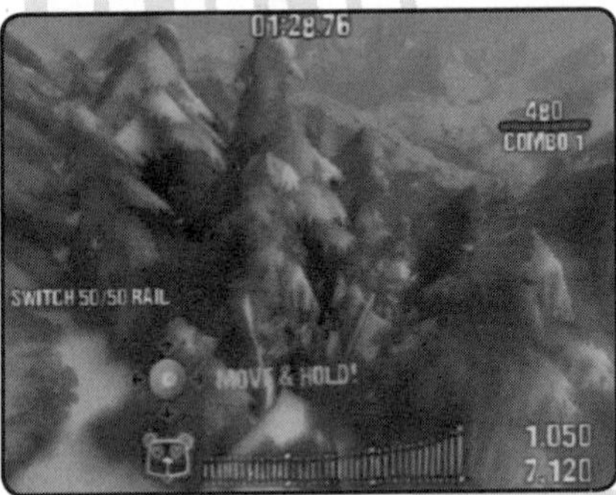

(continued)

SSX On Tour (cont.)

Cheat	*Code*
$99,000,000 (The Tour)	LOOTSNOOT
All Characters (Quick Play)	ROADIEROUNDUP
All Attributes (The Tour)	POWERPLAY
All Movies (The Tour)	THEBIGPICTURE
All Reward Clothing (The Tour)	FLYTHREADS
All Tricks (The Tour)	JACKALOPESTYLE
Infinite Boost (All Modes)	ZOOMJUICE
Unlock Mitch Koobski (Quick Play)	MOREFUNTHANONE
Unlock Nigel (Quick Play)	THREEISACROWD

Insider Tip
Repeating tricks actually costs you points. Try to vary your tricks as much as possible during a run, or even plan a series of tricks to attempt. One other effect of the All Tricks cheat is that the tricks help graphics appear every time you do a trick.

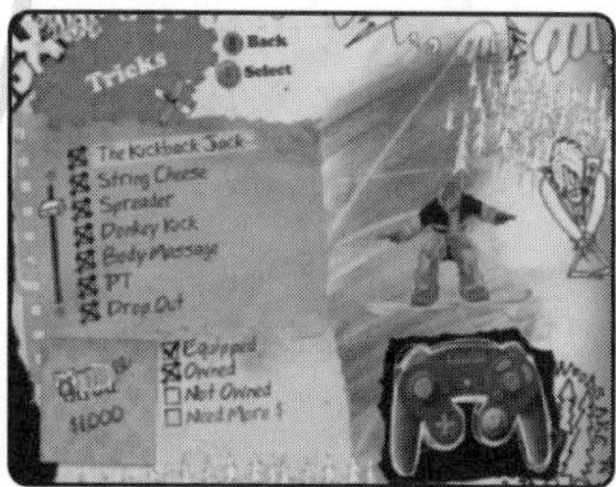

Tak: The Great Juju Challenge

Unlockable Bonuses
In Tak: The Great Juju Challenge, you collect bugs, crystals, and fruit, and combine them in different proportions to access bonuses. Recipe cards scattered through the levels tell you what to mix, but the recipes below aren't shown in the game. Once you're in the Juju Realm, access the Juju Potions and Blessings screen, select the Universal Card option, and enter the recipes below.

Bonus	*Bugs*	*Crystals*	*Fruit*
Magic Particles	24	40	11
More Magic Particles	48	57	57
Bonus Music Track 1	67	8	20
Bonus Music Track 2	6	18	3
Bonus Sound Effects	20	17	5
Bonus Sound Effects 2	50	84	92
Juju Concept Art	33	22	28
Vehicle Concept Art	11	55	44
World Concept Art	83	49	34

2K Sports NBA 2K8

Have a Ball . . . and a Couple of Secret Teams and Jerseys

Sport a new look on the court or elevate your game by unlocking a hidden team. At the 2K Sports NBA 2K8 Main Menu, choose Features, and then Codes and enter the following:

Unlock the 2008 All Star NBA jerseys	haeitgyebs
Unlock the 2K Sports Team	2ksports
Unlock the ABA Ball	payrespect
Unlock the NBA 2K Team	nba2k
Unlock the second road game Indiana Pacers jerseys	cpares
Unlock the St. Patrick's Day jerseys	uclerehanp
Unlock the Valentine's Day jerseys	amcnreo
Unlock the Visual Concepts Team	vcteam

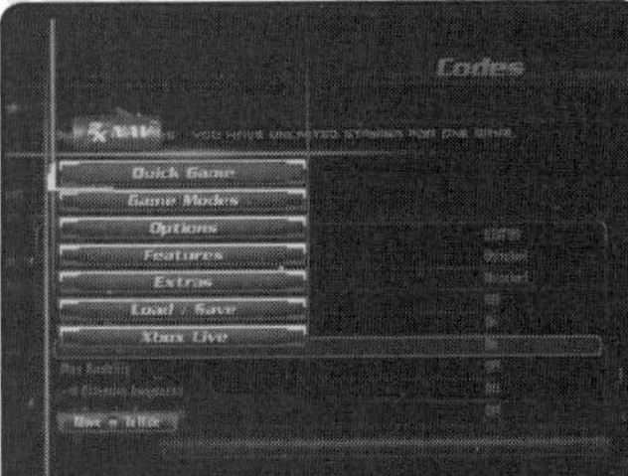

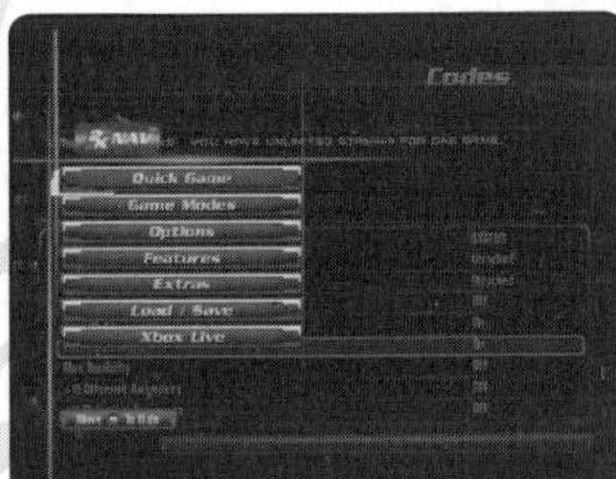

2K Sports NHL 2K8

Unlock All the New Reebok Edge NHL Jerseys!

While some games make you input one code for each team jersey, 2K Sports NHL 2K8 lets you unlock all of the new Reebok Edge NHL hockey jerseys with one code. Choose Features at the Main Menu, then select Unlock 2007-2008 Uniforms and finally choose Enter Password. Pay close attention to the uppercase and lowercase letters when you enter this password:

S6j83RMk01

Cars Mater-National Championship

Tune-up Your Racing Performance

From the Main Menu choose Options, then select Cheat Codes and enter the following codes. Pay close attention to the differences between the letter "O" and the number "0" in some license plate codes. If you mess up entering a code, you'll hear a siren informing you to try again, or that particular code was already entered.

Improve acceleration	0TO200X
Infinite turbo boost	ZZOOOOM
Unlock all art	BUYTALL
Unlock all color combinations for all cars	PAINTIT
Unlock all color combinations for the Lightning McQueen car	NCEDUDZ
Unlock Arcade Mode courses, mini-games and story mode locations	PLAYALL
Unlock Expert level	VRYFAST

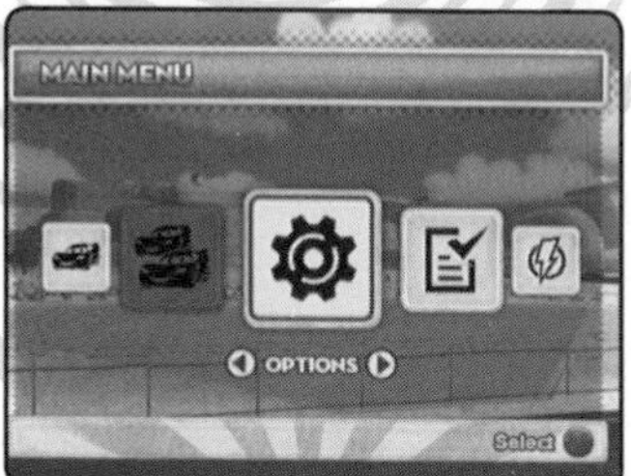

LEGO Star Wars: The Complete Saga

Cantina Codes

You can unlock the following ships and characters at the Cantina with the following codes. If you enter a code correctly, you'll see a message confirming which ship or character you unlocked. Remember you'll need to buy them from the Character menu if you have enough credits.

Admiral Ackbar	ACK646
Battle Droid (Commander)	KPF958
Boss Nass	HHY697
Captain Tarpals	QRN714
Count Dooku	DDD748
Disguise Skill	BRJ437
Ewok	EWK785
Force Grapple Leap Skill	CLZ738
General Grievous	PMN576
Greedo	ZZR636
IG-88	GIJ989
Imperial Guard	GUA850
Imperial Shuttle	HUT845
Jango Fett	KLJ897
Ki-Adi Mundi	MUN486
Luminara	LUM521

(continued)

Wii Xbox 360 Xbox GC PS3 PS2 DS GBA PSP

LEGO Star Wars: The Complete Saga (cont.)

Padmé	VBJ322
R2-Q2	EVILR2
Sandtrooper	CBR954
Stormtrooper	NBN431
Taun We	PRX482
TIE Fighter	DBH897
TIE Interceptor	INT729
Droid TriFighter	AAB123
Vulture Droid	BDC866
Watto	PLL967
Zam Wesell	584HJF
Zam's Airspeeder	UUU875

MLB 07: The Show

Unlock the Silver and Gold Era Teams
Add legendary pros to your team lineup by entering the following code on the direction buttons at the game's Main menu screen: Left, Up, Right, Down, Down, Left, Up, Down

Insider Tip
Like real baseball, these codes take a little bit of practice and timing before you hit them.

Big Heads and a Big Baseball (and Back Again)
To give all of the players big heads and enlarge the baseball, pause the game (tap START) while your player is pitching or batting and enter the following code on the direction buttons: Left, Right, Up, Up, Left, Up, Up, Left

To change the size of the ball back to normal, pause the game again (press START) and enter this code on the direction buttons: Left, Up, Down, Right, Left, Left, Up, Down

Your Big Break
If you need to add the maximum amount of break to your pitches, pause the game (press START) and enter this code on the direction buttons: Right, Up, Right, Down, Up, Left, Left, Down

Major League Baseball 2K7

Big League Cheats

To activate cheats, go to the My 2K7 Menu screen and select Enter Cheat Code. After entering a cheat, you'll still need to make it active. Return to the My 2K7 menu to turn the selected cheats on and off.

Cheat	Code
Boost Team Power for one inning	mightymick
Unlock everything	Derek Jeter
Mighty Mick (Boost Hit Ability for hitters 3, 4 and 5 in your lineup)	triplecrown
Add Mickey Mantle for Pinch Hitting	phmantle
Big Blast--hit huge home runs cheat	m4murder
Mickey Mantle available as a free agent	themick
Unlock arcade games	Game On

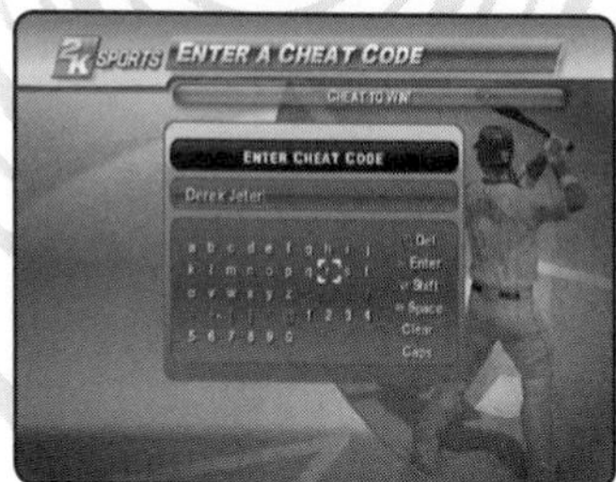

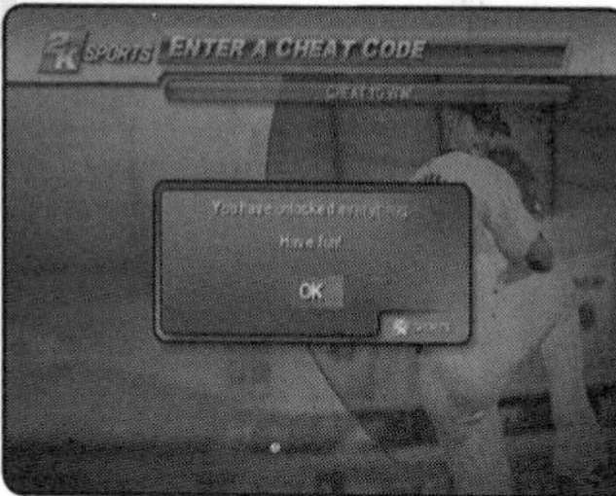

MX vs. ATV Untamed

Unleash Untamed Codes

To unlock extras for your Untamed rides, choose the Cheats option on the Main Menu and enter the following:

Cheat	Code
Unlock all riding gear made by Fox	CRAZYLIKEA
Unlock all handlebar options	NOHANDS

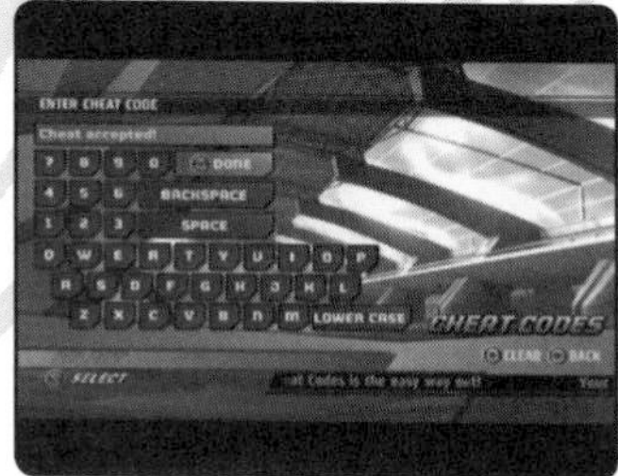

Wii Xbox 360 Xbox GC PS3 PS2 DS GBA PSP

More Cars and Fantasy Features

After you start a game, go to the Main menu and select EA Sports Extras, then choose Cheat Codes and enter the following cheats:

Cheat	*Code*
Unlock All Chase Mode Cars	checkered flag
Unlock EA Sports Car	EA SPORTS CAR
Unlock Fantasy Drivers	race the pack
Unlock Wal-Mart Car	walmart everyday

As you enter each code correctly, the game gives you a "Cheat Code Accepted" message.

NBA 07

Jersey Codes for the Trophy Room

To enter a code, choose Options on the Main menu and then check out the Trophy Room. Select Team Jerseys and press the Square button to enter these codes:

Cheat	*Code*
Unlock Charlotte Bobcats 2006 Uniform	JKL846ETK5
Unlock Eastern All Stars 2007 Uniform	5F89RE2H8G
Unlock New Jersey Nets 2006 Uniform	NB79D965D2
Unlock New Orleans/Oklahoma Hornets 2007 Uniform	EL2E3T8H58
Unlock Utah Jazz 2006 Uniform	228GG7585G
Unlock Washington Wizards 2006 Uniform	PL5285F37F
Unlock Western All Stars 2007 Uniform	2H5E89EH8C

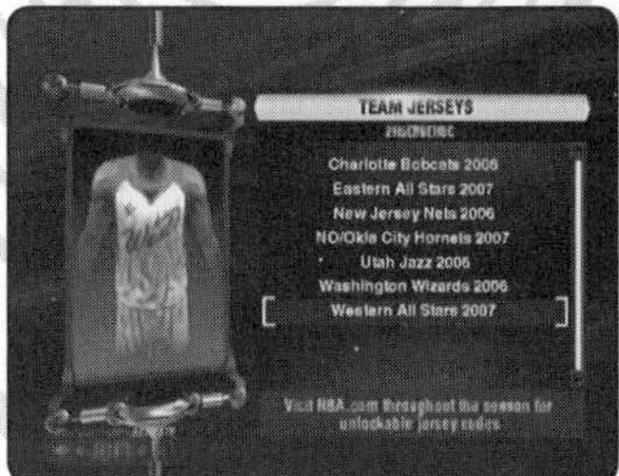

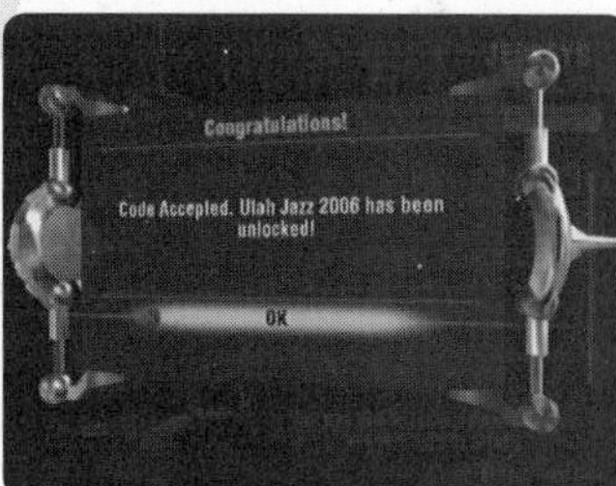

NBA Live 08

New Shoes for Your Team

From the Main Menu, choose My NBA Live 07, then EA Sports Extras. Select the option for NBA Codes and add the following to walk off with these new shoes:

Adidas Duncan Stealth All-Star	FE454DFJCC
Adidas Gil Zero All-Star	23DN1PPOG4

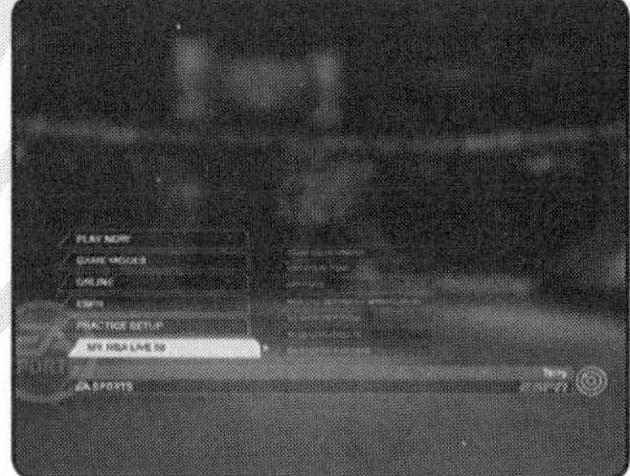

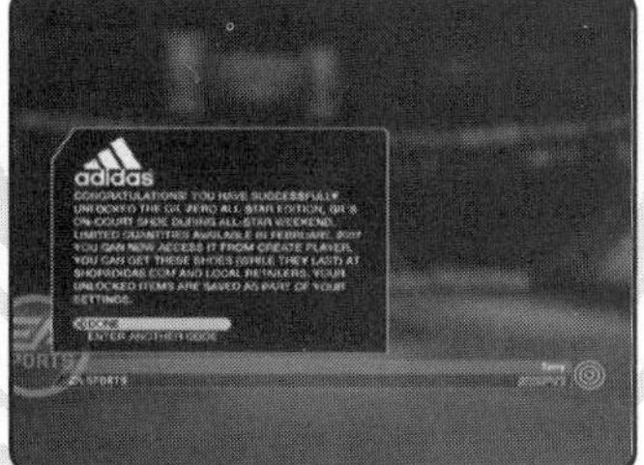

Need for Speed Carbon

Unlockable Upgrades, Vinyls, and More

You don't need speed to unlock these infinite bonuses and logo vinyls, but you do need smooth and even button pushing on the direction pad. Enter these codes on the Main menu:

Cheat	*Code*
Unlocks Castrol Cash	Down, Up, Left, Down, Right, Up, Square, Triangle
Infinite Nitrous Upgrade	Left, Up, Left, Down, Left, Down, Right, Square
Infinite Speedbreaker Upgrade	Down, Right, Right, Left, Right, Up, Down, Square
Unlocks NFS Carbon Logo Vinyls	Right, Up, Down, Up, Down, Left, Right, Square
Unlocks NFS Carbon Special Vinyls	Up, Up, Down, Down, Down, Down, Up, Square

Insider Tip

Entering codes in the PS3 version is easier than on most platforms, but if you have continued problems, try entering a menu like "My Cars" and then returning to the Main menu to try again.

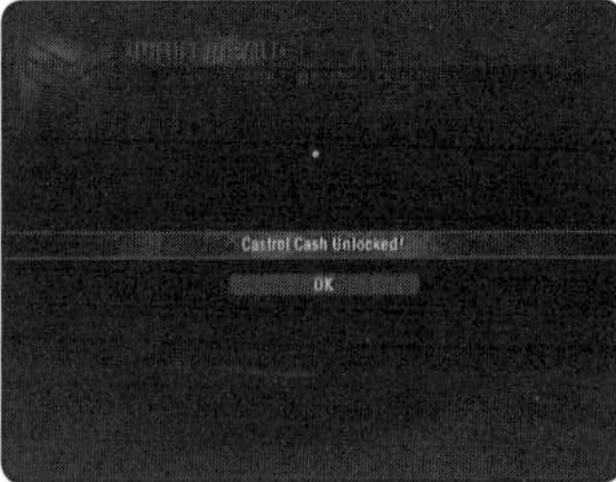

And Now a Code from Our Sponsors . . .

Unlike other Need For Speed titles where codes are entered from the Main Menu, you must enter the Need For Speed Prostreet codes from the Career Menu. Once you start a Career mode game and have access to EA Nation online, you'll be able to select the Code entry option and add these cool cars, cash, and tune-ups:

Add $10,000 to your spending money	CASHMONEY
Add another $10,000 and bonus cars	REGGAME
Add five repair tokens	SAFETYNET
Unlock the Castrol Syntec vinyls	CASTROLSYNTEC
Unlock the Coke Zero Golf GTI	ZEROZEROZERO
Unlock the Energizer vinyls	ENERGIZERLITIUM
Unlock the classic Chevelle SS	HORSEPOWER
Unlock the Audi TT	ITSABOUTYOU
Unlock the Dodge Viper SRT10	WORLDSLONGESTLASTING

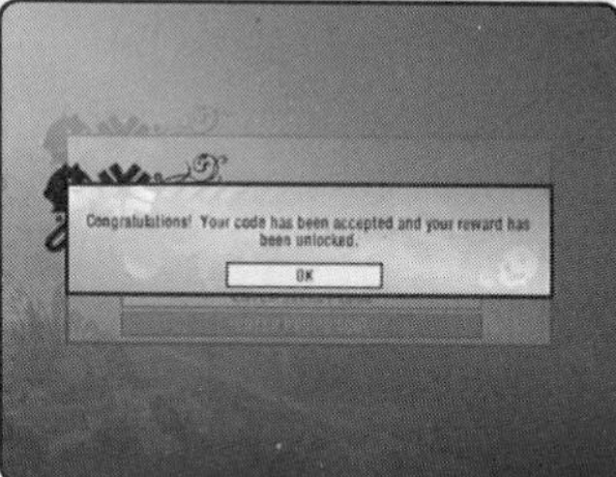

Insider Tip:
Last time we checked and verified all this stuff, the above codes still worked after the latest patch from EA games, so you're ready to roll!

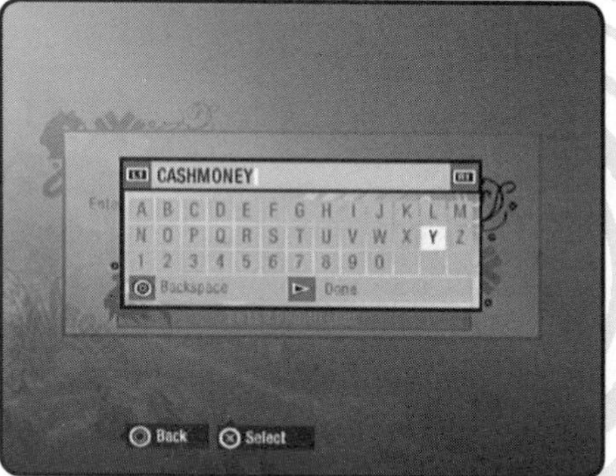

Wii
Xbox 360
Xbox
GC
PS3
PS2
DS
GBA
PSP

NHL 08

Hit the Ice with New Gear
At the 2007 NHL All-Star game, the NHL adopted highly breathable Reebok Edge jerseys for the 2008 hockey season, but gamers needed a special code to unlock the authentic look in their EA Sports NHL 08 games. From the Main Menu choose My NHL 08 and then select the RBK Edge option and enter the following code:

New 2008 Reebok uniforms	h3oyxpwksf8ibcgt

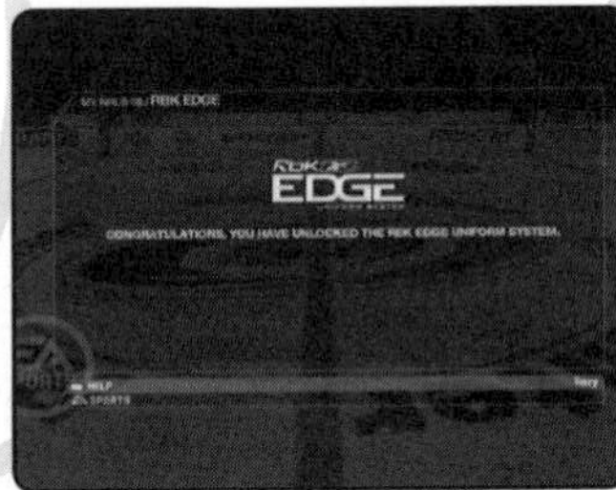

Tiger Woods PGA Tour 07

These Guys Are Good, but Now You're Better
From the Main Menu choose Options, then Password and enter these codes:

Create big heads in the gallery	TENGALLONHAT
Unlock Bridgestone sponsorship	SHOJIRO
Unlock Cobra sponsorship	SNAKEKING
Unlock course memberships	ELDRICK
Unlock EA Sports sponsorship	INTHEGAME
Unlock Graffalloy sponsorship	JUSTSHAFTS
Unlock MacGregor sponsorship	MACTEC
Unlock Mizuno sponsorship	RIHACHINRZO

Tiger Woods PGA Tour 07 (cont.)

Unlock Nike sponsorship	JUSTDOIT
Unlock Oakley sponsorship	JANNARD
Unlock PGA Tour sponsorship	LIGHTNING
Unlock Ping sponsorship	SOLHEIM
Unlock Precept sponsorship	GUYSAREGOOD
Unlock Taylormade sponsorship	MRADAMS
Unlock team mode players	GAMEFACE

Tiger Woods PGA Tour 08

Unlock It All!

Wayne Rooney might rule the Old Trafford pitch, but how well can he putt at Pebble Beach? Find out for yourself. From the Main Menu, select EA Sports Extras and enter the following passwords at the Password Menu. Remember to press the R2 button to switch all letters to UPPERCASE!

Add infinite funds to your golf account	CREAM
Unlock all Courses	GREENSFEES
Unlock all Golfers	ALLSTARS
Unlock Manchester United Star Wayne Rooney	PLAYFIFA08

Ape Escape 3

Secret Monkey Codes

Normally if you want to uncover a Rare Monkey Code, you will have to buy a hint book at the bookstore in the game Shopping Area and read it in your Gallery, but you can use these handy codes and save your money for other cool stuff. To enter a Secret Monkey Code, press L1, L2, R1, and R2 at the same time on the Game Title screen and then press START. You should see a password entry screen. Now enter these codes and head for the television programs where the monkeys are located.

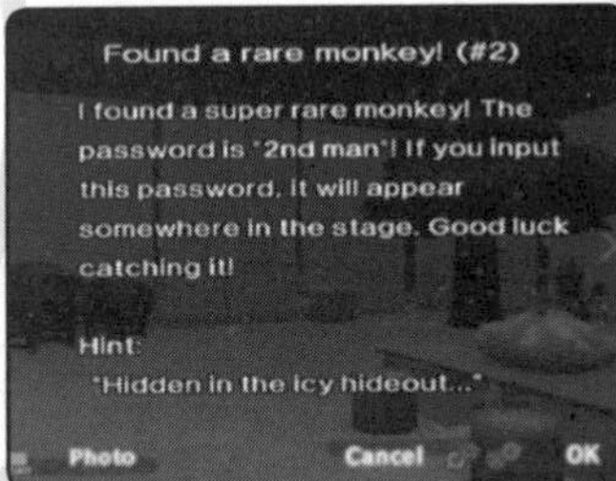

Cheat	*Code*
Dark Master on the Kung-Fu Alley Program	blackout
Pipotron Blue on the Airplane Squadron Program	coolblue
Pipotron Red on the Toytown Program	redmon
Pipotron Yellow on the Winterville Program	yellowy
SAL-1000* on the Saru-mon's Castle Program	grobyc
SAL-3000* on the Space TV Fortress Program	SAL3000
Shimmy on the Winterville Program	2nd man
Spork on the Hide n' Seek Forest Program	krops

Insider Tip
The rare monkeys (marked with an asterisk) can't be caught until you have the Super Monkey Morph!

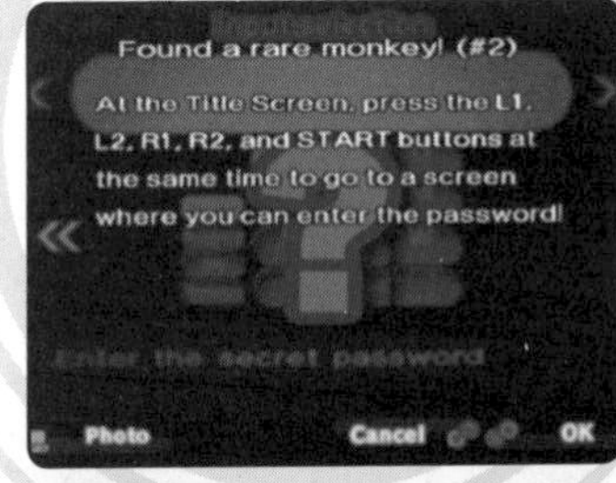

Unlockable Secret Movie

If you don't want to monkey around looking for hidden simians with Secret Monkey Codes, check out this secret movie tape for your home theater. To enter this code, press L1, L2, R1, and R2 at the same time on the Game Title screen. You should see a password entry screen where you can enter this code:

2 snakes

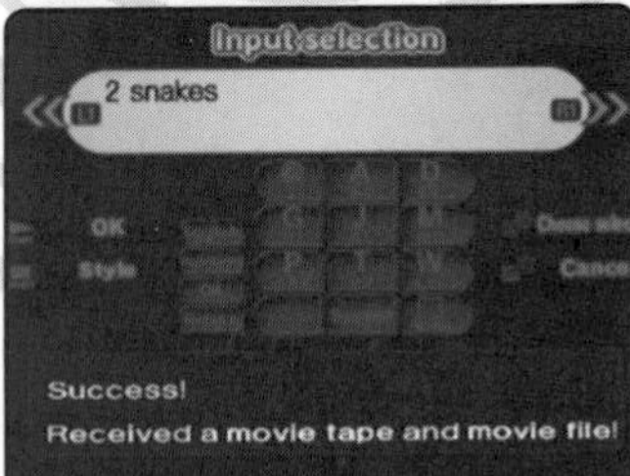

ATV Offroad Fury 2

Unlock Everything You Could Ever Want
Go to the Profile Editor menu and select Unlock Items. Now choose Cheats and enter the following codes:

Cheat	*Code*
Unlock everything in the game	IGIVEUP
Unlock all ATV models	SHOWROOM
Unlock all game modes	GAMEON
Unlock all tracks	TRLBLAZR
Unlock all equipment	THREADS
Unlock all championship events	GOLDCUPS
Unlock San Jacinto Isles	GABRIEL
Disable or enable your ability to wreck after jumps	FLYPAPER
Add 1000 points to your profile	GIMMEPTS
Enable or disable aggressive AI riders	EATDIRT
Disable or enable stop action replay camera	STOPCAM
Enable or disable Wheelies-for-Points feature	GETONUP
Enable or disable all-out mode for AI riders	BRINGIT

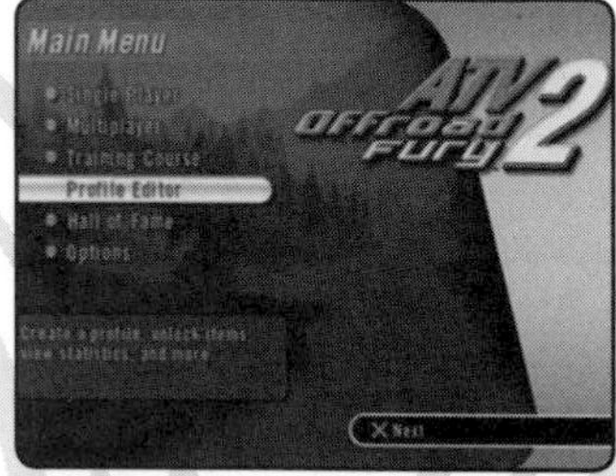

Insider Tip
You can enter more than one code before playing your game, but remember, if you enable a game feature that you decide that you don't like, go back and enter the same code again to disable it.

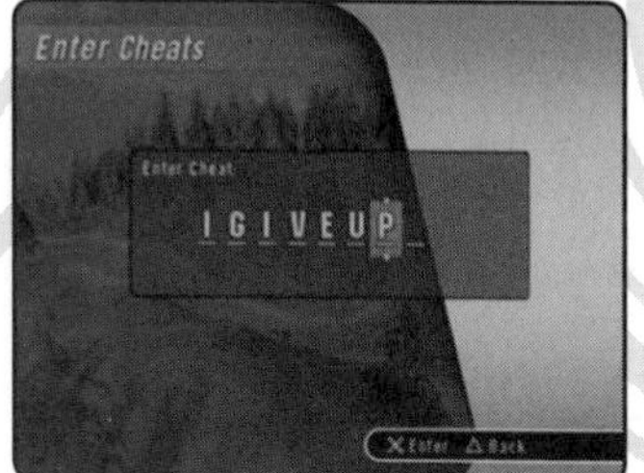

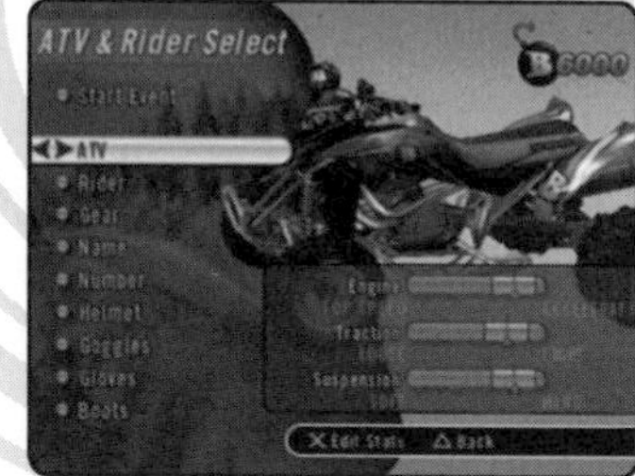

ATV Offroad Fury 4

Unlockable Bonuses

You can enter these codes at the Cheat menu in your Player Profile options. To enter an exclamation point (!) press the R2 Button or move your cursor over to the Symb icon on the screen and press X to select a new list of symbols. Now enter these special codes:

Cheat	*Code*
Earn 75,000 credits	!MegaWedge!
Unlock all sponsors	uDunGud
Unlock all tracks	TraxAhoy

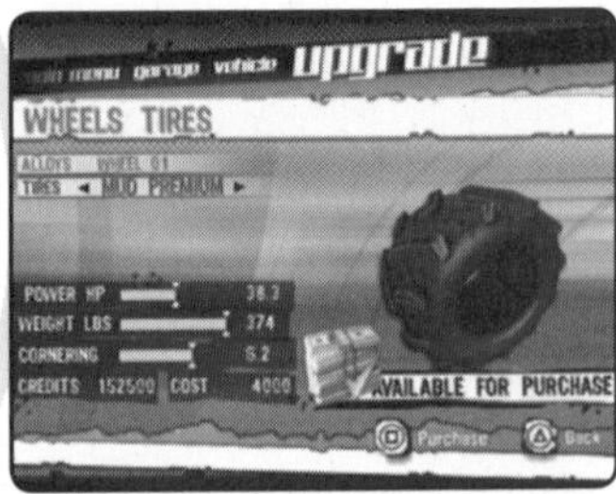

Insider Tips

Remember that these codes are case sensitive, so press the L2 Button or point the cursor to the CAP icon and press X to switch between upper- and lowercase.

Sometimes one code is all you need to use to have fun. You can earn more than 75,000 credits per cheat code if you keep entering it again and again.

Avatar: The Last Air Bender—The Burning Earth

Zip Code Cheats

If you want to deal double damage or browse the gallery art, these zip code cheats will take you there. From the Main Menu, select the Cheats option and enter the following five-digit codes:

Cheat	Code
Activate double damage	90210
Activate unlimited health	65049
Activate unlimited special attacks	66206
Max-level upgrade	89121
Unlock all bonus games	99801
Unlock all gallery items	85061
Unlock one-hit dishonor	28260

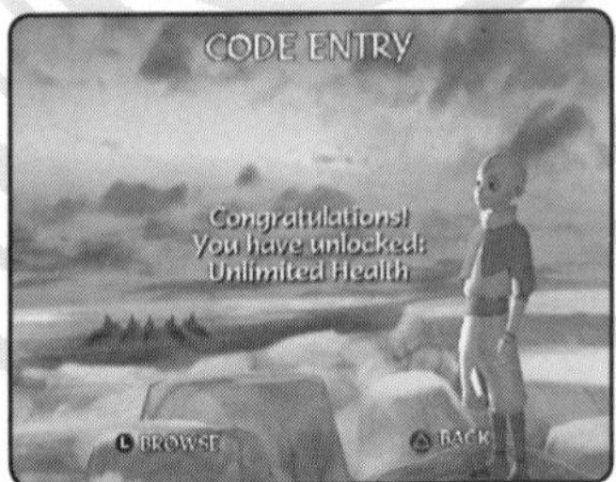

Barnyard

Unlockable Bonuses and Antics
To unlock Bonus Items, such as concept artwork and test animations of the characters, go to the Main menu, hold R1 and R2 and press Triangle, Circle, X, Square, Square, X, Circle, Triangle.

To unlock the Antics (which are actually mini-games) go to the Main menu, hold R1 and R2 and press Triangle, Square, X, Circle, Circle, X, Square, Triangle.

Max Out Your Gopher Bucks and Knapsack Items
To rack up 9,999 Gopher Bucks, hold R1 and R2 during normal gameplay and press X, X, Square, Square, Square, Square, Triangle, Square.

To award yourself all the Flower Power and Knapsack items, hold R1 and R2 during normal gameplay and press X, X, Triangle, Circle, Square, Square, Circle, Triangle.

Bratz: Forever Diamondz

Extra Blingz, Gift Sets, and More
Before you'll be able to scoop up some free blingz, you'll have to make it through the tutorial tasks and then return to the Bratz office. Once there, access the Cheat Computer to enter the following codes. If you enter a code correctly, you'll see a confirmation message.

Cheat	*Code*
1000 Blingz and Some Free Stuff	SIZZLN
2000 Blingz	FLAUNT
Gift Set A	STYLIN
Gift Set B	SKATIN
Gift Set C	JEWELZ
Gift Set E	DIMNDZ
Pet Treats	TREATZ

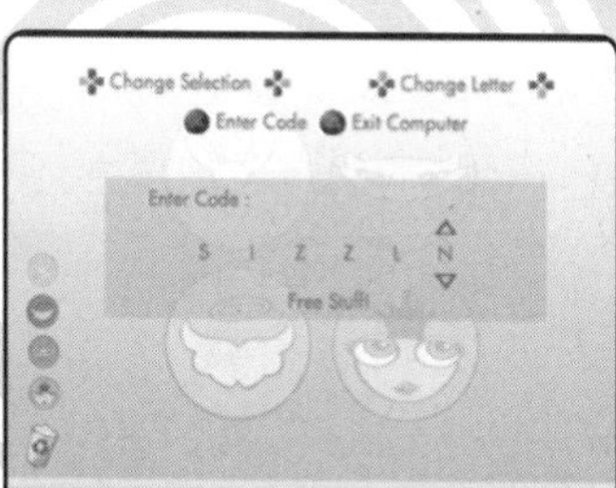

Insider Tip
These codes can only be used once, so don't get greedy!

Bratz: Rock Angelz

Office Cheats

Enter these codes on the office orange Cheat Computer after the Bratz decide to go into the publishing business:

Cheat	Code
Change Cameron	STYLIN
Change Dylan	MEYGEN
Change Koby	PRTPRN
Change London Boy	BLINGZ
Change Paris Boy	ROCKIN
Earn 1000 Blingz	YASMIN
Earn 2000 Blingz	PHOEBE
Earn 2100 Blingz	DANCIN
Earn 3000 Blingz	WAYFAB
Earn 6000 Blingz	HOTTIE
Unlock Party Jewelry	KOOLKT

Cheat	Code
Unlock Party Outfit	MODELS
Unlock New Party Outfit	RUNWAY
Unlock Ringtone 12	BLAZIN
Unlock Ringtone 14	BNYBOO
Unlock Ringtone 15	FIANNA
Unlock Ringtone 16	ANGELZ

Insider Tip
You can only enter a Rock Angelz code once, so spend those Blingz wisely!

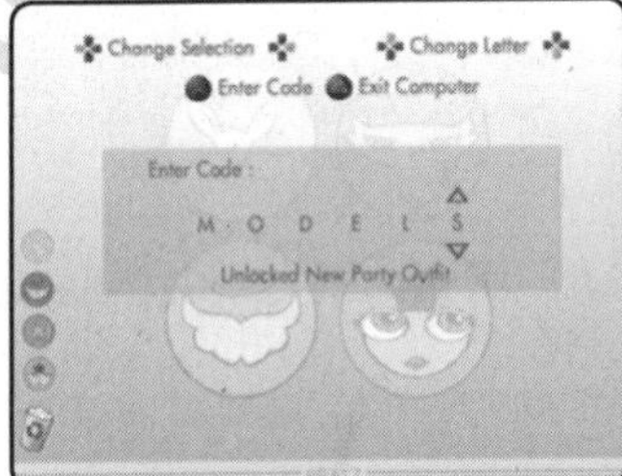

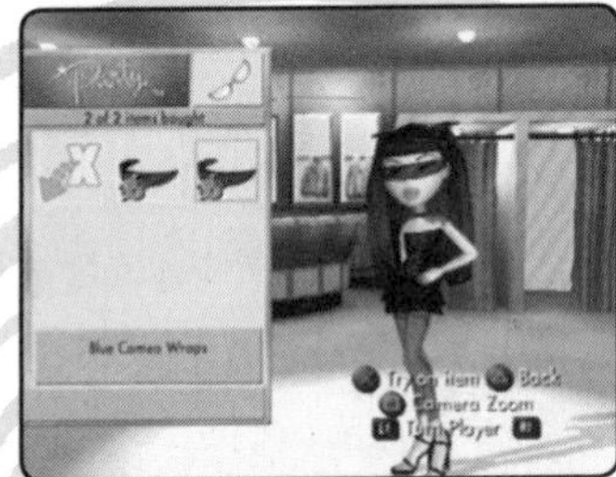

Cars

Unlockable Turbo, Tracks, and Mini-Games

Choose the Options menu and then select Cheat Codes and spell out these names on the license plates. If you mess up on a code, you'll hear a siren. Give it another try! If you enter a code correctly, you'll exit the Cheat Codes screen. Keep in mind that codes are not saved with your profile, and must be entered every time you turn on the game.

(continued)

Cars (cont.)

Cheat	*Code*
Boost at the Start of a Race	IMSPEED
Unlimited Turbo	VROOOOM
Unlock All Cars	YAYCARS
Unlock All Paint Jobs	R4MONE
Unlock Tracks and Mini-Games	MATTL66
Unlock Tracks, Mini-Games, and Paint Jobs	IF900HP
Unlock Mater's Speedy Circuit and Mater's Countdown Clean-Up	TRGTEXC
Unlock All Videos	WATCHIT
Unlock All Concept Art	CONC3PT

Insider Tip
Note that MATTL66 and IF900HP unlock all arcade tracks except Mater's Speedy Circuit (one of the Road Races) and Mater's Countdown Clean-Up (one of the Mini-Games).

Cars Mater-National Championship

Turbocharge Your Driving Fun!
From the Main Menu choose Options, then select Cheat Codes and enter the following codes. Pay close attention to the differences between the letter "O" and the number "0" in some license plate codes. If you mess up entering a code, you'll hear a siren informing you to try again, or that the code is already entered.

Cheat	*Code*
Improve acceleration	0TO200X
Infinite turbo boost	ZZOOOOM
Unlock all art	BUYTALL
Unlock all color combinations for all cars	PAINTIT
Unlock all color combinations for the Lightning McQueen car	NCEDUDZ
Unlock Arcade Mode courses, mini-games and story mode locations	PLAYALL
Unlock Expert level	VRYFAST

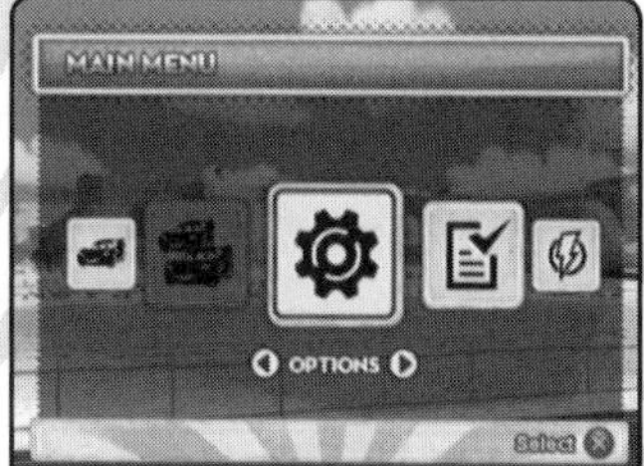

Disney's Extreme Skate Adventure

Extreme Unlocks
To enter these unlocks, choose Options at the Main menu and then select Cheat Codes and enter the following:

Cheat	*Code*
All characters	friendsofbob
All items	supercharger
All stages	extremepassport
Meter always full	sweetthreads

Remember to enter these codes in lowercase letters. If you do everything right, you should hear a yell.

Catch a Music Video
To view a special music video, choose Options at the Main menu and then select Cheat Codes and enter the following:

Cheat	*Code*
Lion King music video	savannah
Tarzan music video	nugget
Toy Story music video	marin

Remember to enter these codes in lowercase letters. If you do everything right, you should hear a yell. To see the new videos, choose Movies at the Main menu.

Finding Nemo

No Longer a Fish Out of Water
The codes for Finding Nemo are powerful, but there's a trick to getting them to work. You must enter these codes at the New Game screen and finish the code before the game demo starts. If you enter a code correctly, you'll see the word "Cheat!" appear. Once you enter the codes, go to the Stage Select menu (the place where you can choose the stages that you already explored). Now press START and you'll see the Cheat option on the screen. Depending on how many cheats you entered, you'll need to press right or left to choose the one you want.

Access all levels:
Triangle, Triangle, Triangle, Square, Square, Circle, Square, Triangle, Circle, Square, Triangle, Square, Triangle, Square, Triangle, Circle, Triangle, Triangle

(continued)

Invincibility:
Triangle, Square, Square, Circle, Circle, Circle, Triangle, Triangle, Square, Square, Square, Circle, Circle, Circle, Circle, Square, Triangle, Circle, Circle, Circle, Square, Circle, Triangle, Circle, Circle, Triangle, Circle, Square, Circle, Circle, Circle, Triangle

View end credits:
Triangle, Square, Circle, Triangle, Triangle, Square, Circle, Triangle, Square, Circle, Triangle, Square, Square, Circle, Triangle, Square, Circle, Triangle, Square, Circle, Circle, Triangle, Square, Circle

Unlock bonus level:
Triangle, Square, Circle, Circle, Square, Triangle, Triangle, Square, Circle, Circle, Square, Triangle, Triangle, Circle, Square, Triangle, Square, Circle, Circle, Square, Triangle

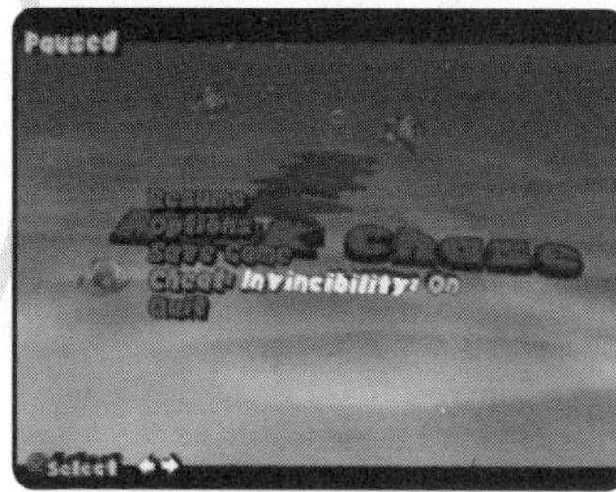

Frogger: Ancient Shadow

Unlockable Level Advances, Costumes, and More
At the Main menu, select Secret Code and then enter one of the following codes.

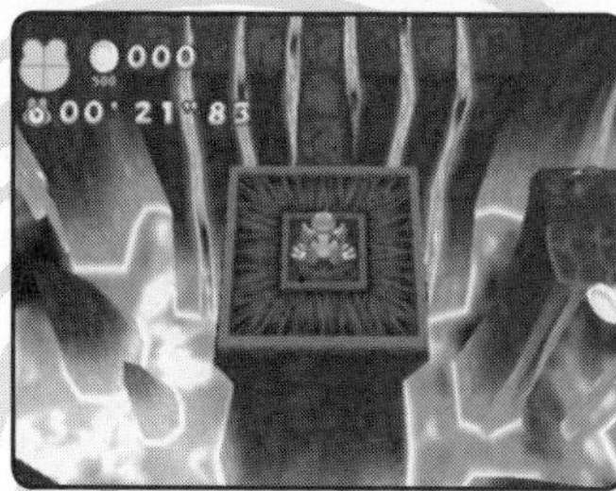

Hop Ahead

Cheat	*Code*
Berry starts at Dr. Wani's Mansion Level 1	Lily, Lumpy, Lily, Berry
Berry starts at Dr. Wani's Mansion Level 2	Dr. Wani, Frogger, Frogger, Finnius
Berry starts at Doom's Temple Level 1	Dr. Wani, Lily, Dr. Wani, Lily
Berry starts at Doom's Temple Level 2	Lily, Lily, Lily, Frogger
Berry starts at Doom's Temple Level 3	Berry, Frogger, Frogger, Frogger
Berry starts at Elder Ruins Level 1	Dr. Wani, Dr. Wani, Lily, Lily
Berry starts at Elder Ruins Level 2	Frogger, Finnius, Berry, Frogger
Berry starts at Sealed Heart Level 1	Lumpy, Dr. Wani, Lily, Lily
Berry starts at Sealed Heart Level 2	Lumpy, Frogger, Frogger, Lily

(continued)

Frogger: Ancient Shadow

Hidden Artwork

Cheat	*Code*
Frogger on the Moon	Finnius, Finnius, Finnius, Finnius
Swamp of Froggerstein Poster	Frogger, Frogger, Frogger, Frogger
Super Berry in the City	Berry, Berry, Berry, Berry
Game Event Scene 06	Dr. Wani, Frogger, Dr. Wani, Frogger
Game Event Scene 14	Berry, Berry, Berry, Dr. Wani
Mr. Shibazaki Art Gallery 01	Dr. Wani, Dr. Wani, Dr. Wani, Dr. Wani
Mr. Shibazaki Art Gallery 02	Lumpy, Frogger, Berry, Lily
Mr. Shibazaki Art Gallery 03	Dr. Wani, Frogger, Lily, Finnius

Unlockable Costumes

Cheat	*Code*
Bird's Nest Costume	Lily, Lily, Lily, Lily
Lobster Costume	Finnius, Dr. Wani, Lumpy, Frogger
Masted Ship Costume	Lumpy, Lumpy, Lumpy, Lumpy
Skull Costume	Frogger, Lumpy, Lily, Frogger

(continued)

Frogger: Ancient Shadow (cont.)

Unlockable Letters

Cheat	*Code*
John's letter with seed	Dr. Wani, Berry, Lily, Finnius
WHC Inc. letter with seed	Berry, Frogger, Frogger, Lumpy
Dr. Wani letter with seed	Finnius, Lumpy, Berry, Lumpy
Opart letter with seed	Lumpy, Frogger, Lumpy, Berry
Secret Admirer letter with seed	Frogger, Dr. Wani, Lily, Dr. Wani

Insider Tip
If you don't know which character is which on the code screen, play a little Story Mode and you'll soon recognize all the faces!

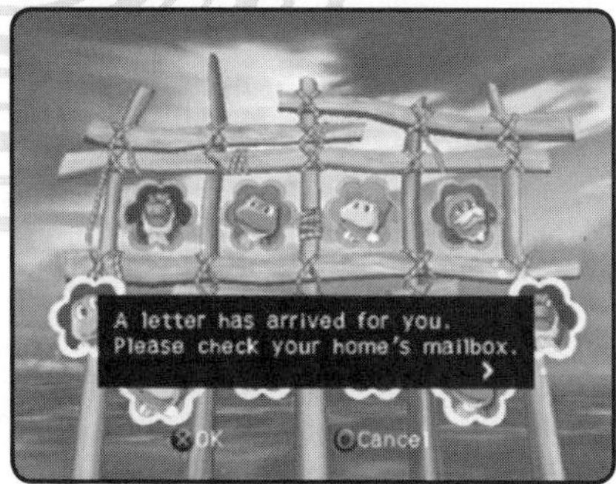

Gretzky NHL 06

Unlock It All
You could play a couple of seasons before you unlocked every trick and secret in Gretzky NHL 06, or you could have everything with one simple code. At the Main menu, choose Features and then Challenges, followed by Unlockables. Press START at the Unlockables to access the special keyboard, then enter this code: CONHEOSL

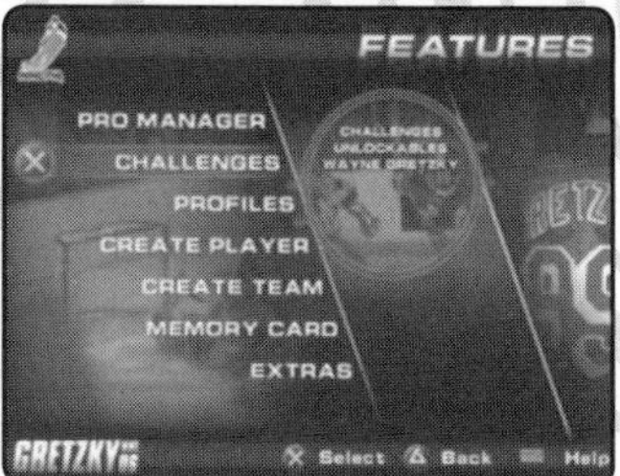

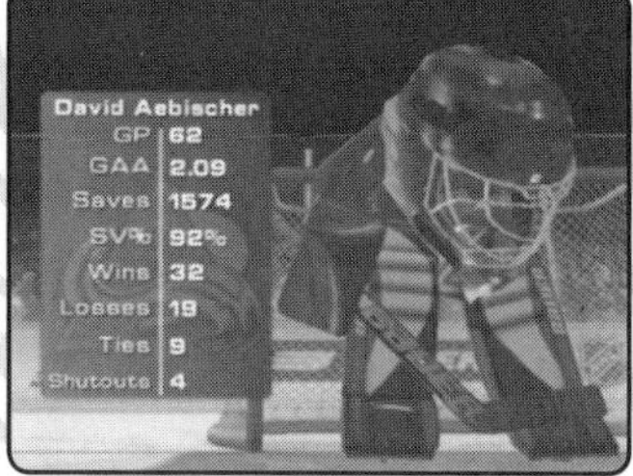

Hot Shots Golf Fore!

Unlock All Courses for Purchase

To enter a code, choose Options on the Main menu and then select the Password option near the bottom of the menu. Just remember that after you unlock the courses, you'll need to use your game points to purchase the courses at the shop.

Cheat	*Code*
Bagpipe Classic Course	CRCNHZ
Blue Lagoon Country Club	WVRJQS
Day Dream Golf Course	OQUTNA
Mini-Golf 2 Course	RVMIRU
Silk Road Classic Course	ZKOGJM
United Forest Golf Course	UIWHLZ
Western Valley Country Club	LIBTFL
Wild Green Country Club	YZLOXE

Unlock All Caddies for Purchase

To enter a code, choose Options on the Main menu and then select the Password option near the bottom of the menu. You can use these codes to unlock all the caddies in the game, but you'll need to use your game points to purchase the caddies at the shop.

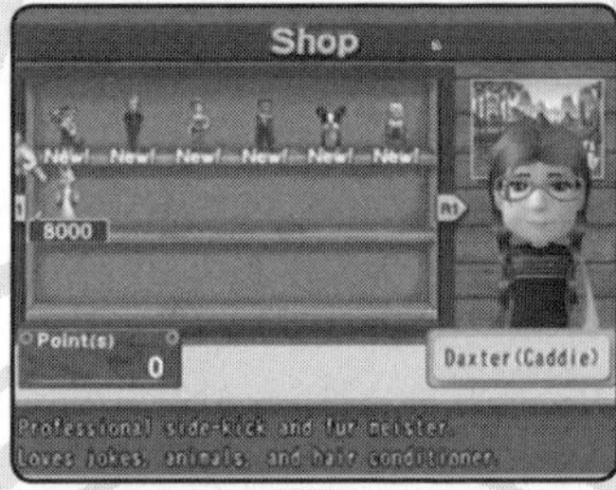

Cheat	*Code*
Caddie Clank	XCQGWJ
Caddie Daxter	WSIKIN
Caddie Kayla	MZIMEL
Caddie Kaz	LNNZJV
Caddie Mochi	MYPWPA
Caddie Simon	WRHZNB
Caddie Sophie	UTWIVQ

Unlock All Opponents for Single Player Mode

To unlock all the Vs. Mode opponents for play in Single Play Mode, enter this code at the Password feature on the Options menu:

REZTWS

20% Off Shop Items

To reduce shop price items by 20%, enter this code at the Password feature on the Options menu: MKJ3FQ

(continued)

Unlockable Items

If you want a specific item, you might score it for free with these codes:

Cheat	*Code*
Capsule 1	WXAFSJ
Capsule 2	OEINLK
Capsule 3	WFKVTG
Capsule 4	FCAVDO
Capsule 5	YYPOKK
Capsule 6	GDQDOF
Capsule 7	HHXKPV
Capsule 8	UOKXPS
Capsule 9	LMIRYD
Capsule 10	MJLJEQ
Capsule 11	MHNCQI
100t Hammer Club	NFSNHR
Big Air Club	DLJMFZ
Infinity Club	RZTQGV
Pinhole Club	DGHFRP
Beginner's Ball	YFQJJI
Big Air Ball	CRCGKR
Infinity Ball	DJXBRG
Pin Hole Ball	VZLSGP
Sidespin Ball	JAYQRK
Turbo Spin Ball	XNETOK
Lin's Outfit	BBLSKQ
Mike's Outfit	YKCFEZ
Phoebe's Outfit	GJBCHY
Mel's Outfit	ARFLCR

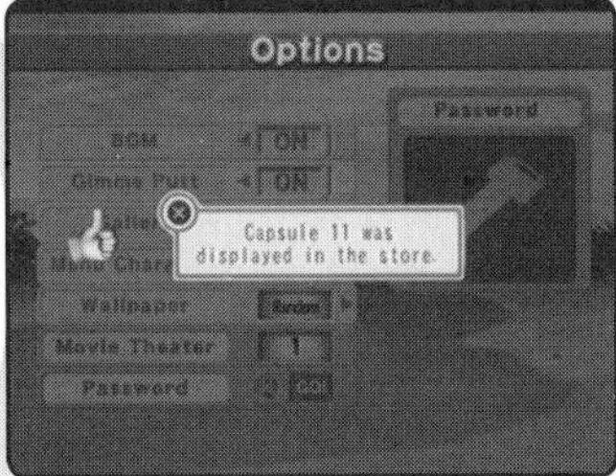

You'll need to own these clubs before you can use their upgrade codes:

Cheat	*Code*
Upgrade 100t Hammer Club to mid-level	BVLHSI
Upgrade 100t Hammer Club from mid- to top-level	MSCRUK
Upgrade Big Air Club to mid-level	TOSXUJ
Upgrade Big Air Club from mid- to top-level	JIDTQI
Upgrade Infinity Club to mid-level	WTGFOR
Upgrade Infinity Club from mid- to top-level	EIPCUL

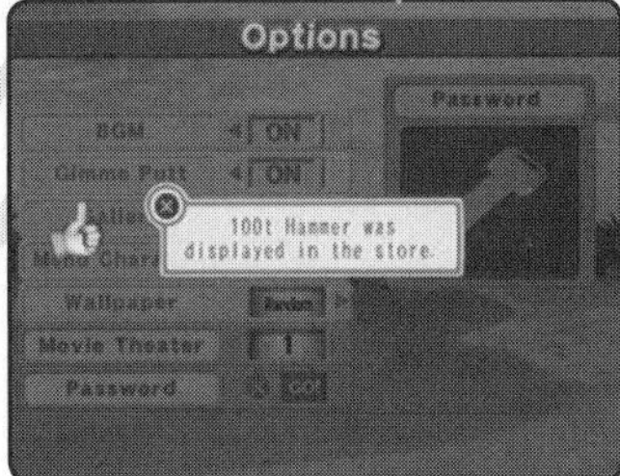

Wii Xbox 360 Xbox GC PS3 PS2 DS GBA PSP

Ice Age 2: The Meltdown

Pause and Unlock!
Unlocking these codes will require some fast fingers and a little memorization. Start a game and then press START to pause. Now enter these codes:

Cheat	*Code*
Unlock All Bonuses	Down, Left, Up, Down, Down, Left, Right, Right
Unlimited Energy	Down, Left, Right, Down, Down, Right, Left, Down
Unlimited Health	Up, Right, Down, Up, Left, Down, Right, Left
Unlimited Pebbles	Down, Down, Left, Up, Up, Right, Up, Down
Unlock Level Select	Up, Right, Right, Left, Right, Right, Down, Down

Insider Tips
Don't be surprised if you have to practice a dozen or so times before the rainbow-colored Unlock message flashes on the screen.

If you enter a code correctly, you'll see a message telling you what you've unlocked. If you enter a code correctly a second time, you'll actually turn the cheat off.

To access new unlocked levels, choose Level Select on the Pause menu.

LEGO Star Wars II: The Original Trilogy

Unlockable Characters and Ships
To unlock characters and ships for use in Free Play (replay) mode, go to the bar in the Cantina, select the Enter Codes option, and type in the following codes. If you enter a code correctly, you'll see a message telling you what you've unlocked, and you can then buy it in the Characters menu, as long as you have enough credits. Remember that you must complete a stage at least once to enable Free Play for that stage, and that ships are available in certain stages only.

Cheat	*Code*
Beach Trooper	UCK868
Ben Kenobi's Ghost	BEN917
Bespin Guard	VHY832
Bib Fortuna	WTY721
Boba Fett	HLP221
Death Star Trooper	BNC332
Ewok	TTT289
Gamorrean Guard	YZF999
Gonk Droid	NFX582
Grand Moff Tarkin	SMG219
Greedo	NAH118
Han Solo (with hood)	YWM840

(continued)

Cheat	Code
IG-88	NXL973
Imperial Guard	MMM111
Imperial Officer	BBV889
Imperial Shuttle Pilot	VAP664
Imperial Spy	CVT125
Jawa	JAW499
Lobot	UUB319
Palace Guard	SGE549
Rebel Pilot	CYG336
Rebel Trooper (Hoth)	EKU849
Sandtrooper	YDV451
Skiff Guard	GBU888
Snowtrooper	NYU989
Stormtrooper	PTR345
The Emperor	HHY382
TIE Fighter	HDY739
TIE Fighter Pilot	NNZ316
TIE Interceptor	QYA828
Tusken Raider	PEJ821
Ugnaught	UGN694

Insider Tip:
Depending on the console, Star Wars II: The Original Trilogy also has a few extra tricks. For example on the PlayStation 2 version, you can unlock these festive disguise options for purchase in the Extras menu at the Cantina.

Red Santa Hat	CL4U5H
Red Nose Disguise	NBP398
Glasses and White Beard	TYH319

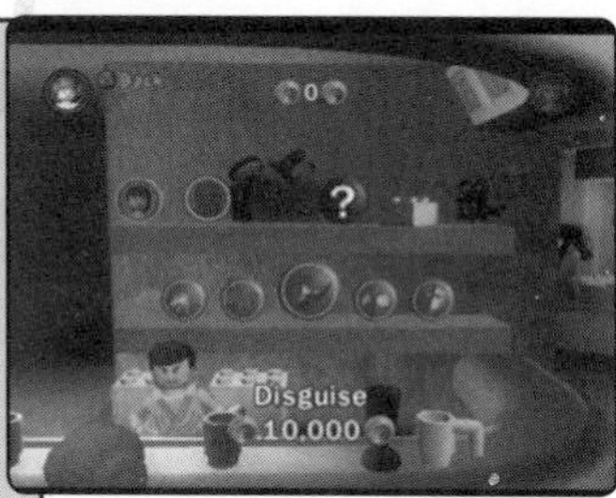

Le Mans 24 Hours

Unlock Cars, Courses, and Championships
Start a new game in Championship mode and then enter the following codes as your name. You don't have to play in Championship mode after entering a name, but you do need to select END on the name menu to input the unlock. Just press the Triangle button to exit back to the main menu, and then repeat with the other codes until you have all the stuff you need.

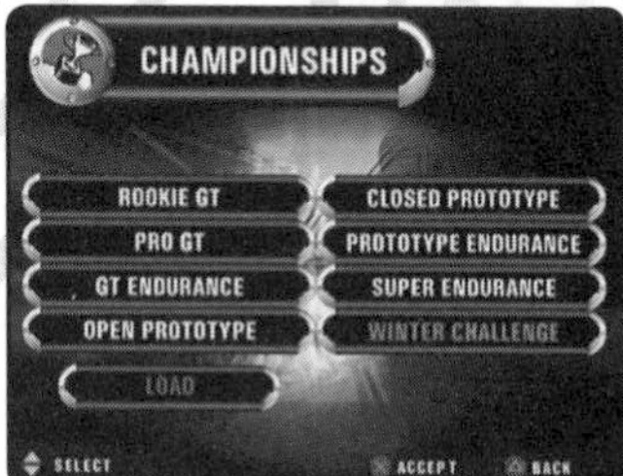

(continued)

Le Mans 24 Hours (cont.)

Cheat	*Code*
Unlock All Cars	ACO
Unlock All Championship Races	NUMBAT
Unlock Le Mans Course	WOMBAT
Unlock All Tracks	SPEEDY
See the Game Credits	HEINEY

Madden NFL 2005

Unlockable Madden Cards
At the Main menu, select My Madden and then choose Madden Cards and go to the Madden Codes section on the menu. Now carefully enter the following codes (everything should be UPPERCASE), and there are no zeros—just letter Os! If you enter an incorrect code, go back and check it against these:

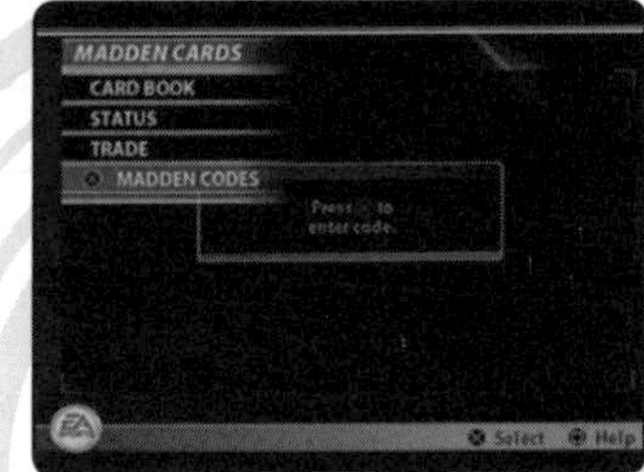

Cheat	*Code*
Your rival gets three downs, not four	Z28X8K
You get five downs	P66C4L
Unlock the Aloha Bowl stadium	G67F5X
Increase your chances for a defensive interception by 75%	J33IBF
Unlimited passing range	B61A8M
Unlimited field goal kicking range	I76X3T
You earn four award points per interception, nine points per sack	M89S8G
Your opponent must move the ball 15 yards for a first down	V65J8P
You just need five yards for a first down	O72E9B
Increase your opponent's fumble chances by 75%	R14B8Z
Increase your chance to break a tackle by 75%	L96J7P
Your opponent's QB throws lob passes	D57R5S
You can't fumble or throw an interception	X78P9Z
Your QB can't be sacked	Y59R8R
Increase the dive distance on your team by 75%	D59K3Y
Narrow the uprights for your opponent	V34L6D
Your opponent will fumble if he jukes during the half	L48G1E

(continued)

Super Bowl Dreams and Legendary Teams

At the Main menu, select My Madden and then choose Madden Cards and go to the Madden Codes section on the menu. Now carefully enter the following codes (everything should be UPPERCASE), and there are no zeros—just letter Os! If you enter an incorrect code, go back and check it against these:

Cheat	Code
Unlock Super Bowl XXXIX Stadium (Jacksonville)	D58F1B
Unlock Super Bowl XL Stadium (Detroit)	O85P6I
Unlock Super Bowl XLI Stadium (Miami)	P48Z4D
Unlock Super Bowl XLII Stadium (Phoenix)	T67R1O

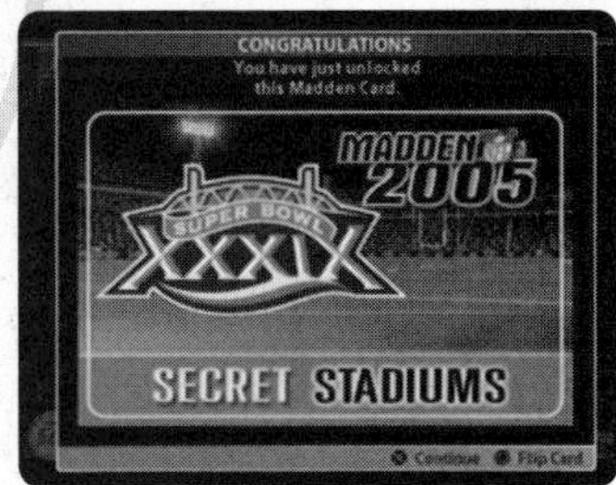

Cheat	Code
Unlock 1958 Colts team	P74X8J
Unlock 1966 Packers team	G49P7W
Unlock 1968 Jets team	C24W2A
Unlock 1970 Browns team	G12N1I
Unlock 1972 Dolphins team	R79W6W
Unlock 1974 Steelers team	R12D9B
Unlock 1976 Raiders team	P96Q8M
Unlock 1978 Dolphins team	G97U5X
Unlock 1980 Raiders team	K71K4E
Unlock 1981 Chargers team	Y27N9A
Unlock 1982 Redskins team	F56D6V

Cheat	Code
Unlock 1983 Raiders team	D23T8S
Unlock 1984 Dolphins team	X23Z8H
Unlock 1985 Bears team	F92M8M
Unlock 1986 Giants team	K44F2Y
Unlock 1988 '49ers team	F77R8H
Unlock 1990 Eagles team	G95F2Q
Unlock 1991 Lions team	I89F4I
Unlock 1992 Cowboys team	I44A1O
Unlock 1993 Bills team	Y66K3O
Unlock 1977 Broncos team	O18T2A

Madden NFL 06

Player Gold Cards and 25% Ratings Boosts

At the Main menu, select My Madden and then choose Madden Cards and go to the Madden Codes section on the menu. Now carefully enter the following codes (everything should be UPPERCASE), and mind your zeros and letter Os!

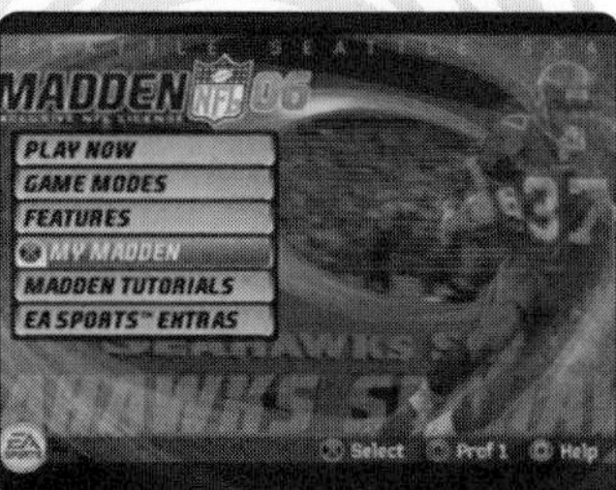

Cheat	*Code*
Champ Bailey	7L8C2W
Ronde Barber	7R7V2E
Bertrand Berry	7U4M9B
Anquan Boldin	7T3V5K
Derrick Brooks	7Q6X4L
Michael Clayton	7T1G2Y
Larry Fitzgerald	7T6B5N
Rex Grossman	6W5J6Z
Tommie Harris	7A7Z2G
Chad Johnson	7D1B2H
Rudi Johnson	7D1X8K
Thomas Jones	6X7W2O
Olin Kreutz	6Z9X5Y
Ashley Lelie	7J8F4J
J.P. Losman	7D8S6J
John Lynch	1A2D9F

Cheat	*Code*
Anthony McFarland	7S4C4D
Willis McGahee	7E3G7Y
Donovan McNabb	8Q2J2X
Lawyer Milloy	7H9E8L
Eric Moulds	7F5B2Y
Carson Palmer	7C6U4H
Jake Plummer	7J3Y7F
Simeon Rice	7Q6F4G
Brian Simmons	7D5W8J
Takeo Spikes	7H3B2Y
Lee Suggs	7P5G3N
LaDainian Tomlinson	7U6B3L
Brian Urlacher	6Y5Z6H
D.J. Williams	7O1J3F
Al Wilson	7K5C8V
Kellen Winslow Jr.	7Q2E4S

(continued)

Madden NFL 06 (cont.)

Super Bowl Venues

At the Main menu, select My Madden and then choose Madden Cards and go to the Madden Codes section on the menu. Now carefully enter the following codes (everything should be UPPERCASE), and there are no zeros—just letter Os! If you enter an incorrect code, go back and check it against these:

Cheat	*Code*
Unlock Super Bowl XL Stadium (Detroit)	4F9D2B
Unlock Super Bowl XLI Stadium (Miami)	4F9D2H
Unlock Super Bowl XLII Stadium (Phoenix)	4I1V6T
Unlock Super Bowl XLIII Stadium (Tampa)	4F3D7E
Unlock the Aloha Stadium (Hawaii)	4I1V6K

Madden NFL 07

Madden Card Codes

At the Main menu, select My Madden and then choose Madden Cards and go to the Madden Codes section on the menu. Now carefully enter the following codes (everything should be UPPERCASE, so hit the Caps button), and mind your zeros and letter Os!

Cheat	*Code*
You won't make a mistake—no interceptions or fumbles for a half	XL7SP1
Your QB is on target and he'll enjoy 100% accuracy	WROA0R
Lame Duck Card—the other team will lob passes for a half	5LAW00

(continued)

Madden NFL 07 (cont.)

Cheat	Code
'58 Colts	B57QLU
'66 Packers	1PL1FL
'68 Jets	MIE6WO
'70 Browns	CL2TOE
'72 Dolphins	NOEB7U
'74 Steelers	YOOFLA
'77 Broncos	C8UM7U
'78 Dolphins	VIU0O7
'80 Raiders	NLAPH3
'81 Chargers	COAGI4
'82 Redskins	WL8BRI
'83 Raiders	H0EW7I

Cheat	Code
'84 Dolphins	M1AM1E
'85 Bears	QOETO8
'86 Giants	ZI8S2L
'88 '49ers	SP2A8H
'90 Eagles	2L4TRO
'91 Lions	J1ETRI
'92 Cowboys	W9UVI9
'93 Bills	DLA3I7
'94 '49ers	DR7EST
'96 Packers	F8LUST
'98 Broncos	FIES95
'99 Rams	S9OUSW

Cheat	Code
Super Bowl XLI Stadium (Miami)	RLA9R7
Super Bowl XLII Stadium (Glendale, AZ)	WRLUF8
Super Bowl XLIII Stadium (Tampa)	NIEV4A
Super Bowl XLIV Stadium (Miami)	M5AB7L
Bears pump up crowd	B1OUPH
Bengals cheerleader	DRL2SW
Bills cheerleader	1PLUYO
Broncos cheerleader	3ROUJO
Browns pump up crowd	T1UTOA
Buccaneers cheerleader	S9EWRI
Cardinals cheerleader	57IEPI

Cheat	Code
Chargers cheerleader	F7UHL8
Chiefs cheerleader	PRI5SL
Colts cheerleader	1R5AMI
Cowboys cheerleader	Z2ACHL
Dolphins cheerleader	C5AHLE
Eagles cheerleader	PO7DRO
Falcons cheerleader	37USPO
'49ers cheerleader	KL0CRL
Giants pump up crowd	C4USPI
Jaguars cheerleader	MIEH7E
Jets pump up crowd	COLUXI
Lions pump up crowd	3LABLU
Packers pump up crowd	4HO7VO
Panthers cheerleader	F2IASP

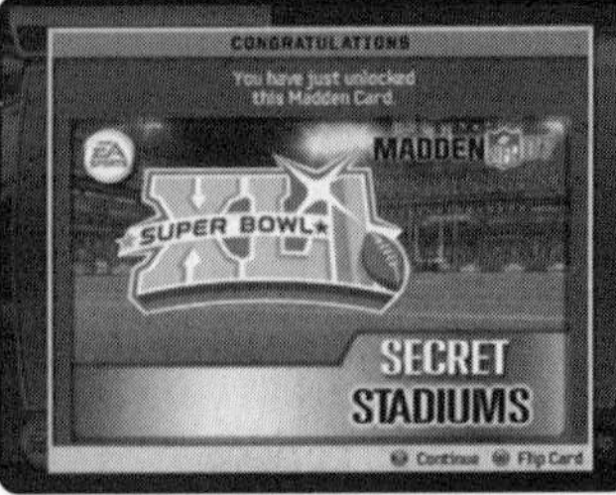

Unlockable Extras

Whether you want to race the truck or race number 3 as Dale Earnhardt Sr., these are the best codes in the game. From the Fight to the Top Main menu, access the Edit Driver menu, then enter the following first and last names.

Cheat	*First Name*	*Last Name*
Instant $10 million in Fight to the Top Mode	Walmart	Money
Max out Fan Level in Fight to the Top Mode	Super	Star
Max out Prestige Level in Fight to the Top Mode	MeMyself	AndI
Max out Team Prestige in Fight to the Top Mode	All	ForOne
Race as Dale Earnhardt Sr.	The	Intimidator
Race as Jarrett in the UPS Truck	Race	TheTruck
Unlock All Chase Plates in Fight to the Top Mode	Gimme	Gimmie
Unlock the Wal-Mart cars, raceway, and custom car	Walmart	Exclusive

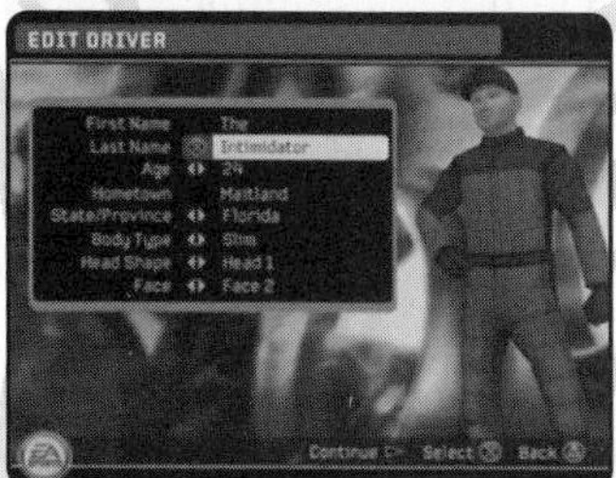

Remember that these codes are case-sensitive! Also, once you use the codes, you can race as either Dale in the other game modes, but not in Fight to the Top.

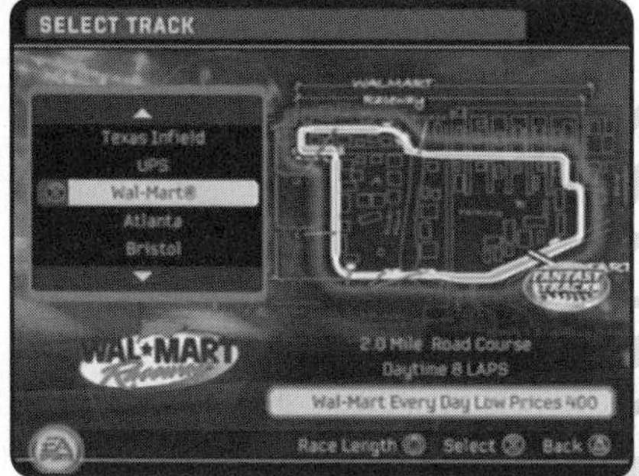

Wii
Xbox 360
Xbox
GC
PS3
PS2
DS
GBA
PSP

NBA 2K5

24/7 Items Unlocked

Need unlimited spending money for cool customizations? Check out this trick. Just keep in mind that the code unlocks items, not the stages. You'll still need to play and win to unlock those places. Begin a 24/7 game and enter the following name for your character:

RAY GRAHAM

After you add the name, check out the 24/7 Items menu at your home. Use the L1 and R1 Buttons to scroll through the list of options (and check out the cool bunny slippers).

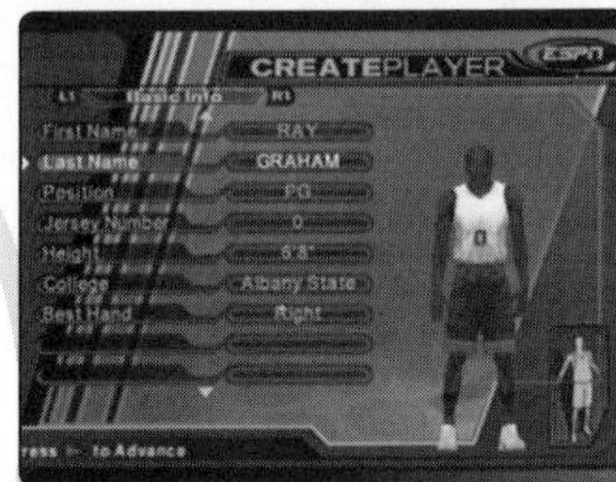

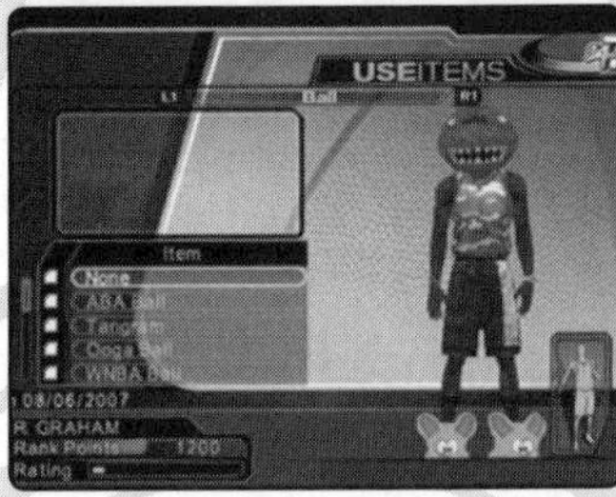

NBA Ballers and NBA Ballers: Phenom

VS Lineup Codes

The trick to entering NBA Ballers Phenom codes is knowing where to enter them. Look for the VS screen showing the three basketballs next to the pictures of the players. To enter these codes, the first number in the three-digit code is how many times you press the Square button, the second number is how many times you press the Triangle button, and the last digit is how many times you press the Circle button. To finish off the code, press any direction pad button before the game loads.

Cheat	*Square*	*Triangle*	*Circle*
Ally-Oop Ability	7	2	5
Alternate Gear	1	2	3
Baby Ballers	4	2	3
Better Free Throws	3	1	7
Big Head on Player	1	3	4
Double Juice Replenish	4	3	1
Kid Ballers	4	3	3
Super Block Ability	1	2	4
Young Ballers	4	4	3

Unlockable Features

Use these codes to unlock the best features in the game. Go to the My NBA Live option on the Main menu and then select NBA Codes to enter a code.

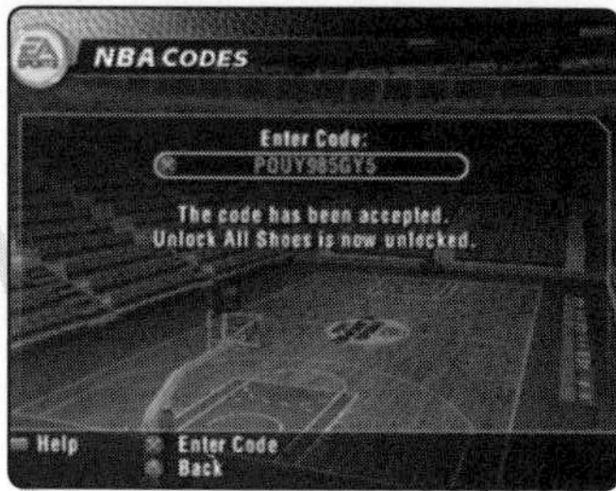

Cheat	*Code*
Earn 15,000 NBA Store Points	87843H5F9P
Unlock all hardwood classics jerseys	725JKUPLMM
Unlock all NBA gear	ERT9976KJ3
Unlock all shoes	POUY985GY5
Unlock all team gear	YREY5625WQ

Hidden Characters

You can also unlock hidden characters in the game in the Create Player option on the Roster Management menu. Enter these names as the last name of the player (choose BIO to access the Name menu), then look for these players in the free agent pool.

Cheat	*Code*
Mario Austin	POSNEGHX
Malick Badiane	SKENXIDO
Sani Becirovic	ZXCCVDRI
Matt Bonner	BBVDKCVM
Carlos Delfino	SDFGURKL
Jermaine Dupri	SOSODEF
Andreas Glyniadakis	POCKDLEK
Kyle Korver	OEISNDLA
James Lang	NBVKSMCN
Paccelis Morlende	QWPOASZX
Aleksander Pavlovic	WHSUCPOI
Rick Rickert	POIKJMN
Sofoklis Schortsanitis	IOUBFDCJ
Nedzad Sinanovic	ZXDSDRKE
Tommy Smith	XCFWQASE
Szymon Szewczyk	POIOIJIS
Remon Van de Hare	ITNVCJSD
Xue Yuyang	WMZKCOI

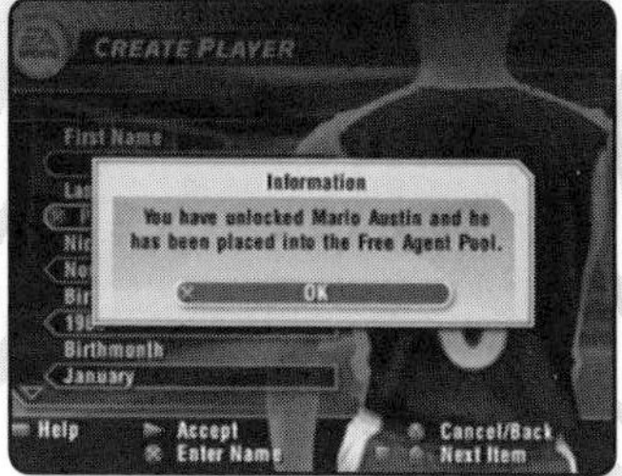

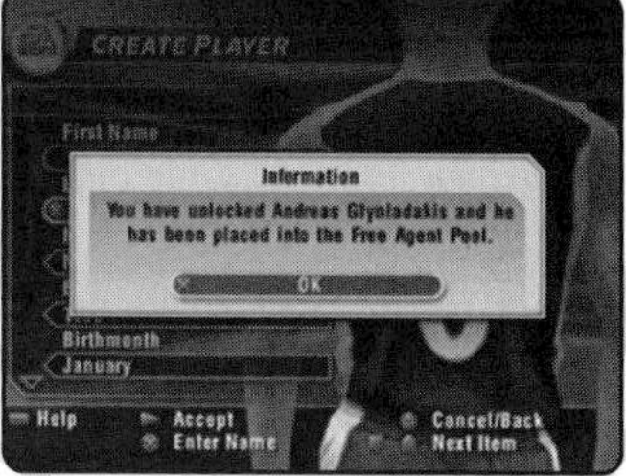

Wii Xbox 360 Xbox GC PS3 PS2 DS GBA PSP

NBA Live 08

Adidas Shoes for You

Will new shoes improve your game? Probably not, but these items will add some variety to your game. From the Main Menu, choose My NBA Live, then NBA Codes. Now enter the following codes and you'll walk off with new shoes:

Adidas TS Lightswitch Gil Agent Zero shoe	ADGILLIT6BE
Adidas TS Lightswitch Gil Cuba shoe	ADGILLIT4BC
Adidas TS Lightswitch Gil Black President shoe	ADGILLIT7BF
Adidas TS Lightswitch Gil Customize shoe	ADGILLIT5BD
Adidas TS Lightswitch Gil GilWood	ADGILLIT1B9
Adidas TS Lightswitch (Away) Shoe	ADGILLIT0B8
Adidas TS Lightswitch (Home) Shoe	ADGILLIT2BA

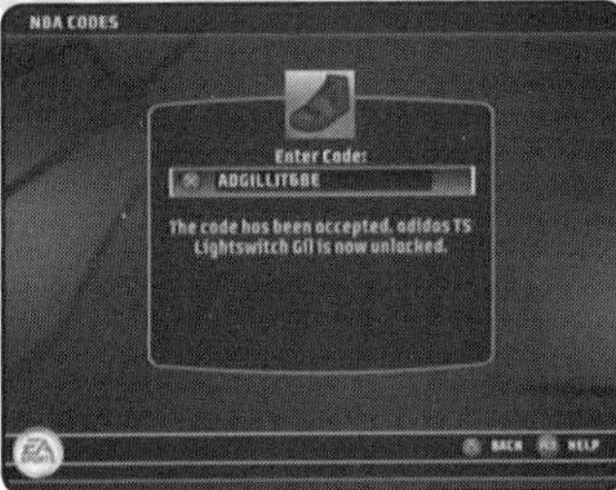

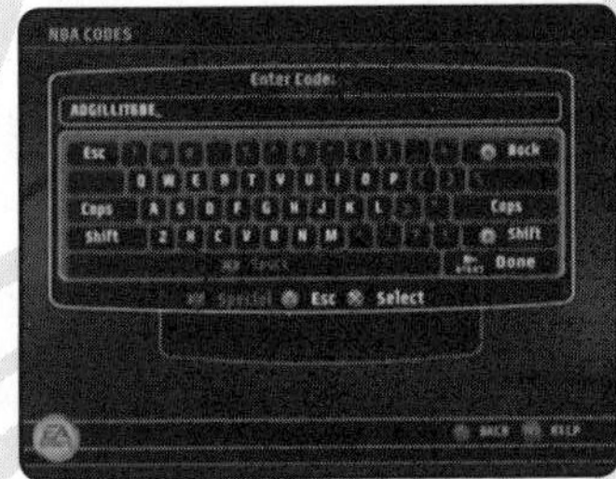

NBA Street

Versus Screen Codes

Versus Screen codes are not hard to enter, but you have to have the code ready before time runs out. The first number in the codes below is how many times you need to press the Square button, the second number is how many times you press the Triangle button, the third number his how many times you press the Circle button, and the fourth number is how many times you press the X button. After you have a code entered (and before time runs out) press the Right button on the direction pad and you should see a message that will verify that you entered the code right.

Cheat	*Square*	*Triangle*	*Circle*	*X*
ABA Ball	0	1	1	0
ABA Socks	4	4	4	4
Alley-oops Disabled	3	4	1	2

(continued)

NBA Street (cont.)

Cheat	*Square*	*Triangle*	*Circle*	*X*
Beach Ball	0	1	1	2
Big Head	4	1	2	1
Disable Cheats	1	1	1	1
Dunks Disabled	3	0	1	2
EA Big Ball	0	1	4	0
Easy Shots	2	1	3	0
Fewer Blocks	3	1	2	3
Fewer Gamebreakers	1	3	4	2
Gamebreakers Disabled	1	4	4	2
Infinite Turbo	2	0	3	0
Juice Disabled	1	4	4	3
Medicine Ball	0	1	1	3
Mega Dunks	3	0	1	0
More Gamebreakers	1	4	3	2
No Auto Replays	1	2	1	1
No Shot Clock	4	4	0	3
No Two-Point Shots	3	3	0	3
NuFX Ball	0	1	3	0
Reduced Steals	3	1	4	0
Soccer Ball	0	2	1	0
Tiny Heads	4	2	4	2
Tiny Players	4	0	4	0
Volley Ball	0	1	1	4
WNBA Ball	0	1	2	0

Unlockable Players

You can also unlock the following players on the Versus screen with these codes:

Cheat	*Square*	*Triangle*	*Circle*	*X*
Unlock Athletic Joe	1	2	0	1
Unlock Captain Quicks	3	0	2	1
Unlock Mad Handles	3	2	1	0
Unlock Springtime Joe	1	1	0	1
Unlock Summertime Joe	1	0	0	1

Need for Speed Carbon

Unlockable Extras

While you don't need a lot of speed to unlock these infinite bonuses and logo vinyls, you will need smooth and even button pushing on the direction pad. Enter these codes on the Main menu:

Cheat	*Code*
Infinite Nitrous	Left, Up, Left, Down, Left, Down, Right, Square
Infinite SpeedBreaker	Down, Right, Right, Left, Right, Up, Down, Square
Castrol Cash Unlocked	Down, Up, Left, Down, Right, Up, Square, Triangle
Carbon Logo Vinyls	Right, Up, Down, Up, Down, Left, Right, Square
Special Logo Vinyls	Up, Up, Down, Down, Down, Down, Up, Square

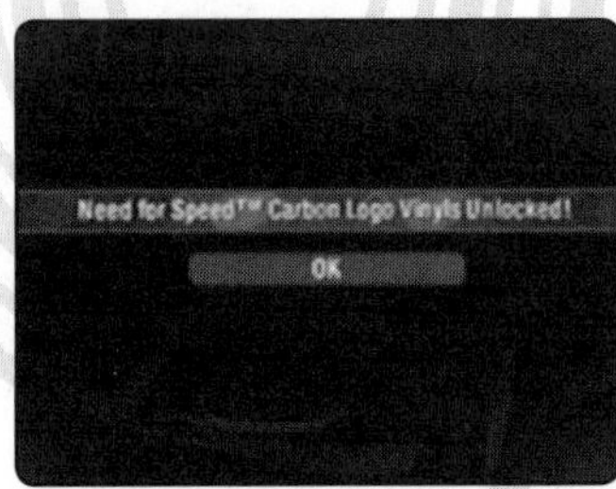

Need For Speed ProStreet

Promotion Codes and Spending Money

Add a new ride or customize your look with these codes. Select the Code Entry option in the Main Menu and check your spelling. You'd be surprised at how many street racers misspell lithium.

Add $10,000 to your spending money	cashmoney
Add another $10,000 to your spending money	reggame
Add five repair tokens	safetynet
Unlock the Castrol Syntec vinyls	castrolsyntec
Unlock the Coke Zero Golf GTI	zerozerozero
Unlock the Energizer vinyls	energizerlithium
Unlock the classic Chevelle SS	horsepower
Unlock the Audi TT	itsaboutyou
Unlock the Progressive vinyls	leipzig
Unlock the Mitsubishi Lancer Evolution	mitsubishigofar
Unlock the Dodge Viper SRT10	worldslongestlasting
Unlock four cars (240 SX, GTO, Chevy, Viper)	unlockallthings

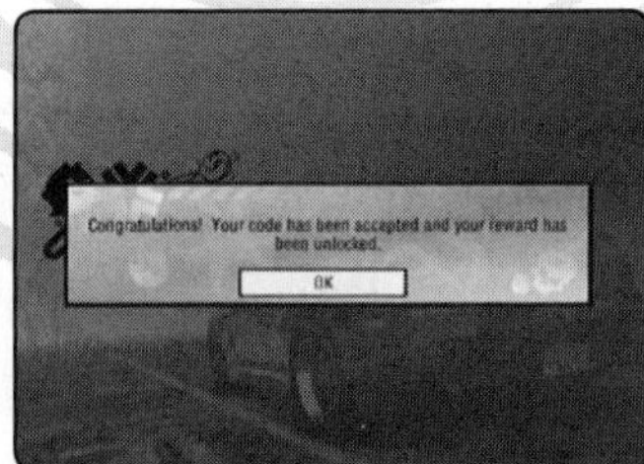

Need for Speed Underground

Unlock All Tracks

Enter these codes at the Main menu:

Cheat	*Code*
Open all Circuit mode tracks	Down, R1, R1, R1, R2, R2, R2, Square
Open all Sprint mode tracks	Up, R2, R2, R2, R1 Down, Down, Down
Open all Drag mode tracks	Right, Square, Left, R1, Square, L1, L2, R2
Open all Drift mode tracks	Left, Left, Left, Left, Right, R2, R1, L2

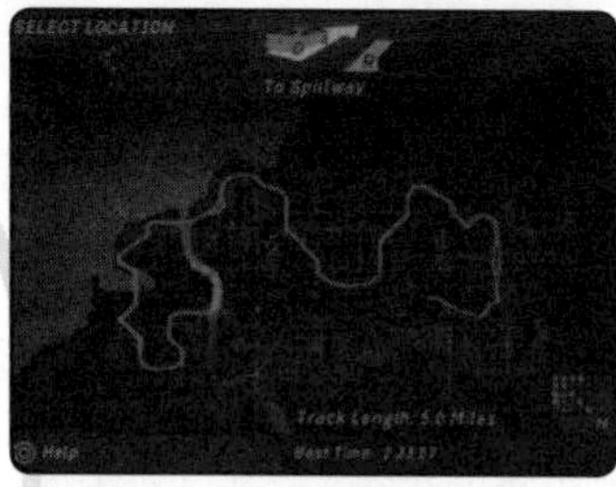

You'll have to check the Game Mode Tracks to verify that the code worked.

Need for Speed Underground 2

Unlockable Sponsor Cars

Enter these codes at the Press Start title screen:

Car	*Code*
Lincoln Navigator	Up, Right, Up, Up, Down, Right, Down, Right
Hummer H2	Up, Left, Up, Up, Down, Left, Down, Left
Mitsubishi Eclipse	Up, Down, Right, Up, Left, Down, Right, Right
Lexus	Up, Down, Left, Up, Left, Up, Right, Left

Be sure to enter these codes on the direction pad, not with the analog stick. If you enter the code correctly, you'll hear a chime that sounds just like the tone you hear when you choose a Game menu selection. Unlock more than one car and you can race against a friend in Split Screen mode.

Custom Vinyls

Unlock the Sponsor vinyls by entering these codes at the Press Start title screen. Access the features at the Career mode graphics shop.

Cheat	*Code*
Unlock the Best Buy Sponsor Vinyl	Up, Down, Up, Down, Down, Up, Right, Left
Unlock the Burger King Vinyl	Up, Up, Up, Down, Up, Up, Left
Unlock the Unique Vinyl	Down, Up, Down, Left, L1, L1, L1, Down

Insider Tip

Never found a graphics shop in Career mode? Wait until you see an e-mail from Rachel about the graphic shop north of the casinos in South Market. Look for a dead end and drive beyond the construction roadblocks to a red light, and you'll find the shop. Once you locate the graphics shop, you can select it on your GPS mapping system.

NFL Street

To unlock these special game features, you'll need to create a new file name for each unlock feature. Choose the NFL Challenge on the main menu, select Create New when the game prompts you to enter a User ID, and then enter one of these names:

Cheat	*Code*
Unlock all of the playing fields	Travel
Unlock NFL Legends Team	Classic
Unlock the Executioners Team	Excellent

You can also create a new team on the Select Controller menu if you press up or down on the direction pad.

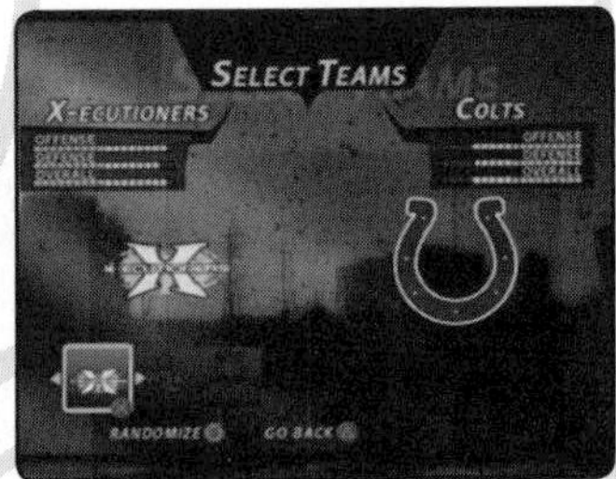

Nightmare Before Christmas: Oogie's Revenge

Costume Codes
During game play, pick a quiet spot away from the attacking fiends. From here, you can unlock the Pumpkin Jack and Santa Jack codes by entering the following on the direction pad and by pressing the tops of the Analog Control Sticks (L3 and R3 buttons): Down, Up, Right, Left, L3, R3

Once you enter the code successfully, you can change to Pumpkin Jack by pressing the L1 button and Santa Jack by pressing the R1 button.

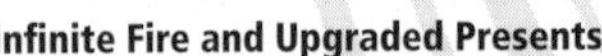

Infinite Fire and Upgraded Presents
Change into Pumpkin Jack by pressing the L1 button and quickly enter the following code: Left, Down, Right, Up, Right, Down, Left, Up

If you did it right, you'll hear the sound of a lid closing (the same noise that you hear when you press START) and the number next to Jack's flame power will change to an infinity symbol.

Change to Santa Jack by pressing the R1 button and enter this code to upgrade the power of your presents: Down, Left, Right, Up, L3, R3

Unlock Everything

Entering this code can be a little complicated, so follow these directions closely:

1. Start the game and choose Single Player at the Main menu.
2. Press the Triangle button to choose License on the Coast 2 Coast screen.
3. Press the X button and scroll down to Edit License on the License Options menu.
4. Choose Enter Name and press X.
5. Hit the Backspace button on the screen to erase the existing license name.
6. Hit the Caps Lock button on the screen.
7. Now enter ENTIRETY as the name on the license in uppercase letters.
8. Hit the Done button on the screen.
9. Press Down on the direction buttons once so the Select Nationality appears at the top of the screen.
10. Now press the Circle button to go back. Do NOT hit the Done button on the screen.

If you entered the code correctly, you'll see all the courses open and you can choose any rival and any car in the game!

Earn a Million OutRun Miles

This code is also complicated, so follow these directions closely:

1. Start the game and choose Single Player at the Main Menu.
2. Press the Triangle button to choose License on the Coast 2 Coast screen.
3. Press the X button and scroll down to Edit License on the License Options menu.
4. Choose Enter Name and press X.
5. Hit the Backspace button on the screen to erase the existing license name.
6. Hit the Caps Lock button on the screen.
7. Now enter MILESANDMILES as the name on the license in uppercase letters.
8. Hit the Done button on the screen.
9. Press Down on the direction buttons once so the Select Nationality appears at the top of the screen.
10. Now press the Circle button to go back. Do NOT hit the Done button on the screen.

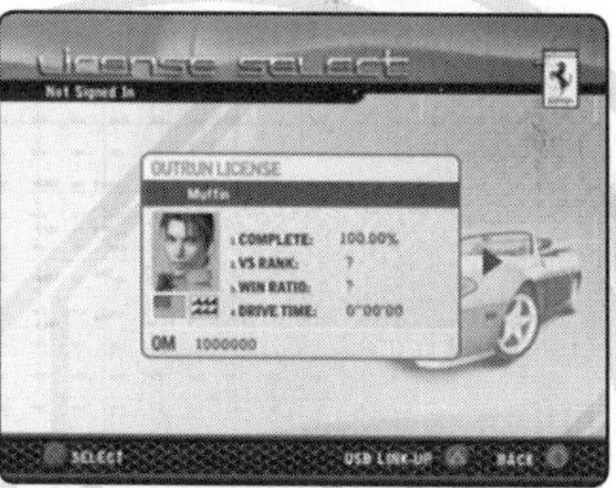

If you entered the code correctly, you'll have a million OutRun miles!

Over the Hedge

Unlock All Levels, Mini-Games, and More

These quick and simple codes can do everything from increasing the amount of health you get from power-ups to unlocking bonus content. To enter any code, pause your game, hold the L1 and R1 buttons, enter the code, and then release L1 and R1.

Cheat	*Code*
Unlock All Levels	Triangle, Circle, Triangle, Circle, Circle, Square
Unlock All Mini-Games	Triangle, Circle, Triangle, Triangle, Square, Square
Unlock All Melee Moves	Triangle, Circle, Triangle, Square, Square, Circle
Inflict Extra Melee Damage	Triangle, Circle, Triangle, Circle, Triangle, Square
More Health from Power-Ups	Triangle, Circle, Triangle, Circle, Square, Triangle
Powered-Up Projectiles	Triangle, Circle, Triangle, Circle, Square, Circle
Unlock Bonus Comic #14	Triangle, Circle, Square, Square, Circle, Triangle
Unlock Bonus Comic #15	Triangle, Triangle, Square, Circle, Square, Circle

If you enter the codes correctly, you'll see the words Cheat Enabled.

Insider Tip

You can enter more than one code while on the Pause screen. Use combined codes like the Extra Melee Damage cheat and Melee Moves Unlock cheat to make the game easier without taking away all of the challenges.

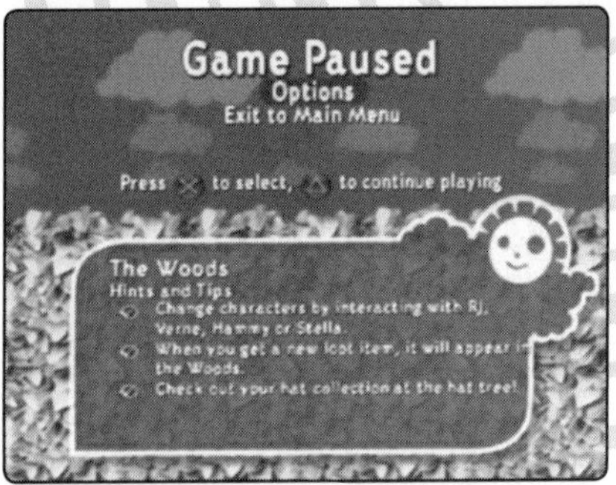

Paris-Dakar Rally

Unlockable Tracks, Cars, and More
If you need a little assistance, try these codes:

Cheat	***Code***
Unlock all tracks	DEADPARROT
Unlock all cars	ILUMBERJACK
Unlock everything	CRUNCHYFROG

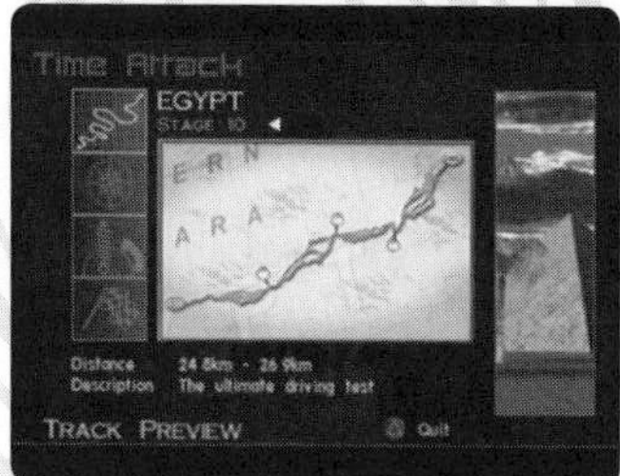

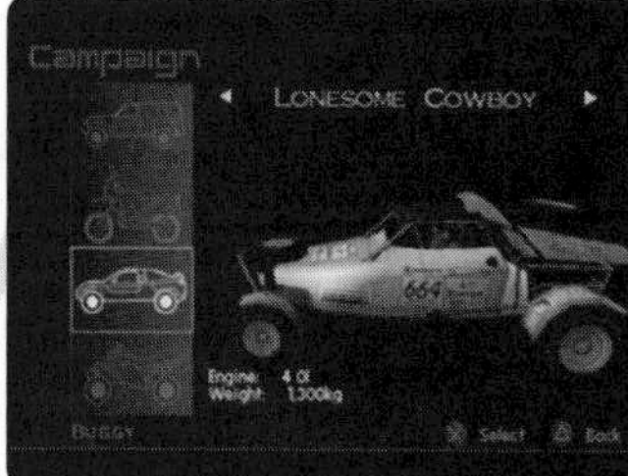

Pinball Hall of Fame The Gottlieb Collection

Code for Old-School Arcade Games
Long before video games, your parents and grandparents plunked down their spare change to play these arcade games—although few of them will never admit it today. Select Enter Code from the Main Menu and enter these three-letter codes:

Unlock the vintage 1932 Play-Boy card-theme pinball game	PKR
Unlock the Xolten fortune teller machine	XTN
Activate Custom Balls at the Option menu	BLZ
Unlock Tournament mode	TMA
Unlock the Love Meter arcade machine	LUV
Unlock the Gottlieb Factory Tour photo album	DGC
Unlock Payout mode	LAS
Activate the Tilt feature at the Option menu	NDG
Activate the Infinite Last Ball feature at the Option menu	INF

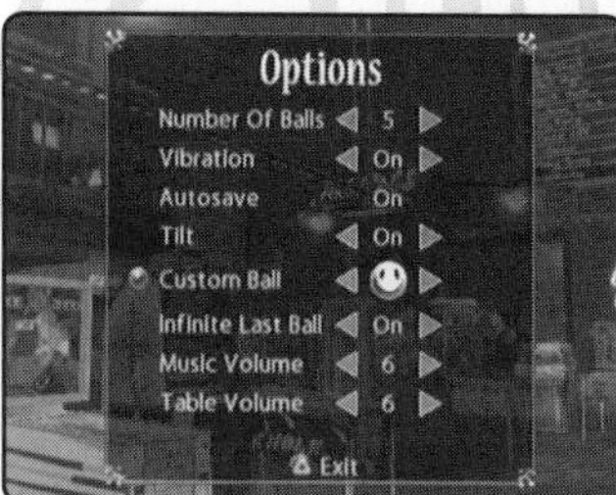

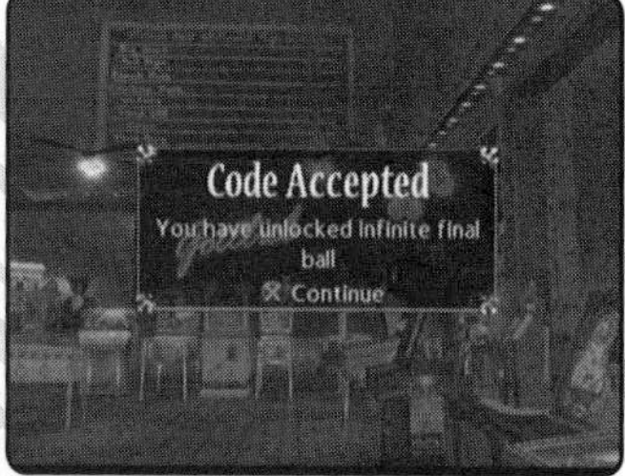

Rampage: Total Destruction

Monstrous Codes

You won't find the Hidden Code screen in Rampage: Total Destruction unless you press the L2 and R2 buttons at the same time at the Main menu. You'll hear a laugh if you enter the following codes correctly.

Cheat	Code
Unlock All Cities	271828
Unlock All Monsters and Cities	141421
Invincible to Attack	986960
Buildings Are Weak	071767
All Upgraded Abilities	011235
Check Out Credits	667302
Open Final Scene	667301
Replay Beginning Scene	667300
Show Game Version in Upper Left Corner	314159
Unlock Demo Mode	082864

Insider Tip

You may need to reset your game after entering in some codes like the Demo mode. To disable other codes, open the Code menu again and enter 000000.

Ratatouille

A Smorgasbord of Secrets

At the Menu, choose Extras and then Gusteau's Shop. At Gusteau's Shop, choose the Secrets option. At this menu you'll see a list of codes that you can buy with Gusteau points, but if you press right on the D-Pad you'll scroll through twenty blank spots for additional codes! Select a code number and then press the X Button to enter the corresponding cheat code.

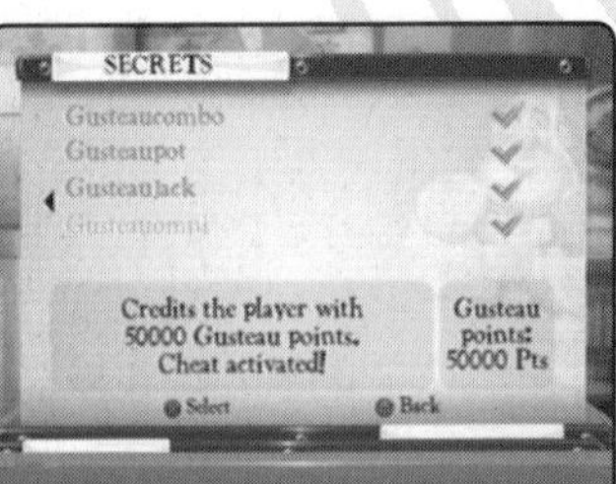

(continued)

Ratatouille (cont.)

Cheat	*Code*
Code 1 unlocks Very Easy game play mode	Pieceocake
Code 2 protects Remy from impact and enemy damage	Myhero
Code 3 plays the Asobo logo	Asobo
Code 4 protects Remy from all damage except from falls and water	Shielded
Code 5 makes Remy undetected by foes	Spyagent
Code 6 gives Remy gas when he jumps	Ilikeonions
Code 7 replaces tail swipe with a head butt!	Hardfeelings
Code 8 unlocks multi-player mode	Slumberparty
Code 9 unlocks all concept art	Gusteauart
Code 10 unlocks the four championship modes	Gusteauship
Code 11 unlocks all minigames in all modes	Mattelme
Code 12 unlocks all videos	Gusteauvid
Code 13 unlocks all bonus art work	Gusteaures
Code 14 unlocks all Dream Worlds in Gusteau's Shop	Gusteaudream
Code 15 unlocks all slides in Gusteau's Shop	Gusteauslide
Code 16 unlocks all single-player minigames	Gusteaulevel
Code 17 unlocks all Gusteau Shop items	Gusteaucombo
Code 18 awards 5,000 Gusteau points	Gusteaupot
Code 19 awards 10,000 Gusteau points	Gusteaujack
Code 20 awards 50,000 Gusteau points	Gusteauomni

It's important to capitalize the first letter in these codes and then keep everything else lowercase. After entering a code, you'll need to highlight the code that you want to use and press the X button to activate it.

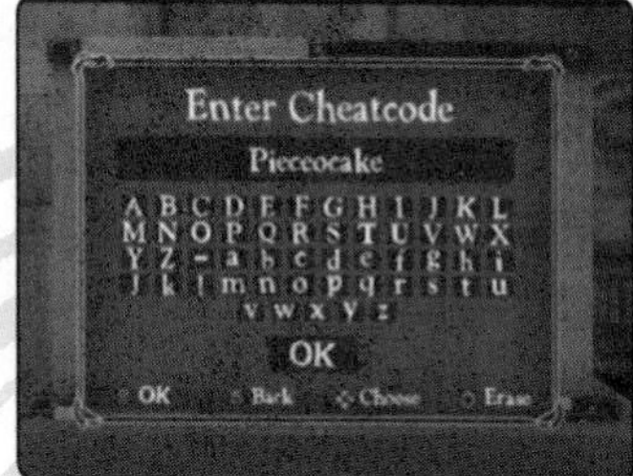

Scooby-Doo! Night of 100 Frights

Rewards for Fast Fingers

While these codes work, you'll need to practice a bit before your fingers are fast enough to enter these quick codes correctly. Start a game and then press START to pause your progress. At the pause screen, press and hold L1, L2, R1, R2 all at the same time. You'll need to hold those buttons down while entering the following codes. If you do it right, you'll hear Scooby cheer.

(continued)

Scooby-Doo! Night of 100 Frights (cont.)

Increased gum, soap, and other power-ups: Circle, Square, Circle, Square, Circle, Square, Square, Square, Circle, Circle, Square, Circle, Circle, Circle

Unlock video cut scenes in Monster Gallery: Square, Square, Square, Circle, Circle, Circle, Square, Circle, Square

See final credits: Square, Circle, Circle, Square, Circle, Square

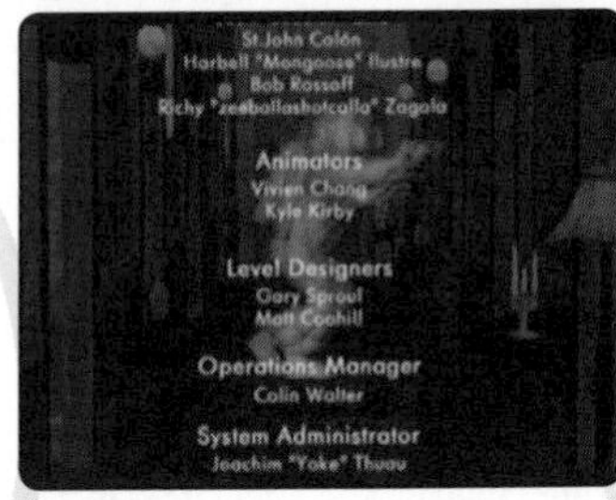

Insider Tip

If a game contains codes that require extra finger speed, start with a simple code first and tackle the hard ones last. Try entering the final credits code several times until you do it right. Now you know how fast you need to press the buttons to unlock the gum, soap, and other power-ups. Luckily, these codes just require pressing the Square and Circle buttons.

Shark Tale

Unlockable Invincibility (and More)!

Start a game and pause it by pressing SELECT. While the game is paused, hold the L1 button and enter the following codes:

Cheat	*Code*
Invincibility	X, O, X, Left, Square, R1, Down, Square, Square
Knock fish off the screen	O, O, O, O, X, O, O, O, O
Replace Pearls with Fish King Coins	O, X, O, O, O, X, O, O

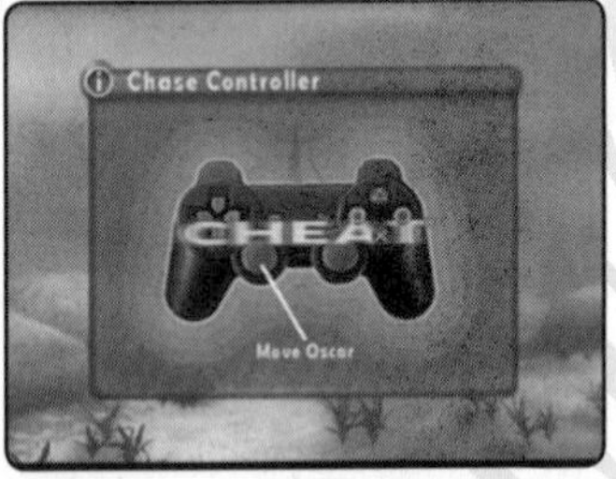

Insider Tips

You'll find that these codes are easy to enter if you pay close attention to which buttons you're holding while entering the codes.

If you find that the invincibility code or another code makes the game too easy, enter the code a second time to disable it.

Shrek 2

Scrapbook Cheats
Start a game and pause it. Select the Scrapbook option on the Pause menu and then enter these codes on the Scrapbook screen:

Cheat	*Code*
Add 1,000 gold coins	Left, Up, X, Circle, Left, Up, X, Circle, Left, Up, X, Circle, Circle, Circle, Circle, Circle, Circle
Refill all health meters	Left, Up, X, Circle, Left, Up, X, Circle, Left, Up, X, Circle, Up, Right, Down, Left, Up
Unlock all levels	Left, Up, X, Circle, Left, Up, X, Circle, Left, Up, X, Circle, Up, Up, Up, Up, Up
Unlock all bonuses	Left, Up, X, Circle, Left, Up, X, Circle, Left, Up, X, Circle, Square, Circle, Square, Circle, Square, Circle

Insider Tips
If you enter the code right, you'll hear one of the characters say a line from the game. You don't have to press the buttons fast to correctly enter a code, so just focus on being accurate.

If you need more than 1,000 gold coins, try entering the Gold Coin code more than once at the Scrapbook screen!

Shrek the Third

10,000 Extra Far Far Coins
If you need a little more purchase power, go to the Gift Shop and enter this code on your controller D-pad: Up, Up, Down, Up, Right, Left

Insider Tip
This code requires a little practice and pacing—it's not the speed of the code, but how smoothly you press each direction on the pad.

(continued)

Shrek the Third (cont.)

Open the Ogre Babies Stage

This code was a secret promotion code that some lucky players received when they bought their Shrek the Third games at certain stores. Open the Main menu and then press the following on your controller D-pad: Left, Down, Right, Up, Right, Right, Right

Secret Costumes

Open the Main menu and then press the following on your controller D-pad:

Cheat	Code
Snorkle Suit	Right, Right, Down, Left, Left, Up, Right
Outback Outfit	Left, Left, Up, Right, Right, Up, Left

Spider-Man

Unbeatable Cheats

You can enter these codes at the Cheats menu by scrolling to Specials at the Main menu screen. You can enter multiple codes at the Cheats menu and combine code effects. If you type in a code right you'll hear the Green Goblin laugh as you select Done.

Cheat	Code
Big head and feet on Spider-Man	GOESTOYOURHEAD
Enemies have big heads	JOELSPEANUTS
Goblin costume on Spider-Man	FREAKOUT
Open all levels, combo moves, and gallery stuff	ARACHNID
Open bonus training levels	HEADEXPLODY
Open level select options	IMIARMAS
Play as a patrol officer	REALHERO

Spider-Man (cont.)

Cheat	*Code*
Play as a scientist	SERUM
Play as a helicopter pilot	CAPTAINSTACEY
Play as a thug	THUGSRUS
Play as a skull gang member	KNUCKLES
Play as Shocker	HERMANSCHULTZ
Skip levels at the pause screen	ROMITAS
Slow motion attacks	DODGETHIS
Switch to first-person perspective	UNDERTHEMASK
Unlimited Goblin Glider energy	CHILLOUT
Unlimited webbing	ORGANICWEBBING

Spider-Man Friend or Foe

Sidekicks and Tech Tokens

Sometimes the fight feels better when you have a sidekick along. While on Nick Fury's flying Helicarrier enter these codes on the direction buttons:

Add 5,000 Tech Tokens to inventory	Up, Up, Down, Down, Left, Right
Unlock Green Goblin sidekick	Left, Down, Right, Right, Down, Left
Unlock Sandman sidekick	Right, Right, Right, Up, Down, Left
Venom sidekick	Left, Left, Right, Up, Down, Down

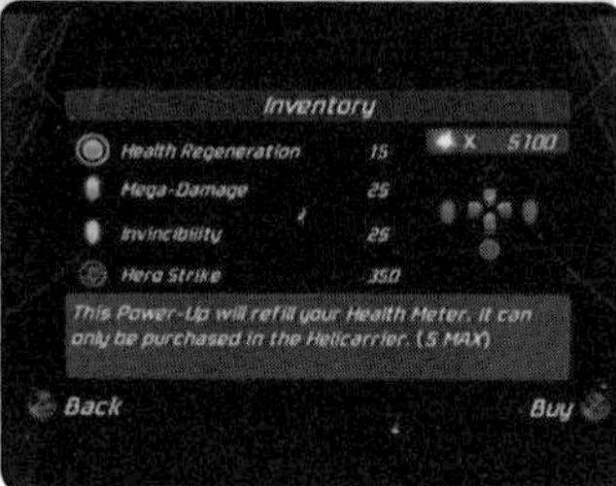

Insider Tip:
It's not necessary to enter the Spider-Man Friend or Foe codes quickly, but you'll need to be accurate. When you enter a code correctly, you'll hear a faint electronic noise.

SpongeBob Squarepants Lights, Camera, PANTS!

Bonus Menu Codes
What are the best bonus codes in Bikini Bottom? From the Main Menu, choose Bonuses and then Rewards. Go to the Codes Menu and enter the following codes on the Shell Keypad:

Unlock Hook, Line and Cheddar mini game	893634
Unlock Silver Story mode difficulty level	486739
Unlock all action figures in the game	977548

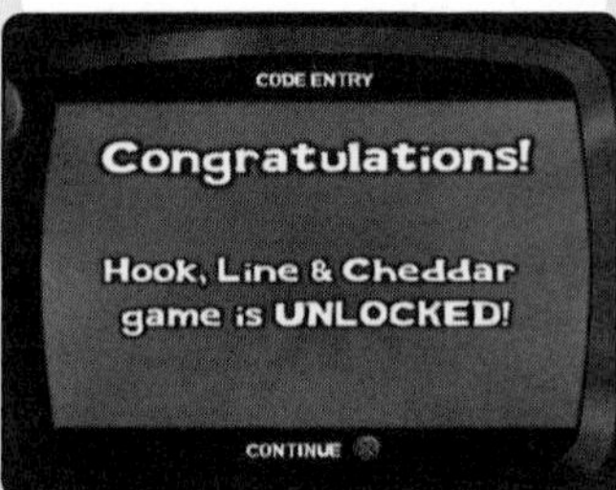

SSX On Tour

Unlockable Clothes, Cash, and Characters
From the Main menu, go to the Extras menu and then to the Cheats menu. All cheats should be typed in using all capital letters. The All Attributes and All Tricks codes award you everything available, without you having to purchase them in the Gear Shop. The Videos found in the Extras menu are separate from the Movies, which are found on the Rewards menu in The Tour mode.

Cheat	*Code*
$99,000,000 (The Tour)	LOOTSNOOT
All Characters (Quick Play)	ROADIEROUNDUP
All Attributes (The Tour)	POWERPLAY
All Movies (The Tour)	THEBIGPICTURE
All Reward Clothing (The Tour)	FLYTHREADS
All Tricks (The Tour)	JACKALOPESTYLE

(continued)

Cheat	*Code*
Infinite Boost (All Modes)	ZOOMJUICE
All Levels Unlocked	BACKSTAGEPASS
Snowball Fight!	LETSPARTY

Insider Tip
To throw a snowball with the Snowball Fight code, press R1 while riding or skiing.

SSX 3

Unlockable Extras
To enter these cheats, press the Square button at the Main menu to access Options, and then choose Enter Cheat. These codes unlock the remaining five cheat characters, but you'll still need to either buy them or accomplish the goals described on the Cheat Characters menu.

Cheat	*Code*
Unlock all artwork	naturalconcept
Unlock all snowboards	graphicdelight
Unlock all peaks	biggerthank7
Unlock all songs	djsuperstar
Unlock all posters	postnobills
Unlock all toys	noqluerequired
Unlock all trading cards	gotitgotitneedit
Unlock all videos	myeyesaredim
Unlock lodge one clothes	shoppingspree
Unlock Brodi cheat character	zenmaster
Unlock Bunny San cheat character	wheresyourtail
Unlock Canhuck cheat character	greatwhitenorth
Unlock Churchill cheat character	tankengine
Unlock Cudmore the Cow cheat character	milkemdaisy

(continued)

Wii

Xbox 360

Xbox

GC

PS3

PS2

DS

GBA

PSP

SSX 3 (cont.)

Cheat	*Code*
Unlock Eddie cheat character	worm
Unlock Gutless cheat character	boneyardreject
Unlock Hiro cheat character	slicksuit
Unlock Luther cheat character	bronco
Unlock Jurgen cheat character	brokenleg
Unlock Marty cheat character	back2future
Unlock Legend cheat character	callhimgeorge
Unlock Stretch cheat character	windmilldunk
Unlock Svelte Luther cheat character	notsosvelte
Unlock Unknown Rider cheat character	finallymadeitin

Insider Tip

As you unlock codes at the Enter Cheat option and press the Done button, you'll hear a musical note that sounds just like the noise you hear when you make a menu selection. If you hear a different tone, it probably means that you made a small mistake. Try entering the code again.

Surf's Up

Boards, Birds, and . . . a Deer?

Select Extras and Cheat Codes from the Main Menu and enter the following codes. When you enter the code correctly, you'll see a "CHEAT ACTIVATED" message. If you enter a code letter incorrectly, hit the Square Button to erase the code letter. Be careful, because choosing "BACK" with the Triangle Button will kick you out of the Cheat Code menu.

Unlock the Astral surfboard	ASTRAL
Unlock the two bonus missions	DONTFALL
Unlock the championship locations	FREEVISIT
Unlock all Leaf Sliding areas	GOINGDOWN
Unlock Tank Evans	IMTHEBEST
Unlock Tatsushi Kobayashi	KOBAYASHI
Unlock the Monsoon surfboard	MONSOON
Unlock all multiplayer levels	MULITPASS
Unlock all surfboards	MYPRECIOUS
Unlock all galleries	NICEPLACE
Unlock Geek	SLOWANDSTEADY
Unlock Elliot	SURPRISEGUEST
Unlock Zeke Topanga	THELEGEND
Unlock Arnold	TINYBUTSTRONG
Unlock the Tiny Shockwave surfboard	TINYSHOCKWAVE
Unlock character customization options	TOPFASHION
Unlocks the videos	WATCHAMOVIE

Thrillville: Off the Rails

In-Game Cheats

Thrillville: Off the Rails codes are easy to input because most of the codes are similar and you have plenty of time to enter each one. You must enter these codes while the game is in progress and you'll hear a small chime when you do it right!

Earn an additional $50,000	Square, Circle, Triangle, Square, Circle, Triangle, X Button
Add an extra 500 Thrill Points	Circle, Square, Triangle, Circle, Square, Triangle, Square
Unlock all Mini-Games	Square, Circle, Triangle, Square, Circle, Triangle, Right D-Pad
Unlock all missions	Square, Circle, Triangle, Square, Circle, Triangle, Square
Unlock all parks	Square, Circle, Triangle, Square, Circle, Triangle, Square
Unlock all rides	Square, Circle, Triangle, Square, Circle, Triangle, Triangle

Tiger Woods PGA TOUR 2005

Unlockable Golfers and Courses

Enter these codes at the Password link on the Options menu. Pay close attention to the uppercase and lowercase letters or the code won't work. If you enter the unlock correctly, you'll hear a voice say, "Oh Yeah!"

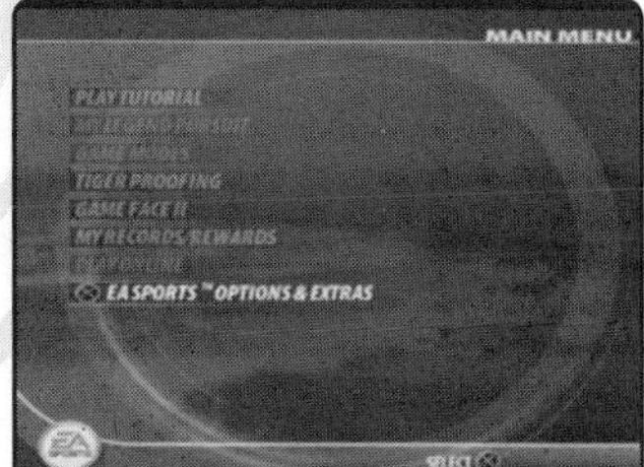

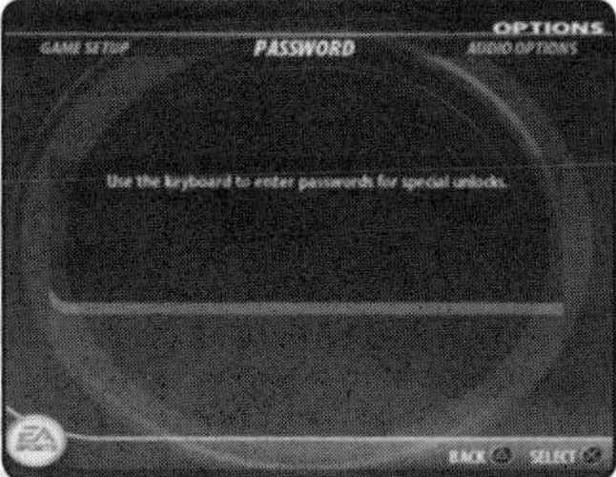

(continued)

Wii
Xbox 360
Xbox
GC
PS3
PS2
DS
GBA
PSP

Tiger Woods PGA TOUR 2005 (cont.)

Cheat	*Code*
Adriana "Sugar" Dulce	SOSWEET
Alastair "Captain" McFadden	NICESOCKS
All courses	THEWORLDISYOURS
All golfers and courses	THEGIANTOYSTER
Aphrodite Papadapolus	TEMPTING
Arnold Palmer	THEKING
Ben Hogan	PUREGOLF
Bev "Boomer" Bouchier	THEBEEHIVE
Billy "Bear" Hightower	TOOTALL
Bunjiro "Bud" Tanaka	INTHEFAMILY
Caesar "The Emperor" Rosado	LANDOWNER
Dion "Double D" Douglas	DDDOUGLAS
Gary Player	BLACKKNIGHT
Hunter "Steelhead" Elmore	GREENCOLLAR
Jack Nicklaus	GOLDENBEAR
Jeb "Shooter" McGraw	SIXSHOOTER
Justin "The Hustler" Timberlake	ALTEREGO
Kendra "Spike" Lovette	ENGLISHPUNK
Raquel "Rocky" Rodgers	DOUBLER
Reginald Weathers	REGGIE
Seve Ballesteros	THEMAGICIAN
The Roof Skill Course	NIGHTGOLFER
The Sunday Tiger with improved stats	NEWLEGEND
Tiffany Williamson	RICHGIRL

Insider Tip
If you already own other EA titles like Madden NFL 2005, Need for Speed Underground, NFL Street, and SSX3, be sure to save those files to the same PS2 Memory Card before you start Career mode in Tiger Woods PGA TOUR 2005. If you do, you'll begin with an extra spending cash bonus!

Tony Hawk's Downhill Jam

Cool Codes to Beat the Uphill Grind
Go to the Main menu, choose Options, select Cheat Codes and enter the following codes:

Cheat	*Code*
Open All Skaters	IMINTERFACING
Open All Boards and Gear	RAIDTHEWOODSHED
Open All Events	ADVENTURESOFKWANG
Open All Movies	FREEBOZZLER

You don't have to toggle any of the open codes at the Toggle Cheats menu.

(continued)

Weird Effects, Amazing Moves, and More
If you spell these codes right, you'll hear a metal door slam. When you enter a cheat code, don't forget to go to the Toggle Cheats menu to activate it!

Cheat	***Code***
Free Boost	OOTBAGHFOREVER
Always Special	POINTHOGGER
Manuals	IMISSMANUALS
Perfect Rail	LIKETILTINGAPLATE

Cheat	***Code***
Perfect Manuals	TIGHTROPEWALKER
Perfect Stats	IAMBOB
First Person Skater	FIRSTPERSONJAM
Shadow Skater	CHIMNEYSWEEP
Demon Skater	EVILCHIMNEYSWEEP
Mini Skater	DOWNTHERABBITHOLE
Giganto-Skater	IWANNABETALLTALL
Invisible Skater	NOWYOUSEEME
Skate as a Work of Art	FOURLIGHTS
Large Birds	BIRDBIRDBIRDBIRD
Especially Large Birds	BIRDBIRDBIRDBIRDBIRD
Tiny People	SHRINKTHEPEOPLE
Display Coordinates	DISPLAYCOORDINATES

Wii Xbox 360 Xbox GC PS3 PS2 DS GBA PSP

Top Gear Dare Devil

Unlock a Blue Paint Job
If you don't like driving the Red Pod in Rome, enter this code at the Main menu and give yourself a new color: Down, Square, Down, R1, Right, Right, Up, Left, Circle, Circle, L2, L1

Activate Motion Blur
You can also activate the Motion Blur gauge by entering this code at the Main menu: Up, Left, Circle, Down, Right, Square, Up, Down, Left, Right, Circle, Square

Now check out the Options menu and you'll see a new Motion Blur bar at the bottom.

Alien Motorists
To change everyday motorists into aliens, enter this code while driving around town: Up, Up, Triangle, Triangle, Left, Circle, Left, Circle, Down, Down, X, X

Yu-Gi-Oh! GX The Beginning of Destiny

Build the Ultimate Deck
You won't be able to enter these passwords until you play the game through May 15th and receive an e-mail message from Chancellor Sheppard about a "Suspicious Facility" on the island. Go to the map screen and you'll find a new location called the Lab. Enter these passwords in the basement of the facility, but remember that you'll still need to rent the cards back at the Academy Shop!

Cheat	*Code*
Ancient Gear Cannon	80045583
Ancient Gear Castle	92001300
Ancient Gear Drill	67829249
Ancient Gear Beast	10509340
Ancient Gear Golem	83104731
Ancient Gear Soldier	56094445
Ancient Gear	31557782
Ancient Lamp	54912977
Ancient Lizard Warrior	43230671
Ancient Telescope	17092736
Andro Sphinx	15013468
Ante	02204140
Anteatereatingant	13250922
Anti-Aircraft Flower	65064143
Anti-Spell	53112492
Apprentice Magician	09156135
Appropriate	48539234
Aqua Madoor	85639257

(continued)

Yu-Gi-Oh! GX The Beginning of Destiny (cont.)

Cheat	*Code*
Aqua Spirit	40916023
Arcane Archer of the Forest	55001420
Archfiend of Gilfer	50287060
Archfiend Soldier	49881766
Archlord Zerato	18378582
Armaill	53153481
Armed Charger	90374791
Armed Dragon Level 10	59464593
Armed Dragon Level 3	00980973
Armed Dragon Level 5	46384672

Cheat	*Code*
Armed Dragon Level 7	73879377
Armed Ninja	09076207
Armed Samurai - Ben Kei	84430950
Armor Axe	07180418
Armor Break	79649195
Armored Glass	36868108
Armored Lizard	15480588
Armored Starfish	17535588
Armored Zombie	20277860
Array of Revealing Light	69296555
Arsenal Bug	42364374
Arsenal Robber	55348096
Arsenal Summoner	85489096
Assault on GHQ	62633180
Astral Barrier	37053871
Asura Priest	02134346
Aswan Apparition	88236094
A-Team: Trap Disposal Unit	13026402
Atomic Firefly	87340664
Attack and Receive	63689843
Attack Reflector Unit	91989718
Aussa the Earth Charmer	37970940
Autonomous Action Unit	71453557
Avatar of the Pot	99284890
Axe Dragonute	84914462

Cheat	*Code*
Axe of Despair	40619825
Axe Raider	48305365
B. Skull Dragon	11901678
B.E.S. Covered Core	15317640
B.E.S. Crystal Core	22790789
B.E.S. Tetran	44954628
Baby Dragon	88819587
Back to Square One	47453433
Backfire	82705573
Backup Soldier	36280194
Bad Reaction to Simochi	40633297
Bait Doll	07165085
Ballista of Rampart Smashing	00242146
Banisher of the Light	6152825
Banisher of the Radiance	94853057
Banner of Courage	10012614
Bark of Dark Ruler	41925941
Barrel Dragon	81480460
Basic Insect	89091579
Battery Charger	61181383
Batteryman AA	63142001
Batteryman C	19733961
Battle Footballer	48094997
Battle Ox	05053103
Battle Steer	18246479
Battle-Scarred	94463200
Battle Warrior	55550921
Bazoo The Soul-Eater	40133511
Beast Fangs	46009906
Beast Soul Swap	35149085
Beastking of the Swamps	99426834
Beautiful Headhuntress	16899564
Beaver Warrior	32452818
Beckoning Light	16255442
Beelze Frog	49522489
Begone, Knave	20374520
Behemoth, the King of All Animals	22996376
Beiige, Vanguard of Dark World	33731070
Berserk Dragon	85605684
Berserk Gorilla	39168895
Beta the Magnet Warrior	39256679
Bickuribox	25655502
Big Bang Shot	61127349
Big Burn	95472621
Big Core	14148099

(continued)

Yu-Gi-Oh! GX The Beginning of Destiny (cont.)

Cheat	*Code*
Big Eye	16768387
Big Insect	53606874
Big Koala	42129512
Big Shield Gardna	65240384
Big Wave Small Wave	51562916
Big-Tusked Mammoth	59380081
Bio-Mage	58696829
Birdface	45547649
Birthright	35539880
Black Illusion Ritual	41426869
Black Luster Ritual	55761792
Black Luster Soldier-Envoy of Beginning	72989439
Black Pendant	65169794
Black Tyranno	38670435
Blackland Fire Dragon	87564352
Blade Knight	39507162
Blade Rabbit	58268433
Blade Skater	97023549
Bladefly	28470714
Blast Held by a Tribute	89041555
Blast Magician	21051146
Blast with Chain	98239899
Blasting the Ruins	21466326
Blazing Inpachi	05464695
Blessings of the Nile	30653113
Blind Destruction	32015116
Blindly Loyal Goblin	35215622
Block Attack	25880422
Blue Eyes Ultimate Dragon	23995346
Blue Eyes White Dragon	89631139
Blue Medicine	20871001
Blue-Eyes White Dragon (not SDK- 001)	80906030
Book of Life	02204140
Book of Moon	14087893
Book of Secret Arts	91595718
Bottomless Shifting Sand	76532077
Bottomless Trap Hole	29401950
Bracchio-raidus	16507828
Brain Control	87910978
Breath of Light	20101223
Bright Castle	82878489
Burning Land	24294108
Burning Spear	18937875
Burst Breath	80163754
Burst Return	27191436
Burst Stream of Destruction	17655904
Buster Blader	78193831
Call of the Haunted	97077563
Call of the Mummy	04861205
Cannon Soldier	11384280
Card Destruction	72892473
Card of Safe Return	57953380
Card Trooper	85087012
Castle of Dark Illusions	00062121
Castle Walls	44209392
Catapult Turtle	95727991
Ceasefire	36468556
Celtic Guardian	90101050
Chain Destruction	01248895
Chain Energy	79323590
Chaos Emperor Dragon-Envoy of The End	82301904
Chimeratech Overdragon	64599569
Chorus of Sanctuary	81380218
Chosen One	21888494
Clay Charge	22479888
Cliff the Trap Remover	06967870
Clown Zombie	92667214
Cocoon of Evolution	40240595
Cold Wave	60682203
Collected Power	07565547
Compulsory Evacuation Device	94192409
Copycat	26376390
Crass Clown	93889755
Crawling Dragon #2	38289717
Crawling Dragon	67494157
Creature Swap	31036355
Crimson Sunbird	46696593
Crush Card Virus	57728570
Curse of Anubis	66742250
Curse of Dragon	28279543

(continued)

Cheat	Code
Curse of Fiend	12470447
Curse of Royal	02926176
Curse of the Masked Beast	94377247
Cyber Dragon	70095154
Cyber End Dragon	01546123
Cyber Harpie Lady	80316585
Cyber Jar	34124316
Cyber Raider	39978267
Cyber Shiled	63224564
Cyberdark Dragon	40418351
Cyberdark Edge	77625948
Cyberdark Horn	41230939
Cyberdark Keel	03019642

Cheat	Code
Cyber-Tech Alligator	48766543
Cyclon Laser	05494820
D.D. Assailant	70074904
D.D. Survivor	48092532
D.D. Warrior	37043180
Damage Condenser	28378427
Dancing Fairy	90925163
Dark Artist	72520073
Dark Avatar	21208154
Dark Balter the Terrible	80071763
Dark Blade	11321183
Dark Chimera	32344688
Dark Coffin	01804528
Dark Core	70231910
Dark Energy	04614116
Dark Eraser	57793869
Dark Jeroid	90980792
Dark Magic Curtain	99789342
Dark Magician Girl	38033121
Dark Magician of Chaos	40737112
Dark Magician	40609080

Cheat	Code
Dark Rabbit	99261403
Dark Sage	92377303
Dark Scorpion Burglars	40933924
Dark Scorpion Combination	20858318
Dark Spirit of the Silent	93599951
Dark World Dealings	74117290
Darkfire Dragon	17881964
Darkness Approaches	80168720
Dark-Piercing Light	45895206
Deal of Phantom	69122763
De-Fusion	95286165
Delinquent Duo	44763025
Delta Attacker	39719977
Desert Sunlight	93747864
Despair from the Dark	71200730
De-Spell	19159413
Destiny Board	94212438
Destiny Draw	45809008
Destiny Hero Disk Commander	56570271
Destiny Hero Dreadmaster	40591390
Destiny Hero Malicious	09411399
Destruction Punch	05616412
Dian Keto the Cure Master	84257639
Dimensionhole	22959079
DNA Surgery	74701381
Don Zaloog	76922029
Dora of Fate	67464807
Dragon Capture Jar	50045299
Dragon Treasure	01435851
Dragon Zombie	66672569
Dragoness the Wicked Knight	70681994
Dragonic Attack	32437102
Dragon's Gunfire	55991637
Dragon's Rage	54178050
Dream Clown	13215230
Driving Snow	00473469
Dunames Dark Witch	12493482
Dungeon Worm	51228280
Dust Barrier	31476755
Dust Tornado	60082869
Earth Chant	59820352
Eatgaboon	42578427
Ectoplasmer	97342942
Ekibyo Drakmord	69954399
Electro-Whip	37820550
Elegant Egotist	90219263

(continued)

Yu-Gi-Oh! GX The Beginning of Destiny (cont.)

Cheat	*Code*
Elemental Absorber	94253609
Elemental Dragon	30314994
Elemental Hero Avian	21844576
Elemental Hero Bladedge	59793705
Elemental Hero Bubbleman	79979666
Elemental Hero Clayman	84327329
Elemental Hero Dark Neos	28677304
Elemental Hero Flame Wingman	35809262
Elemental Hero Grand Neos	48996596
Elemental Hero Rampart Blaster	47737087
Elemental Hero Sparkman	20721928
Elemental Hero Stratos	40044918
Elemental Hero Thunder Giant	61204971
Elemental Mistress Doriado	99414168
Elf's Light	39897277
Embodiment of Apophis	28649820
Enchanting Fitting Room	30531525
Enemy Controller	98045062
Eradicating Aerosol	94716515
Eternal Draught	56606928
Eternal Rest	95051344
Exarion Universe	63749102
Exile of the Wicked	26725158
Exiled Force	74131780
Exodia the Forbidden One	33396948
Fairy Box	21598948
Fairy Meteor Crush	97687912
Fairy's Hand Mirror	17653779
Feather Shot	19394153
Feather Wind	71060915
Feral Imp	41392891
Fiend Kraken	77456781
Final Destiny	18591904
Final Flame	73134081

Cheat	*Code*
Fire Princess	64752646
Fissure	66788016
Flame Cerberus	60862676
Flame Manipulator	34460851
Flame Swordsman	45231177
Flying Kamakiri #1	84834865
Follow Wind	98252586
Foolish Burial	81439173
Forced Requisition	74923978
Forest	87430998
Fusion Gate	24094653
Fusion Sage	26902560
Gaia Power	56594520
Gaia the Dragon Champion	66889139
Gaia the Fierce Knight	06368038
Gamble	37313786
Garoozis	14977074
Gate Guardian	25833572
Gear Golem the Moving Fortress	30190809
Gemini Elf	69140098
Germ Infection	24668830
Giant Flea	41762634
Giant Soldier of Stone	13039848
Giant Trunade	42703248
Gift of the Mystical Elf	98299011
Gigantes	47606319
Gilford the Lightning	36354007
Goblin Fan	04149689
Goblin's Secret Remedy	11868825
Goddess of Whim	67959180
Goddess with the Third Eye	53493204
Gokibore	15367030
Gorgon's Eye	52648457
Graceful Charity	79571449
Graceful Dice	74137509
Grappler	02906250
Gravedigger Ghoul	82542267
Gravekeeper's Assailant	25262697
Gravekeeper's Servant	16762927
Gravekeeper's Spear Soldier	63695531
Graverobber's Retribution	33737664
Gravity Axe – Grarl	32022366
Gravity Bind	85722772
Great Moth	14141448
Great Shogun Shien	63176202
Great White	13429800

(continued)

Cheat	Code
Green Gadget	41172955
Griffore	53829412
Ground Collapse	90502999
Guardian Sphinx	40659562
Gust Fan	55321970
Gust	73079365
Gyakutenno Megami	31122090
Hallowed Life Barrier	88789641
Harpie Lady	76812113
Harpie Lady 1	91932350
Harpie Lady 2	27927359
Harpie Lady 3	54415063
Harpie Lady Sisters	12206212
Harpie's Feather Duster	18144586
Harpie's Hunting Ground	75782277
Harpie's Pet Dragon	52040216
Heart of the Underdog	37562283
Heavy Storm	19613556
Helpoemer	76052811
Hercules Beetle	52584282
Hero Signal	22020907
Hero Spirit	81167171
Hinotama	46130346
Hitotsu-Me Giant	76184692
Horn Imp	69669405
Horn of Light	38552107
Horn of the Unicorn	64047146
Horus the Black Flame Dragon Level 4	75830094
Horus the Black Flame Dragon Level 6	11224103
Horus the Black Flame Dragon Level 8	48229808
House of Adhesive Tape	15083728
Human-Wave Tactics	30353551
Illusionist Faceless Mage	28546905
Imperial Order	61740673

Cheat	Code
Inferno Fire Blast	52684508
Inferno Reckless Summon	12247206
Infinite Cards	94163677
Infinite Dismissal	54109233
Injection Fairy Lily	79575620
Insect Armor with Laser Cannon	03492538
Insect Barrier	23615409
Insect Imitation	96965364
Insect Queen	91512835
Inspection	16227556
Interdimensional Matter Transporter	36261726
Invigoration	98374133
Jam Breeding Machine	21770260
Jam Defender	21558682
Jar of Greed	83968380
Jellyfish	14851496
Jinzo #7	77585513
Jirai Gumo	15401633
Judge Man	30113682
Judgement of Anubis	55256016
Just Desserts	24068492
Kairyu-Shin	76634149
Kazejin	62340868
Killer Needle	88979991
King of Yamimakai	69455834
Kishido Spirit	60519422
Kojikocy	01184620
Koumori Dragon	67724379
Krokodilus	76512652
Kunai with Chain	37390589
Kuriboh	40640057
La Jinn the Mystical Genie of the Lamp	97590747
Labyrinth of Nightmare	66526672
Labyrinth Tank	99551425
Labyrinth Wall	67284908
Larvae Moth	87756343
Laser Cannon Armor	77007920
Last Day of Witch	90330453
Last Will	85602018
Launcher Spider	87322377
Lava Battleguard	20394040
Lava Golem	00102380
Left Arm of the Forbidden One	07902349

(continued)

Yu-Gi-Oh! GX The Beginning of Destiny (cont.)

Cheat	*Code*
Left Leg of the Forbidden One	44519536
Legendary Sword	61854111
Light of Intervention	62867251
Lightning Blade	55226821
Lightning Vortex	69162969
Limiter Removal	23171610
Lord of D.	17985575
Luminous Spark	81777047
Luster Dragon #2	17658803
Luster Dragon (1900/1600)	11091375
Machine Conversion Factory	25769732
Machine King	25769732
Mage Power	46700124
Magic Cylinder	62279055
Magic Drain	59344077
Magic Jammer	77414722
Magic Thorn	53119267
Magical Hats	81210420
Magical Scientist	34206604
Magic-Arm Shield	96008713
Magician of Faith	31560081
Magician's Circle	00050755
Maha Vailo	93013676
Majestic Mech – Goryu	95701283
Major Riot	09074847
Makyura the Destructor	21593977
Malevolent Nuzzler	99597615
Malfunction	06137095
Mammoth Graveyard	40374923
Man-Eater Bug	54652250
Manju of the Ten Thousand Hands	95492061
Masaki the Legendary Swordsman	44287299
Mask of Brutality	82432018

Cheat	*Code*
Mask of Darkness	28933734
Mask of Dispel	20765952
Mask of Restrict	29549364
Mask of the Accursed	56948373
Mask of Weakness	57882509
Masked Dragon	39191307
Masked Sorcerer	10189126
Megamorph	22046459
Mesmeric Control	48642904
Messenger of Peace	44656491
Metal Detector	75646520
Metal Guardian	68339286
Metalmorph	68540058
Metalzoa	50705071
Metamorphosis	46411259
Meteor Black Dragon	90660762
Meteor Dragon	64271667
Meteor of Destruction	33767325
Meteorain	01918087
Michizure	37580756
Millennium Shield	32012841
Milus Radiant	07489323
Mind Control	37520316
Minor Goblin Official	01918087
Mirror Force	44095762
Moai Interceptor Cannons	45159319
Monster Recovery	93108433
Monster Reincarnation	74848038
Monster Tamer	97612389
Mooyan Curry	58074572
Morphing Jar	33508719
Mother Grizzly	57839750
Mountain	50913601
Mucus Yolk	70307656
Muka Muka	46657337
Multiplication of Ants	22493811
Multiply	40703222
Mushroom Man	14181608
Mustering of the Dark Scorpions	68191243
Mysterious Puppeteer	54098121
Mystic Horseman	68516705
Mystic Plasma Zone	18161786
Mystic Probe	49251811
Mystical Elf	15025844
Mystical Moon	36607978
Mystical Space Typhoon	05318639

(continued)

Cheat	Code
Mystik Wok	80161395
Necroface	28297833
Negate Attack	14315573
Neo-Spacian Air Hummingbird	54959865
Neo-Spacian Aqua Dolphin	17955766
Neo-Spacian Flame Scarab	89621922
Nightmare's Steelcage	58775978
Obnoxious Celtic Guard	52077741
Offerings to the Doomed	19230407
Ojama Black	79335209
Ojama Green	12482652
Ojama King	90140980
Ojama Trio	29843091
Ojama Yellow	42941100
Ookazi	19523799
Ordeal of a Traveler	39537362
Order to Charge	78986941
Order to Smash	39019325
Pandemonium	94585852
Panther Warrior	42035044
Paralyzing Potion	50152549
Parrot Dragon	62762898
Pendulum Machine	24433920
Penguin Knight	36039163
Penguin Soldier	93920745
Perfectly Ultimate Great Moth	48579379
Petit Dragon	75356564
Petit Moth	58192742
Pikeru's Circle of Enchantment	74270067
Pineapple Blast	90669991
Polymerization	24094653
Pot of Greed	55144522
Premature Burial	70828912
Prevent Rat	00549481
Princess of Tsurugi	51371017
Prohibition	43711255
Pumpking the King of Ghosts	29155212
Punished Eagle	74703140
Pyramid Energy	76754619
Pyramid Turtle	77044671
Rabid Horseman	94905343
Raigeki	12580477
Raimei	56260110
Rain of Mercy	66719324
Raise Body Heat	51267887

Cheat	Code
Rare Fish	80516007
Raregold Armor	07625614
Raviel, Lord of Phantasms	69890967
Reaper of the Cards	33066139
Reasoning	58577036
Reckless Greed	37576645
Red Gadget	86445415
Red Medicine	38199696
Red-Eyes B. Chick	36262024
Red-Eyes B. Dragon	74677422
Red-Eyes Black Metal Dragon	64335804
Red-Eyes Darkness Dragon	96561011
Reinforcement of the Army	32807846
Reinforcements	17814387
Relinquished	64631466
Reload	22589918
Remove Trap	51482758
Respect Play	08951260
Restructer Revolution	99518961
Return from the Different Dimension	27174286
Reverse Trap	77622396
Right Arm of the Forbidden One	70903634
Right Leg of the Forbidden One	08124921
Ring of Destruction	83555666
Ring of Magnetism	20436034
Riryoku Field	70344351
Robbin' Goblin	88279736
Rock Ogre Grotto #1	68846917
Rogue Doll	91939608
Rope of Life	93382620
Royal Decree	51452091
Royal Magic Library	70791313

(continued)

Yu-Gi-Oh! GX The Beginning of Destiny (cont.)

Cheat	Code
Rude Kaiser	26378150
Ruin, Queen of Oblivion	46427957
Rush Recklessly	70046172
Ryu Kokki	57281778
Ryu-Kishin Powered	24611934
Ryu-Kishin	15303296
Sage's Stone	13604200
Saggi the Dark Clown	66602787
Sakuretsu Armor	56120475
Salamandra	32268901
Sanga of the Thunder	25955164
Sangan	26202165
Sasuke Samurai #2	11760174
Satellite Cannon	50400231
Scapegoat	73915051
Servant of Catabolism	02792265
Seven Tools of the Bandit	03819470
Shadow Ghoul	30778711
Shadow of Eyes	58621589
Share the Pain	56830749
Shield & Sword	52097679
Shift	59560625
Shining Angel	95956346
Shooting Star Bow - Ceal	95638658
Shrink	55713623
Silent Magician Level 4	73665146
Silent Magician Level 8	72443568
Silver Bow and Arrow	01557499
Silver Fang	90357090
Sinister Serpent	08131171
Skill Drain	82732705
Skilled Dark Magician	73752131
Skull Dice	00126218
Skull Invitation	98139712
Skull Lair	06733059
Skyscraper	63035430
Slate Warrior	78636495

Cheat	Code
Snake Fang	00596051
Snatch Steal	45986603
Sogen	86318356
Solemn Judgment	41420027
Solemn Wishes	35346968
Soul of the Pure	47852924
Soul Release	05758500
Soul Resurrection	92924317
Spark Blaster	97362768
Sparks	76103675
Spear Dragon	31553716
Special Hurricane	42598242
Spell Shield Type-8	38275183
Spellbinding Circle	18807108
Spiral Spear Strike	49328340
Spirit Barrier	53239672
Spirit Message "A"	94772232
Spirit Message "I"	31893528
Spirit Message "L"	30170981
Spirit Message "N"	67287532
Spirit Reaper	23205979
Spiritualism	15866454
Spring of Rebirth	94425169
Sprit's Invitation	92394653
Stamping Destruction	81385346
Statue of the Wicked	65810489
Steel Scorpion	13599884
Steel Shell	02370081
Steel Shell	02370081
Stim-Pack	83225447
Stop Defense	63102017
Suijin	98434877
Summoned Skull	70781052
Super Conductor Tyranno	85520851
Super Rejuvenation	27770341
Swamp Battleguard	40453765
Sword Arm of Dragon	13069066
Sword of Dark Destruction	37120512
Sword of the Deep-Seated	98495314
Sword of the Soul-Eater	05372656
Swords of Revealing Light	72302403
Swordstalker	50005633
System Down	18895832
Tailor of the Fickle	43641473
The Cheerful Coffin	41142615
The Dark Door	30606547
The Dragon's Bead	92408984
The Emperor's Holiday	68400115

(continued)

Cheat	Code
The Forceful Sentry	42829885
The Grave of the Enkindling	84136000
The Inexperienced Spy	81820689
The Law of the Normal	66926224
The Little Swordsman of Aile	25109950
The Masked Beast	49064413
The Reliable Guardian	16430187
The Sanctuary in the Sky	56433456
The Shallow Grave	43434803
The Snake Hair	29491031
The Wicked Worm Beast	06285791
Thousand Dragon	41462083
Thousand Energy	05703682
Thousand-Eyes Restrict	63519819
Thunder of Ruler	91781589
Tiger Axe	40907090
Time Machine	80987696
Time Wizard	71625222
Toll	82003859
Toon Alligator	59383041
Toon Summoned Skull	91842653
Torike	80813021
Tragedy	35686187
Trap Dustshoot	64697231
Trap Hole	04206964
Trap Jammer	19252988
Trap Master	46461247
Tremendous Fire	46918794
Triangle Ecstasy Spark	12181376
Tribute Doll	02903036
Tribute to the Doomed	79759861
Tutan Mask	03149764
Twin Swords of Flashing Light - Tryce	21900719
Two-Headed King Rex	94119974
Two-Pronged Attack	83887306
Tyhone	72842870
Type Zero Magic Crusher	21237481
Tyrant Dragon	94568601
UFO Turtle	60806437
Ultimate Offering	80604091
Ultimate Tyranno	15894048
Umi	22702055
Umiiruka	82999629
Upstart Goblin	70368879
Uraby	01784619
Uria, Lord of Searing Flames	06007213
Vampire Genesis	22056710

Cheat	Code
Vampire Lord	53839837
Vengeful Bog Spirit	95220856
Versago the Destroyer	50289460
Vile Germs	39774685
Violet Crystal	15052462
Vorse Raider	14898066
Waboku	12607053
Wall of Illusion	13945283
Wall of Revealing Light	17078030
Wall Shadow	63162310
Warrior Elimination	90873992
Wasteland	23424603
Water Dragon	85066822
Wave Motion Cannon	18992735
White Magical Hat	15160365
Windstorm of Etaqua	59744639
Winged Dragon Guardian of Fortress #1	87796900
Winged Kuriboh	57116033
Witch of the Black Forest	78010363
Wolf	49417509
World Suppression	12253117
X-Head Cannon	62651957
XY-Dragon Cannon	02111707
XYZ-Dragon Cannon	91998119
XZ-Tank Cannon	99724761
Yami	59197169
Y-Dragon Head	65622692
Yellow Gadget	13834120
Yellow Luster Shield	04542651
Zanki	30090452
Zera the Mant	69123138
Z-Metal Tank	64500000
Zoa	24311372
Zombie Warrior	31339260

Wii Xbox 360 Xbox GC PS3 PS2 DS GBA PSP

Advance Wars: Dual Strike

Open the Advance Wars Map
Unlock the special Advance Wars Map in the Design Room with this simple trick:

Go to System menu (flip from the Battle menu with the L or R button) and choose Design Room. Now hold both the L and R buttons as you choose the Map Design feature. You'll unlock a special map where the terrain features spell out the name of the game!

Brain Age

Top Three Results
To see who has the best brains on the block, choose a save file, go to the Mode select screen (across from the Calendar screen), hold the Select button, and tap Graph. You'll be taken to a special menu that allows you to see the top three results in every Brain Age Check test and Training event. See how your scores rank against the competition!

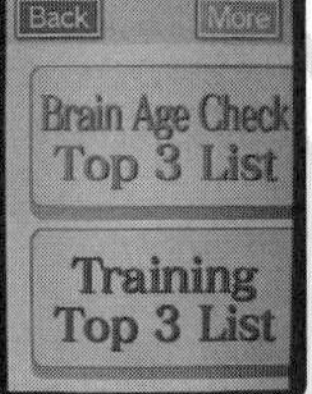

Choose Your Tests
To stack the test deck in your favor, choose a save file, go to the Mode Select screen (across from the Calendar screen), hold the Select button, and tap Brain Age Check. You'll be allowed to choose the three tests you take to measure your current Brain Age.

Cartoon Network Racing

Unlimited Energy, All Power-ups, and More

Depending on the name you choose, you can unlock nifty cheats in Cartoon Network Racing. To change your name, go to the Options menu and select Enter Name. Then choose one of the following codes:

Cheat	*Code*
Activate all Power-ups and hazards in Time Trial Mode	AAARGH
Change Power-ups to petrifying stone blocks	STONEME
Open everything in the game	GIMMIE
See the track from above	IMACOPTER
Unlimited Dumb Missiles	ROCKETMAN
Unlimited energy	SPINACH

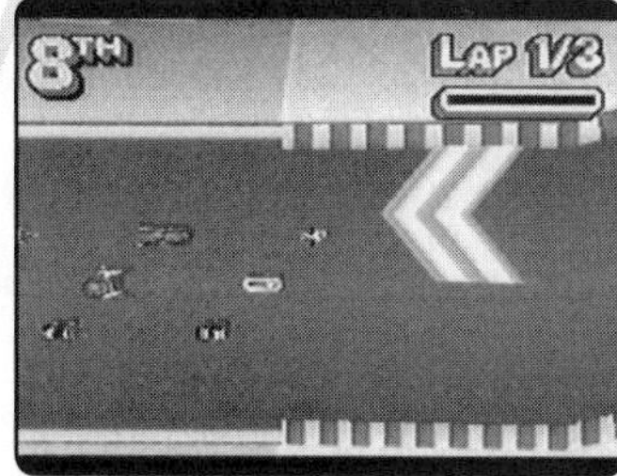

Insider Tip

If you activate a cheat in Cartoon Network Racing, it turns off the save feature, so your best times while using a cheat won't count!

The Chronicles of Narnia: The Lion, The Witch and The Wardrobe

Unlockable Invincibility, Weapons, and More

Enter the following codes on the Title screen to unlock the corresponding cheats. If you enter a code correctly, you'll hear a corresponding sound effect. For example, if you enter the Auto Health Restore code correctly, you'll hear the food collecting/eating sound effect.

Cheat	*Code*
Auto Health Restore	Left, Right, Up, Down, A, A, A, A
Increase Attack Strength	A, Up, B, Down, X, X, Y, Y
Best Weapons	Left, Up, A, B, Right, Down, X, Y
Get Armor	A, X, Y, B, Up, Up, Up, Down
Invincibility	A, Y, X, B, Up, Up, Down, Down
Increase All Stats	Left, B, Up, Y, Down, X, Right, A
Maximum Money	Up, X, Up, X, Down, B, Down, B

(continued)

Insider Tip
These codes work for both new games and saved games, but they do not last beyond your current play session. If you quit your game or turn it off, you'll have to enter the codes before you start your game again.

Code Lyoko

Play As Dark Ulrich
To play as the "dark" version of Ulrich, you must first begin a game, then save it, and exit back to the Main menu. Go to the Load Profile screen, highlight your game file, hold the L and R buttons, and press Up, Left, Right, Y, and X. Begin your saved game as normal. Now when you're in the 3-D exploration areas of the game, Ulrich will wear a more sinister version of his uniform.

Unlock Full Combat Powers and More
This code will grant Ulrich his full combat powers and increase all his items to maximum. In the 3-D exploration areas, pause your game and press Up, Up, Down, Down, Left, Right, Left, Right, B, A, and Start.

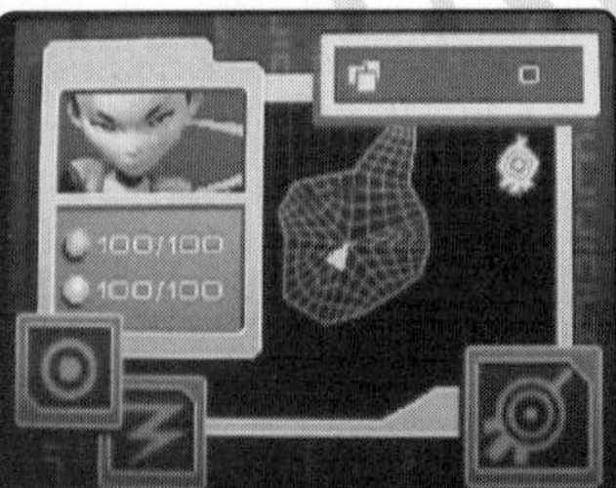

Diddy Kong Racing DS

Picture Prizes
Remember the sand puzzle near the lighthouse where you could draw pictures in the sand? If you use your stylus to connect the stones (like dots) in the right places, you can collect up to four special items.

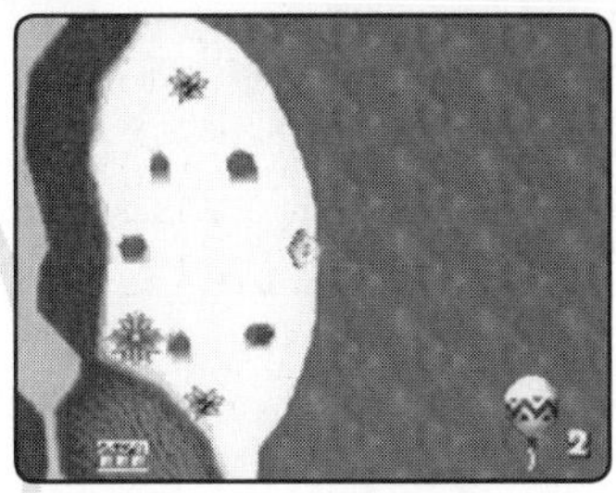

Insider Tip
You can only draw up to four items in the game, so don't squander your artistic talents.

To Earn a:	*Connect the Dots to Make a:*
Scratch and Win Card	big square
Cluster of Coins	big circle
Golden Balloon	balloon with no string attached

After you draw the object on the sand with your stylus, be sure to tap the arrow button in the upper right corner of the touch screen. Then drive or fly right over to pick up the item.

Dragon Booster

Race Ahead with These Passwords
At the Main Menu, choose Password and boost your racing performance with these passwords. Count off each box on the screen from left to right, zigzagging up and down between the rows to match the password number to the appropriate game symbol. When you enter the code correctly, you'll see the word "Success."

Add Super Damage in All City Race	11, 11, 11, 11, 11, 11
Disable Sprint Meter recharge	1, 7, 5, 3, 2, 11
Earn 999,999 Dracles	8, 9, 7, 10, 5, 13
Infinite Sprint Meter power	9, 13, 6, 5, 5, 12
Replace Draculium Bars with sushi in the All City Race	7, 8, 13, 12, 10, 10
Start with Blue Energy Bolt Gear	9, 2, 13, 8, 1, 12
Start with Green Charging Gear	5, 12, 13, 5, 8, 11
Unlock Dragon Booster and Legendary Beau	12, 6, 12, 10, 13, 3
Unlock Dragon-Human Duel vs. Reepyr	1, 9, 3, 6, 5, 2
Unlock Shadow Booster and Shadow Dragon	2, 5, 4, 11, 6, 2
Unlock Skills Competition vs. Wulph	13, 9, 8, 12, 10, 1

Dragon Quest Heroes: Rocket Slime

Unlock Multiplayer Tanks

Once you progress far enough in the game to access the town church, enter these codes when you're inside:

Cheat	*Code*
Multiplayer Nemesis Tank	Y, R, R, Up, L, L, Y, Down, Down, Down, Y, SELECT
Multiplayer Knightro Tank	Y, L, L, Y, R, R, Y, Up, Down, SELECT

Jam Session

Unlock Three Additional Songs!

There are three additional songs hidden on your Jam Session game for Nintendo DS. Normally these songs won't appear in your song list, but if you read the instruction manual, you'll find the songs in the credits. To open the songs, select Free Play mode and then enter the following depending on how you have your Jam Session game configured:

For left-hand control:	Up, Up, Down, Down, Left, Right, Left, Right
For right-hand control:	X, X, B, B, Y, A, Y, A

When you enter the code correctly, you'll hear a guitar chord and the game will return to the song list showing you these new titles:

"I'm Gonna Miss Her" by Brad Paisley
"Needles and Pins" by Tom Petty
"Wild Thing" by Jimmy Hendrix

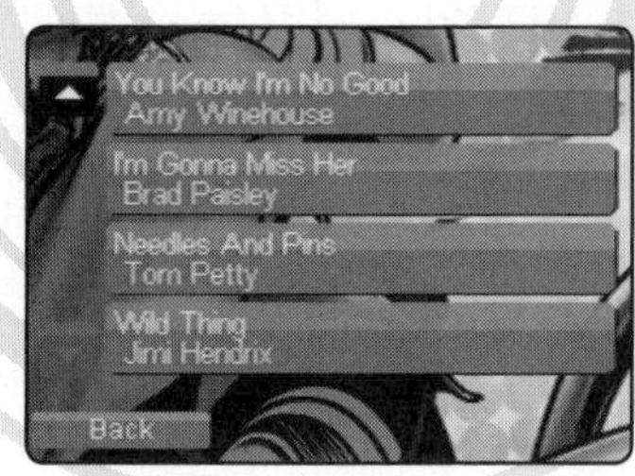

LEGO Star Wars: The Complete Saga

Unlike other LEGO Star Wars games where you input passwords at the Cantina, you'll need to enter these codes at the Main Menu screen:

1,000,000 Studs	START, Right, Up, L Button, Down, Select, L Button, R Button
3,000,000 Studs	START, START, Down, Down, Left, Left, Up, Up, Select
Unlock Bonus Game	Up, Up, Down, L Button, L Button, R Button, R Button
Unlock Debug Menu	Up, Left, Down, Right, Up, Left, Down, Right, Up, Left, Down, Right, R Button, L Button, START, Select

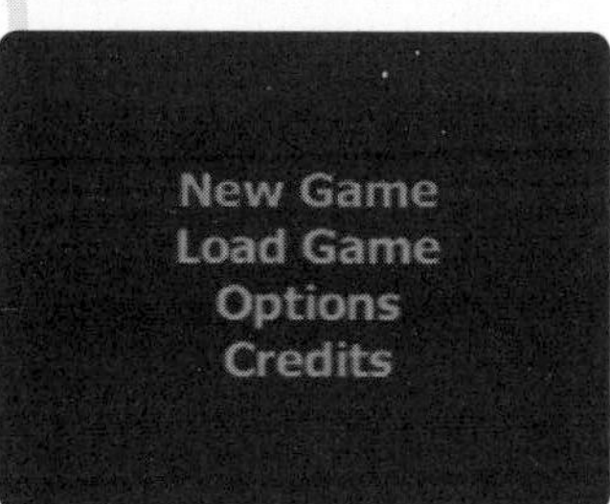

LEGO Star Wars II: The Original Trilogy

Enter these codes at the bar inside the Cantina. Although these codes unlock certain items, you'll still need to buy the items with LEGO Studs.

Unlock all characters	UDLRAB
Unlock all extra features	ABACAB
Unlock all editor clothing	867539
Unlock all editor weapons	BIGGUN
Earn 500,000 LEGO Studs	HGIGHF
Earn 10 LEGO Studs	4PR28U

Wii | Xbox 360 | Xbox | GC | PS3 | PS2 | DS | GBA | PSP

Mario Kart DS

Give Yourself a Head Start
If you don't know the turbo start trick, you might have a tough time in multiplayer races, but there's also another trick you can use if you make a mistake.

To use the turbo acceleration off the starting line, press the acceleration button when you see the number 2 in the countdown to start. If you time it right, you'll get a boost at the beginning of the race and a jump on your rival racers.

If you fall off a cliff or end up being rescued by Lakitu (the cloud-riding guy with the fishing rod) don't hit the acceleration button until the exact moment that he drops you on the track. If your timing is right, you should get a turbo boost that will help you catch up to the field, or even stay ahead of your opponents.

New Super Mario Bros.

Play As Luigi
Start a Mario Game and move your cursor to a save file. After you have the file highlighted, hold the L and the R buttons at the same time and then press the A button. If you did it right, you'll begin the game as Luigi instead of Mario!

Pokémon Diamond

Hatched Eggs in Half the Time
If hatching eggs is taking too long, try adding a Pokémon with Flame Body or Magma Armor to your team. That additional heat speeds up the egg hatching time, so you spend less time counting your Pokémon before they're hatched!

Insider Tip
Try this trick on other Pokémon game versions, too.

Hidden Character Select
Amitie is the main character in this portable puzzler, and she's normally your avatar in the game. However, you can unlock 14 more characters for your use, including Ocean Prince and Popoi, the mischievous black cat. To access the Character Select screen in Single mode, go to Single Puyo Pop, highlight the course you'd like to play, and press X, Down, Up, A.

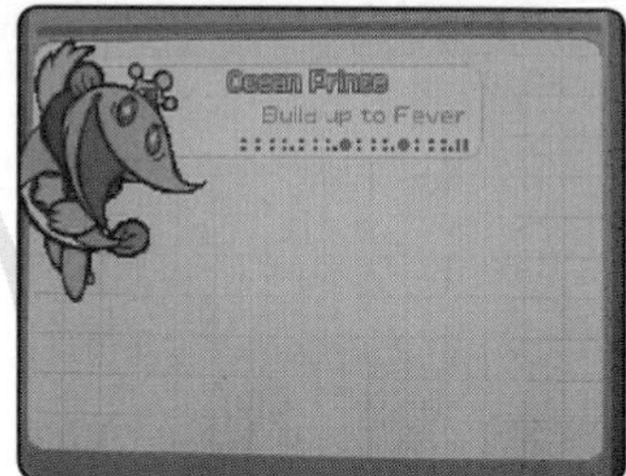

To access the Character Select screen in Endless mode, go to Endless Puyo Pop, highlight the course you'd like to play, and press Up, Down, X, A.

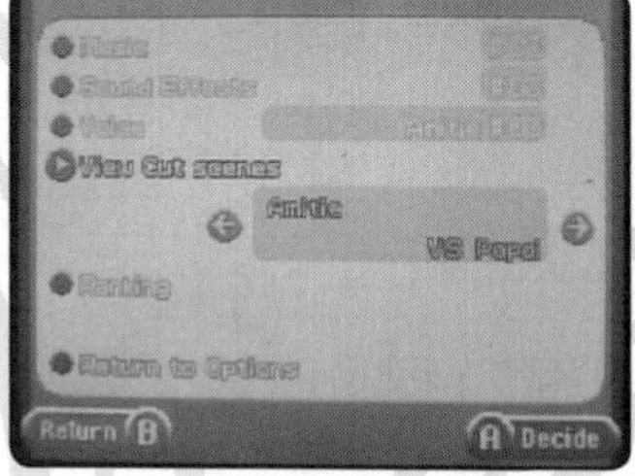

Unlock All Cut Scenes
To unlock all the cut scenes in the game, go to Options, and then to Gallery. Highlight the View Cut Scenes option, then hold X and press Up, Down, Left, Right. You'll be able to view the game's entire storyline in one sitting.

Wii Xbox 360 Xbox GC PS3 PS2 DS GBA PSP

SimCity DS

Add Historical Landmarks to Your Collection!
Before you can add to your collection of historical landmarks, you'll need to select Museum at the Main Menu, choose Landmark Collection and tap on the Password button at the bottom of the screen. Now enter the following passwords:

Landmark	Password
Athens's Parthenon	callas
Austria's St. Stephen's Cathedral	mozart
Barcelona's Sagrada Familia	dali
Bavaria's Neuschwanstein Castle	beethoven
Berlin's Brandenburg Gate	gropius
Berlin's Reichstag	goethe
Chile's Moia	allende
Egyptian Great Pyramids	mahfouz
Egypt's Pharos of Alexandria	zewail
Egypt's Sphinx	haykal
Finland's Helsinki Cathedral	kivi
Hollywood Capitol Records Tower	hemingway
India's Taj Mahal	tagore
Istanbul's Hagia Sofia	ataturk
Japan's Atomic Dome	kawabata
Japan's Daibutsu	mishima
Japan's Edo Castle	shonagon
Japan's Himeji Castle	hokusai
Japan's Kokkai	soseki
Japan's Mt. Fuji	hiroshige
Japan's Shuri Castle	basho
Liverpool Metropolitan Cathedral	austen
Liverpool's Anglican Cathedral	kipling
Liverpool's Royal Liver Building	dickens
London's Big Ben	orwell
London's St. Paul's Cathedral	defoe
London's Trafalgar Square	joyce
London's Westminster Abbey	greene
Lübeck's Holstentor City Gate	durer
Madrid's Palacio Real	cervantes
Melbourne Cricket Grounds	damemelba
Moscow's St. Basil's Cathedral	tolstoy
New York's Statue of Liberty	pollack
New York United Nations	amnesty
New York's Grand Central Station	f.scott
Nintendo's Bowser Castle	hanafuda
Paris's Arc de Triomphe	gaugin
Paris's Conciergerie Palace	rodin
Paris's Eiffel Tower	camus
Paris's Notre Dam Cathedral	hugo
Paris Opera	daumier
Philadelphia's Independence Hall	mlkingjr
San Francisco's Coit Tower	kerouac
San Francisco's Palace of Fine Arts	bunche
St. Louis Gateway Arch	twain
Sweden's Stockholm Palace	bergman
Sydney Opera House	bradman
Taiwan National Museum	yuantlee
Thailand's Rama IX Royal Park	phu
Tower of London	maugham
United States Capitol Building	poe
Washington's Jefferson Memorial	thompson
Washington's Lincoln Memorial	melville
Washington Monument	capote
Washington's Smithsonian Castle	pauling
Washington's White House	steinbeck

- Landmark -
Daibutsu

- Area -
Kamakura, Japan

- Built -
1252

- Comments -
Originally housed inside a wooden temple, which was washed away by a tsunami in 1495.

Note: All passwords for SimCity DS are in lowercase letters.

Instant Armada
Tired of being a mere space cadet? Jump rank and choose any ship for Skirmish mode with this easy unlock code. Enter the following code on the Main menu: Up, Down, Left, Right, Select, Start, Y

If you enter the code correctly, you'll see and hear a confirmation message. You can also use these unlocked ships in Multiplayer mode.

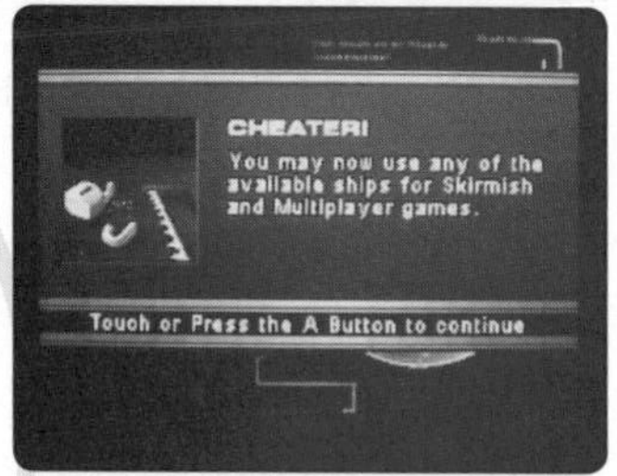

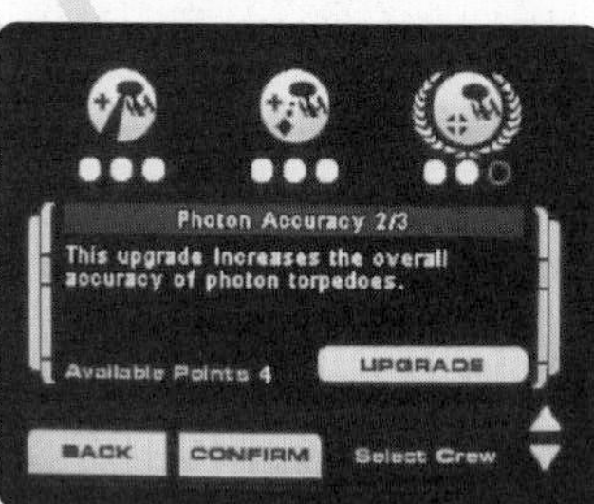

Infinite Crew Upgrades
Load or start your campaign game, then choose "Crew Upgrades" and wait for the crew member descriptions to appear. Now enter the following code: Up, Down, Left, Right, Select, Start, Select

You'll add five crew upgrade points to your score. Need more? Keep entering the code and you'll increase your total by another five points.

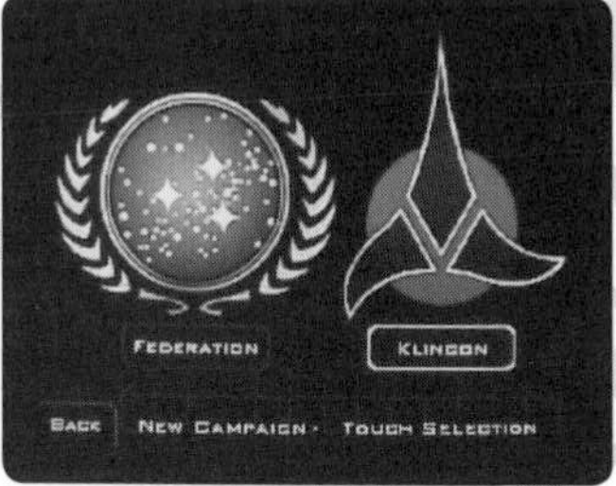

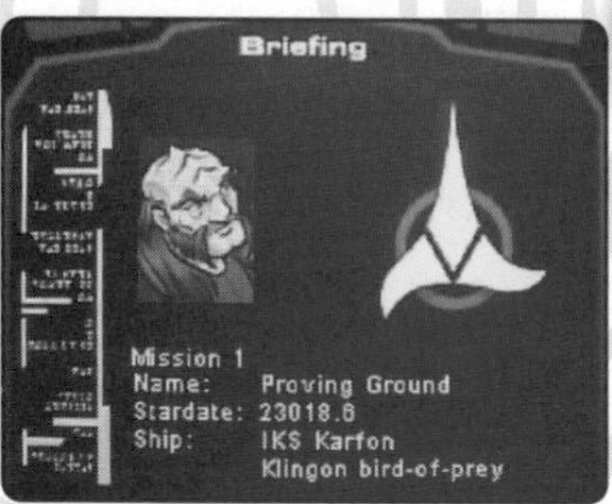

(continued)

Star Trek: Tactical Assault (cont.)

Unlock Your Inner Klingon
Normally you would have to start out as a Starfleet lackey in Star Trek: Tactical Assault, but you can beam off the Federation ships and join the ranks of the Klingon campaign by entering this code on the Main menu: Up, Down, Left, Right, Select, Start, X

Unlock New Missions
If you want to skip ahead to explore new missions, enter the following code on the Main menu: Up, Down, Left, Right, Select, Start, Start

You'll receive a confirmation message if you enter the code correctly. Now enter the Campaign menu and choose Next Mission. Press the R button on the Mission Briefing screen to scroll ahead to new missions.

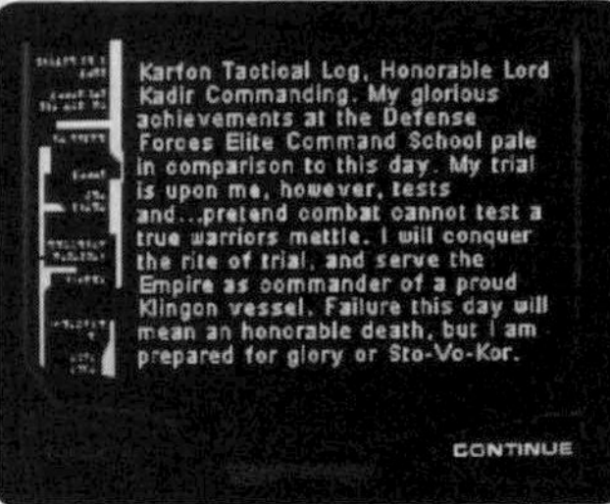

Select Any Ship During a Campaign
You're normally stuck with whichever ship Starfleet or the Klingon High Command sees fit to give you for a given mission. To be able to choose any ship for any mission, enter the following code on the Main menu: Up, Down, Left, Right, Select, Start, B

If you enter the code correctly, you'll see and hear a confirmation message. Now enter the Campaign menu and choose Next Mission. On the Mission Briefing screen, press Up and Down on the directional pad to scroll through all the Federation, Klingon, Romulan, and Orion vessels.

Note that the Orion Heavy Cruiser is the last ship on the list, and if you select it, you won't be able to scroll back through the list. If you don't want the Orion Heavy Cruiser, go back to the previous screen, and then return to the Mission Briefing screen and try again.

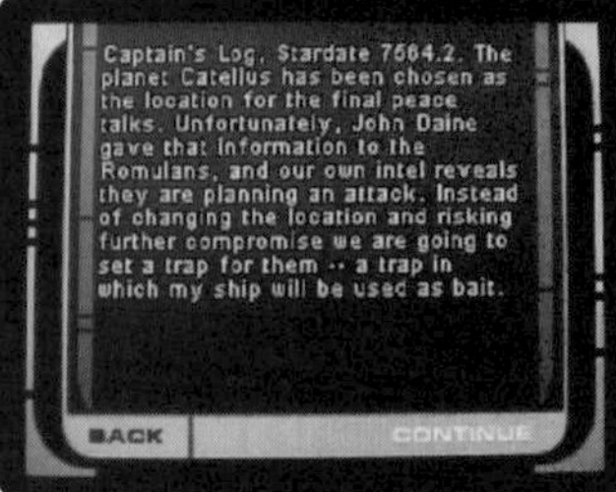

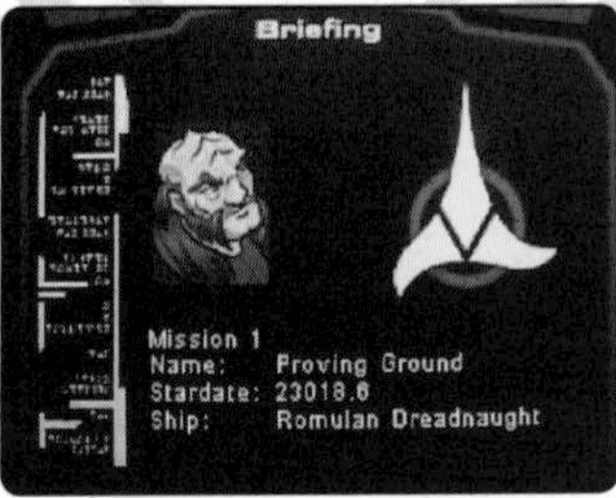

Super Princess Peach

Unlockable Mini-Game
To access a special mini-game, simply hold the R button and press Start on the Title screen. In this challenge, you must use the stylus to guide Toad around and push other Toads off the screen. What's a little strange is that all the other Toads are bawling their eyes out!

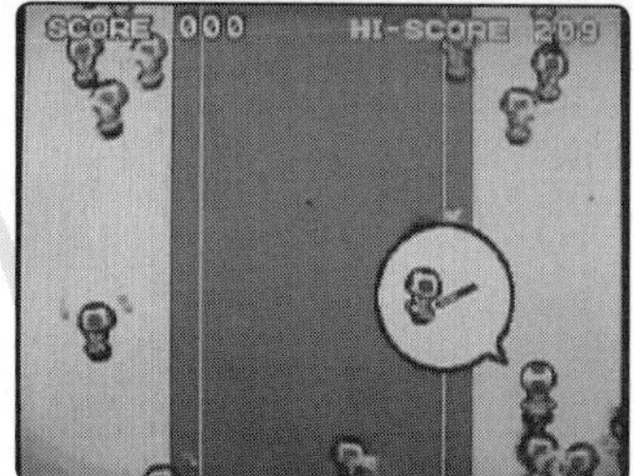

Insider Tip
Instead of moving around a lot and trying to forcibly shove the Toads off the screen, the best thing to do is just stand near the edge of the screen. It's far easier to push the Toads back just as they are entering or leaving the screen than it is to shove them across a wide space. In fact, even the slightest brush against a Toad as he's walking off the screen is enough to get you a point, so take advantage.

Teenage Mutant Ninja Turtles 3: Mutant Nightmare

Pizza Party Power-Ups
It's well known that the Teenage Mutant Ninja Turtles' favorite food of all time is pizza. With this password, they won't have to wait for the delivery guy. When creating or continuing a game, go to the Options screen and then to the Input Password screen. Type in the password DDRMLRDS to change all the health power-ups into slices of cheesy goodness. If you enter the password correctly, you'll hear the Turtles yell, "Yeah!"

(continued)

Wii
Xbox 360
Xbox
GC
PS3
PS2
DS
GBA
PSP

Teenage Mutant Ninja Turtles 3: Mutant Nightmare (cont.)

Holiday Icons
One of your primary goals in each stage is to collect the alien Crystals. These passwords will change them into icons representing different holidays. If you enter a password correctly, you'll hear the Turtles yell, "Yeah!"

Icon	***Password***
Easter Egg	SRDSLLMS
Jack-O'-Lantern	DRSSMRLD
Santa Claus Head	LLDMSRMD

> **Insider Tip**
> At the Title screen, press Up, Up, Down, Down, Left, Right, Left, Right, B, A to hear the Turtles' signature yell, "Cowabunga!"

Tony Hawk's Downhill Jam

Cheats for Sale!
You can buy cheats, but only if you know the right words to enter at the Skateshop. Choose Buy Stuff and then Enter Code to add a code. If you enter a code correctly, you'll get a message that says, "New Goodie Unlocked!"

Cheat	***Code***
Activate Mirror Mode Courses	MIRRORBALL
Access Abominable Snowman Gear	BIGSNOWMAN
Access Always Snowskate Cheat	SNOWSK8T
Access Zombie Gear	ZOMBIEALIVE

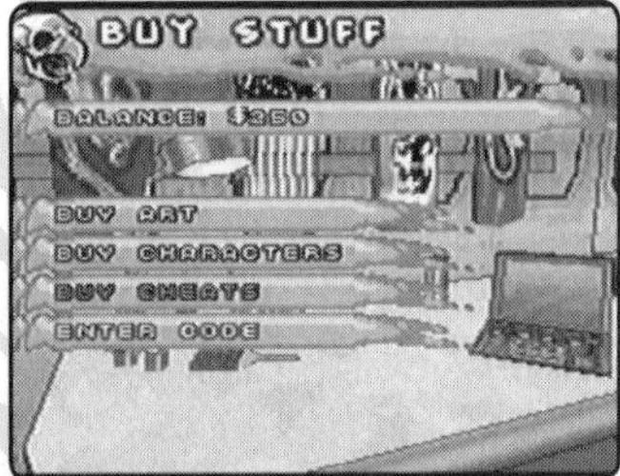

> **Insider Tip**
> Remember that you can't buy your cheats until you complete World Tour Mode.

Create a Winning Hand!

Use these passwords at the Shop menu, but remember that these codes will only work for cards that are already in your deck! If you're not sure which cards you already have, go to the Duelist menu and choose Card List.

Cheat	*Code*
4-Starred Ladybug of Doom	83994646
7 Colored Fish	23771716
A Cat of Ill Omen	24140059
A Deal with Dark Ruler	06850209
A Feather of the Phoenix	49140998
A Feint Plan	68170903
A Hero Emerges	21597117
A Legendary Ocean	00295517
A Man with Wdjat	51351302
A Rival Appears!	05728014
A Wingbeat of Giant Dragon	28596933
Abare Ushioni	89718302
Absolute End	27744077
Absorbing Kid from the Sky	49771608
Abyss Soldier	18318842
Abyssal Designator	89801755
Acid Rain	21323861
Acid Trap Hole	41356845
Acrobat Monkey	47372349
Adhesion Trap Hole	62325062
Adhesive Explosive	53828396
Aegis of Gaia	47060347
After the Struggle	25345186
Agido	16135253
Airknight Parshath	18036057
Aitsu	48202661
Alkana Knight Joker	06150044
Allure Queen Level 3	87257460
Allure Queen Level 5	23756165
Allure Queen Level 7	50140163
Alpha the Magnet Warrior	99785935
Altar for Tribute	21070956
Amazoness Archer	91869203
Amazoness Archers	67987611
Amazoness Blowpiper	73574678
Amazoness Chain Master	29654737
Amazoness Paladin	47480070
Amazoness Swordswoman	94004268
Amazoness Tiger	10979723
Amoeba	95174353
Amphibian Beast	67371383
Amphibious Bugroth	64342551
Amplifier	00303660
An Owl of Luck	23927567
Ancient Elf	93221206

Cheat	*Code*
Ancient Gear Beast	10509340
Ancient Gear Cannon	80045583
Ancient Gear Castle	92001300
Ancient Gear Drill	67829249
Ancient Gear Golem	83104731
Ancient Gear Soldier	56094445
Ancient Gear	31557782
Ancient Lamp	54912977
Ancient Lizard Warrior	43230671
Ancient Telescope	17092736
Andro Sphinx	15013468
Ante	02204140
Anteatereatingant	13250922
Anti-Aircraft Flower	65064143
Anti-Spell	53112492
Apprentice Magician	09156135
Appropriate	48539234
Aqua Madoor	85639257
Aqua Spirit	40916023
Arcane Archer of the Forest	55001420

(continued)

Yu-Gi-Oh! World Championship 2007 (cont.)

Cheat	Code
Archfiend of Gilfer	50287060
Archfiend Soldier	49881766
Archlord Zerato	18378582
Armaill	53153481
Armed Charger	90374791
Armed Dragon Level 10	59464593
Armed Dragon Level 3	00980973
Armed Dragon Level 5	46384672
Armed Dragon Level 7	73879377
Armed Ninja	09076207
Armed Samurai - Ben Kei	84430950
Armor Axe	07180418
Armor Break	79649195
Armored Glass	36868108
Armored Lizard	15480588
Armored Starfish	17535588
Armored Zombie	20277860
Array of Revealing Light	69296555
Arsenal Bug	42364374
Arsenal Robber	55348096
Arsenal Summoner	85489096
Assault on GHQ	62633180
Astral Barrier	37053871
Asura Priest	02134346
Aswan Apparition	88236094
A-Team: Trap Disposal Unit	13026402
Atomic Firefly	87340664
Attack and Receive	63689843
Attack Reflector Unit	91989718
Aussa the Earth Charmer	37970940
Autonomous Action Unit	71453557
Avatar of the Pot	99284890
Axe Dragonute	84914462
Axe of Despair	40619825
Axe Raider	48305365
B. Skull Dragon	11901678
B.E.S. Covered Core	15317640

Cheat	Code
B.E.S. Crystal Core	22790789
B.E.S. Tetran	44954628
Baby Dragon	88819587
Back to Square One	47453433
Backfire	82705573
Backup Soldier	36280194
Bad Reaction to Simochi	40633297
Bait Doll	07165085
Ballista of Rampart Smashing	00242146
Banisher of the Light	6152825
Banisher of the Radiance	94853057
Banner of Courage	10012614
Bark of Dark Ruler	41925941
Barrel Dragon	81480460
Basic Insect	89091579
Battery Charger	61181383
Batteryman AA	63142001
Batteryman C	19733961
Battle Footballer	48094997
Battle Ox	05053103
Battle Steer	18246479
Battle-Scarred	94463200
Battle Warrior	55550921
Bazoo The Soul-Eater	40133511
Beast Fangs	46009906
Beast Soul Swap	35149085
Beastking of the Swamps	99426834
Beautiful Headhuntress	16899564
Beaver Warrior	32452818
Beckoning Light	16255442
Beelze Frog	49522489
Begone, Knave	20374520
Behemoth, the King of All Animals	22996376
Beiige, Vanguard of Dark World	33731070
Berserk Dragon	85605684
Berserk Gorilla	39168895
Beta the Magnet Warrior	39256679
Bickuribox	25655502
Big Bang Shot	61127349
Big Burn	95472621
Big Core	14148099
Big Eye	16768387
Big Insect	53606874
Big Koala	42129512
Big Shield Gardna	65240384

(continued)

Cheat	Code
Big Wave Small Wave	51562916
Big-Tusked Mammoth	59380081
Bio-Mage	58696829
Birdface	45547649
Birthright	35539880
Black Illusion Ritual	41426869
Black Luster Ritual	55761792
Black Luster Soldier- Envoy of Beginning	72989439
Black Pendant	65169794
Black Tyranno	38670435
Blackland Fire Dragon	87564352
Blade Knight	39507162
Blade Rabbit	58268433
Blade Skater	97023549
Bladefly	28470714
Blast Held by a Tribute	89041555
Blast Magician	21051146
Blast with Chain	98239899
Blasting the Ruins	21466326
Blazing Inpachi	05464695
Blessings of the Nile	30653113
Blind Destruction	32015116
Block Attack	25880422
Blue Eyes Ultimate Dragon	23995346
Blue Eyes White Dragon	89631139
Blue Medicine	20871001
Blue-Eyes White Dragon (not SDK-001)	80906030
Book of Life	02204140
Book of Moon	14087893
Book of Secret Arts	91595718
Bottomless Shifting Sand	76532077
Bottomless Trap Hole	29401950
Bracchio-raidus	16507828
Brain Control	87910978
Breath of Light	20101223
Bright Castle	82878489
Burning Land	24294108
Burning Spear	18937875
Burst Breath	80163754
Burst Return	27191436
Burst Stream of Destruction	17655904
Buster Blader	78193831
Call of the Haunted	97077563
Call of the Mummy	04861205
Cannon Soldier	11384280
Card Destruction	72892473
Card of Safe Return	57953380

Cheat	Code
Card Trooper	85087012
Castle of Dark Illusions	00062121
Castle Walls	44209392
Catapult Turtle	95727991
Ceasefire	36468556
Celtic Guardian	90101050
Chain Destruction	01248895
Chain Energy	79323590
Chaos Emperor Dragon-Envoy of The End	82301904
Chimeratech Overdragon	64599569
Chorus of Sanctuary	81380218
Chosen One	21888494
Clay Charge	22479888
Cliff the Trap Remover	06967870
Clown Zombie	92667214
Cocoon of Evolution	40240595
Cold Wave	60682203
Collected Power	07565547
Compulsory Evacuation Device	94192409
Crass Clown	93889755
Crawling Dragon	67494157
Crawling Dragon #2	38289717
Creature Swap	31036355
Crimson Sunbird	46696593
Crush Card Virus	57728570
Curse of Anubis	66742250
Curse of Dragon	28279543
Curse of Fiend	12470447
Curse of Royal	02926176
Curse of the Masked Beast	94377247
Cyber Dragon	70095154
Cyber End Dragon	01546123
Cyber Harpie Lady	80316585

(continued)

Yu-Gi-Oh! World Championship 2007 (cont.)

Cheat	Code
Cyber Raider	39978267
Cyber Shiled	63224564
Cyberdark Dragon	40418351
Cyberdark Edge	77625948
Cyberdark Horn	41230939
Cyberdark Keel	03019642
Cyber-Tech Alligator	48766543
Cyclon Laser	05494820
D.D. Assailant	70074904
D.D. Survivor	48092532
D.D. Warrior	37043180
Damage Condenser	28378427
Dancing Fairy	90925163
Dark Artist	72520073
Dark Avatar	21208154
Dark Balter the Terrible	80071763
Dark Blade	11321183
Dark Chimera	32344688
Dark Coffin	01804528
Dark Core	70231910
Dark Energy	04614116
Dark Eraser	57793869
Dark Jeroid	90980792
Dark Magic Curtain	99789342
Dark Magician Girl	38033121
Dark Magician of Chaos	40737112
Dark Magician	40609080
Dark Rabbit	99261403
Dark Sage	92377303
Dark Scorpion Burglars	40933924
Dark Scorpion Combination	20858318
Dark Spirit of the Silent	93599951
Dark World Dealings	74117290
Darkfire Dragon	17881964
Darkness Approaches	80168720
Dark-Piercing Light	45895206
Deal of Phantom	69122763
De-Fusion	95286165
Delinquent Duo	44763025
Delta Attacker	39719977
Desert Sunlight	93747864
Despair from the Dark	71200730
De-Spell	19159413
Destiny Board	94212438
Destiny Draw	45809008
Destiny Hero Disk Commander	56570271
Destiny Hero Dreadmaster	40591390
Destiny Hero Malicious	09411399

Cheat	Code
Destruction Punch	05616412
Dian Keto the Cure Master	84257639
Dimensionhole	22959079
DNA Surgery	74701381
Don Zaloog	76922029
Dora of Fate	67464807
Dragon Capture Jar	50045299
Dragon Treasure	01435851
Dragon Zombie	66672569
Dragoness the Wicked Knight	70681994
Dragonic Attack	32437102
Dragon's Gunfire	55991637
Dragon's Rage	54178050
Dream Clown	13215230
Driving Snow	00473469
Dunames Dark Witch	12493482
Dungeon Worm	51228280
Dust Barrier	31476755
Dust Tornado	60082869
Earth Chant	59820352
Eatgaboon	42578427
Ectoplasmer	97342942
Ekibyo Drakmord	69954399
Electro-Whip	37820550
Elegant Egotist	90219263
Elemental Absorber	94253609
Elemental Dragon	30314994
Elemental Hero Avian	21844576
Elemental Hero Bladedge	59793705
Elemental Hero Bubbleman	79979666
Elemental Hero Clayman	84327329
Elemental Hero Dark Neos	28677304
Elemental Hero Flame Wingman	35809262

(continued)

Cheat	Code
Elemental Hero Grand Neos	48996596
Elemental Hero Rampart Blaster	47737087
Elemental Hero Sparkman	20721928
Elemental Hero Stratos	40044918
Elemental Hero Thunder Giant	61204971
Elemental Mistress Doriado	99414168
Elf's Light	39897277
Embodiment of Apophis	28649820
Enchanting Fitting Room	30531525
Enemy Controller	98045062
Eradicating Aerosol	94716515
Eternal Draught	56606928
Eternal Rest	95051344
Exarion Universe	63749102
Exile of the Wicked	26725158
Exiled Force	74131780
Exodia the Forbidden One	33396948
Fairy Box	21598948
Fairy Meteor Crush	97687912
Fairy's Hand Mirror	17653779
Feather Shot	19394153
Feather Wind	71060915
Feral Imp	41392891
Fiend Kraken	77456781
Final Destiny	18591904
Final Flame	73134081
Fire Princess	64752646
Fissure	66788016
Flame Cerebrus	60862676
Flame Manipulator	34460851
Flame Swordsman	45231177
Flying Kamakiri #1	84834865
Follow Wind	98252586
Foolish Burial	81439173
Forced Requisition	74923978

Cheat	Code
Forest	87430998
Fusion Gate	24094653
Fusion Sage	26902560
Gaia Power	56594520
Gaia the Dragon Champion	66889139
Gaia the Fierce Knight	06368038
Gamble	37313786
Garoozis	14977074
Gate Guardian	25833572
Gear Golem the Moving Fortress	30190809
Gemini Elf	69140098
Germ Infection	24668830
Giant Flea	41762634
Giant Soldier of Stone	13039848
Giant Trunade	42703248
Gift of the Mystical Elf	98299011
Gigantes	47606319
Gilford the Lightning	36354007
Goblin Fan	04149689
Goblin's Secret Remedy	11868825
Goddess of Whim	67959180
Goddess with the Third Eye	53493204
Gokibore	15367030
Gorgon's Eye	52648457
Graceful Charity	79571449
Graceful Dice	74137509
Grappler	02906250
Gravedigger Ghoul	82542267
Gravekeeper's Assailant	25262697
Gravekeeper's Servant	16762927
Gravekeeper's Spear Soldier	63695531
Graverobber's Retribution	33737664
Gravity Axe - Grarl	32022366
Gravity Bind	85722772
Great Moth	14141448
Great Shogun Shien	63176202
Great White	13429800
Green Gadget	41172955
Griffore	53829412
Ground Collapse	90502999
Guardian Sphinx	40659562
Gust Fan	55321970
Gust	73079365
Gyakutenno Megami	31122090
Hallowed Life Barrier	88789641
Harpie Lady	76812113

(continued)

Yu-Gi-Oh! World Championship 2007 (cont.)

Cheat	Code
Harpie Lady 1	91932350
Harpie Lady 2	27927359
Harpie Lady 3	54415063
Harpie Lady Sisters	12206212
Harpie's Feather Duster	18144586
Harpie's Hunting Ground	75782277
Harpie's Pet Dragon	52040216
Heart of the Underdog	37562283
Heavy Storm	19613556
Helpoemer	76052811
Hercules Beetle	52584282
Hero Signal	22020907
Hero Spirit	81167171
Hinotama	46130346
Hitotsu-Me Giant	76184692
Horn Imp	69669405
Horn of Light	38552107
Horn of the Unicorn	64047146
Horus the Black Flame Dragon Level 4	75830094
Horus the Black Flame Dragon Level 6	11224103
Horus the Black Flame Dragon Level 8	48229808
House of Adhesive Tape	15083728
Human-Wave Tactics	30353551
Illusionist Faceless Mage	28546905
Imperial Order	61740673
Inferno Fire Blast	52684508
Inferno Reckless Summon	12247206
Infinite Cards	94163677
Infinite Dismissal	54109233
Injection Fairy Lily	79575620
Insect Armor with Laser Cannon	03492538
Insect Barrier	23615409

Cheat	Code
Insect Imitation	96965364
Insect Queen	91512835
Inspection	16227556
Interdimensional Matter Transporter	36261726
Invigoration	98374133
Jam Breeding Machine	21770260
Jam Defender	21558682
Jar of Greed	83968380
Jellyfish	14851496
Jinzo #7	77585513
Jirai Gumo	15401633
Judge Man	30113682
Judgment of Anubis	55256016
Just Desserts	24068492
Kairyu-Shin	76634149
Kazejin	62340868
Killer Needle	88979991
King of Yamimakai	69455834
Kishido Spirit	60519422
Kojikocy	01184620
Koumori Dragon	67724379
Krokodilus	76512652
Kunai with Chain	37390589
Kuriboh	40640057
La Jinn the Mystical Genie of the Lamp	97590747
Labyrinth of Nightmare	66526672
Labyrinth Tank	99551425
Labyrinth Wall	67284908
Larvae Moth	87756343
Laser Cannon Armor	77007920
Last Day of Witch	90330453
Last Will	85602018
Launcher Spider	87322377
Lava Battleguard	20394040
Lava Golem	00102380
Left Arm of the Forbidden One	07902349
Left Leg of the Forbidden One	44519536
Legendary Sword	61854111
Light of Intervention	62867251
Lightning Blade	55226821
Lightning Vortex	69162969
Limiter Removal	23171610
Lord of D.	17985575
Luminous Spark	81777047

(continued)

Cheat	Code
Luster Dragon #2	17658803
Luster Dragon (1900/1600)	11091375
Machine Conversion Factory	25769732
Machine King	25769732
Mage Power	46700124
Magic Cylinder	62279055
Magic Drain	59344077
Magic Jammer	77414722
Magic Thorn	53119267
Magical Hats	81210420
Magical Scientist	34206604
Magic-Arm Shield	96008713
Magician of Faith	31560081
Magician's Circle	00050755
Maha Vailo	93013676
Majestic Mech - Goryu	95701283
Major Riot	09074847
Makyura the Destructor	21593977
Malevolent Nuzzler	99597615
Malfunction	06137095
Mammoth Graveyard	40374923
Man-Eater Bug	54652250
Manju of the Ten Thousand Hands	95492061
Masaki the Legendary Swordsman	44287299
Mask of Brutality	82432018
Mask of Darkness	28933734
Mask of Dispel	20765952
Mask of Restrict	29549364
Mask of the Accursed	56948373
Mask of Weakness	57882509
Masked Dragon	39191307
Masked Sorcerer	10189126
Megamorph	22046459
Mesmeric Control	48642904
Messenger of Peace	44656491
Metal Detector	75646520
Metal Guardian	68339286
Metalmorph	68540058
Metalzoa	50705071
Metamorphosis	46411259
Meteor Black Dragon	90660762
Meteor Dragon	64271667
Meteor of Destruction	33767325
Meteorain	01918087
Michizure	37580756
Millennium Shield	32012841
Milus Radiant	07489323

Cheat	Code
Mind Control	37520316
Minor Goblin Official	01918087
Mirror Force	44095762
Moai Interceptor Cannons	45159319
Monster Recovery	93108433
Monster Reincarnation	74848038
Monster Tamer	97612389
Mooyan Curry	58074572
Morphing Jar	33508719
Mother Grizzly	57839750
Mountain	50913601
Mucus Yolk	70307656
Muka Muka	46657337
Multiplication of Ants	22493811
Multiply	40703222
Mushroom Man	14181608
Mustering of the Dark Scorpions	68191243
Mysterious Puppeteer	54098121
Mystic Horseman	68516705
Mystic Plasma Zone	18161786
Mystic Probe	49251811
Mystical Elf	15025844
Mystical Moon	36607978
Mystical Space Typhoon	05318639
Mystik Wok	80161395
Necroface	28297833
Negate Attack	14315573
Neo-Spacian Air Hummingbird	54959865
Neo-Spacian Aqua Dolphin	17955766
Neo-Spacian Flame Scarab	89621922
Nightmare's Steelcage	58775978
Obnoxious Celtic Guard	52077741
Offerings to the Doomed	19230407
Ojama Black	79335209

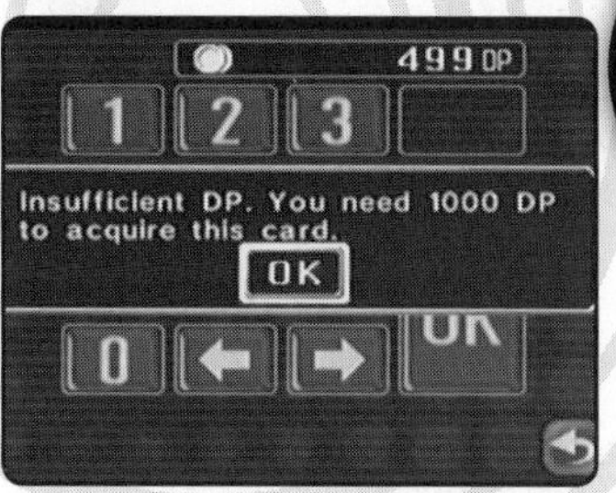

(continued)

Wii
Xbox 360
Xbox
GC
PS3
PS2
DS
GBA
PSP

Yu-Gi-Oh! World Championship 2007 (cont.)

Cheat	Code
Ojama Green	12482652
Ojama King	90140980
Ojama Trio	29843091
Ojama Yellow	42941100
Ookazi	19523799
Ordeal of a Traveler	39537362
Order to Charge	78986941
Order to Smash	39019325
Pandemonium	94585852
Panther Warrior	42035044
Paralyzing Potion	50152549
Parrot Dragon	62762898
Pendulum Machine	24433920
Penguin Knight	36039163
Penguin Soldier	93920745
Perfectly Ultimate Great Moth	48579379
Petit Dragon	75356564
Petit Moth	58192742
Pikeru's Circle of Enchantment	74270067
Pineapple Blast	90669991
Polymerization	24094653
Pot of Greed	55144522
Premature Burial	70828912
Prevent Rat	00549481
Princess of Tsurugi	51371017
Prohibition	43711255
Pumpking the King of Ghosts	29155212
Punished Eagle	74703140
Pyramid Energy	76754619
Pyramid Turtle	77044671
Rabid Horseman	94905343
Raigeki	12580477
Raimei	56260110
Rain of Mercy	66719324
Raise Body Heat	51267887
Rare Fish	80516007
Raregold Armor	07625614
Raviel, Lord of Phantasms	69890967
Reaper of the Cards	33066139
Reasoning	58577036
Reckless Greed	37576645
Red Gadget	86445415
Red Medicine	38199696
Red-Eyes B. Chick	36262024
Red-Eyes B. Dragon	74677422
Red-Eyes Black Metal Dragon	64335804
Red-Eyes Darkness Dragon	96561011
Reinforcement of the Army	32807846
Reinforcements	17814387
Relinquished	64631466
Reload	22589918
Remove Trap	51482758
Respect Play	08951260
Restructer Revolution	99518961
Return from the Different Dimension	27174286
Reverse Trap	77622396
Right Arm of the Forbidden One	70903634
Right Leg of the Forbidden One	08124921

Cheat	Code
Ring of Destruction	83555666
Ring of Magnetism	20436034
Riryoku Field	70344351
Robbin' Goblin	88279736
Rock Ogre Grotto #1	68846917
Rogue Doll	91939608
Rope of Life	93382620
Royal Decree	51452091
Royal Magic Library	70791313
Rude Kaiser	26378150
Ruin, Queen of Oblivion	46427957
Rush Recklessly	70046172
Ryu Kokki	57281778
Ryu-Kishin Powered	24611934
Ryu-Kishin	15303296
Sage's Stone	13604200

(continued)

Cheat	Code
Saggi the Dark Clown	66602787
Sakuretsu Armor	56120475
Salamandra	32268901
Sanga of the Thunder	25955164
Sangan	26202165
Sasuke Samurai #2	11760174
Satellite Cannon	50400231
Scapegoat	73915051
Servant of Catabolism	02792265
Seven Tools of the Bandit	03819470
Shadow Ghoul	30778711
Shadow of Eyes	58621589
Share the Pain	56830749
Shield & Sword	52097679
Shift	59560625
Shining Angel	95956346
Shooting Star Bow - Ceal	95638658
Shrink	55713623
Silent Magician Level 4	73665146
Silent Magician Level 8	72443568
Silver Bow and Arrow	01557499
Silver Fang	90357090
Sinister Serpent	08131171
Skill Drain	82732705
Skilled Dark Magician	73752131
Skull Dice	00126218
Skull Invitation	98139712
Skull Lair	06733059
Skyscraper	63035430
Slate Warrior	78636495
Snake Fang	00596051
Snatch Steal	45986603
Sogen	86318356
Solemn Judgment	41420027
Solemn Wishes	35346968
Soul of the Pure	47852924
Soul Release	05758500
Soul Resurrection	92924317
Spark Blaster	97362768
Sparks	76103675
Spear Dragon	31553716
Special Hurricane	42598242
Spell Shield Type-8	38275183
Spellbinding Circle	18807108
Spiral Spear Strike	49328340
Spirit Barrier	53239672
Spirit Message "A"	94772232
Spirit Message "I"	31893528
Spirit Message "L"	30170981

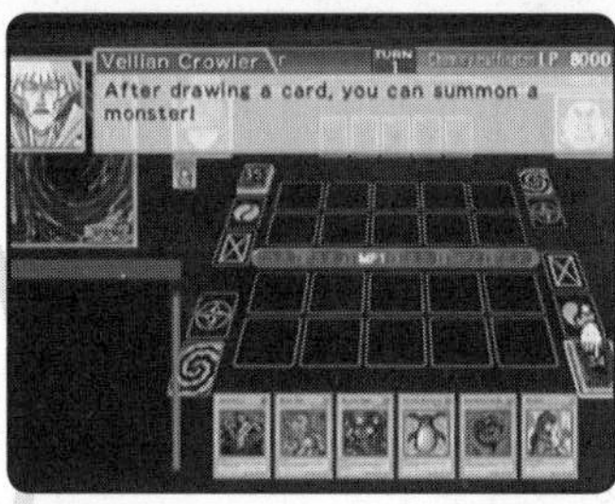

Cheat	Code
Spirit Message "N"	67287532
Spirit Reaper	23205979
Spiritualism	15866454
Spring of Rebirth	94425169
Spirit's Invitation	92394653
Stamping Destruction	81385346
Statue of the Wicked	65810489
Steel Scorpion	13599884
Steel Shell	02370081
Stim-Pack	83225447
Stop Defense	63102017
Suijin	98434877
Summoned Skull	70781052
Super Conductor Tyranno	85520851
Super Rejuvenation	27770341
Swamp Battleguard	40453765
Sword Arm of Dragon	13069066
Sword of Dark Destruction	37120512
Sword of the Deep-Seated	98495314
Sword of the Soul-Eater	05372656
Swords of Revealing Light	72302403
Swordstalker	50005633
System Down	18895832
Tailor of the Fickle	43641473
The Cheerful Coffin	41142615
The Dark Door	30606547
The Dragon's Bead	92408984
The Emperor's Holiday	68400115
The Forceful Sentry	42829885
The Grave of the Enkindling	84136000
The Inexperienced Spy	81820689
The Law of the Normal	66926224
The Little Swordsman of Aile	25109950
The Masked Beast	49064413

(continued)

Yu-Gi-Oh! World Championship 2007 (cont.)

Cheat	*Code*
The Reliable Guardian	16430187
The Sanctuary in the Sky	56433456
The Shallow Grave	43434803
The Snake Hair	29491031
The Wicked Worm Beast	06285791
Thousand Dragon	41462083
Thousand Energy	05703682
Thousand-Eyes Restrict	63519819
Thunder of Ruler	91781589
Tiger Axe	40907090
Time Machine	80987696
Time Wizard	71625222
Toll	82003859
Toon Alligator	59383041
Toon Summoned Skull	91842653
Torike	80813021

Cheat	*Code*
Tragedy	35686187
Trap Dustshoot	64697231
Trap Hole	04206964
Trap Jammer	19252988
Trap Master	46461247
Tremendous Fire	46918794
Triangle Ecstasy Spark	12181376
Tribute Doll	02903036
Tribute to the Doomed	79759861
Tutan Mask	03149764
Twin Swords of Flashing Light - Tryce	21900719
Two-Headed King Rex	94119974
Two-Pronged Attack	83887306
Tyhone	72842870
Type Zero Magic Crusher	21237481
Tyrant Dragon	94568601
UFO Turtle	60806437

Cheat	*Code*
Ultimate Offering	80604091
Ultimate Tyranno	15894048
Umi	22702055
Umiiruka	82999629
Upstart Goblin	70368879
Uraby	01784619
Uria, Lord of Searing Flames	06007213
Vampire Genesis	22056710
Vampire Lord	53839837
Vengeful Bog Spirit	95220856
Versago the Destroyer	50289460
Vile Germs	39774685
Violet Crystal	15052462
Vorse Raider	14898066
Waboku	12607053
Wall of Illusion	13945283
Wall of Revealing Light	17078030
Wall Shadow	63162310
Warrior Elimination	90873992
Wasteland	23424603
Water Dragon	85066822
Wave Motion Cannon	18992735
White Magical Hat	15160365
Windstorm of Etaqua	59744639
Winged Dragon Guardian of Fortress #1	87796900
Winged Kuriboh	57116033
Witch of the Black Forest	78010363
Wolf	49417509
World Supression	12253117
X-Head Cannon	62651957
XY-Dragon Cannon	02111707
XYZ-Dragon Cannon	91998119
XZ-Tank Cannon	99724761
Yami	59197169
Y-Dragon Head	65622692
Yellow Gadget	13834120
Yellow Luster Shield	04542651
Zanki	30090452
Zera the Mant	69123138
Z-Metal Tank	64500000
Zoa	24311372
Zombie Warrior	31339260

Yu-Gi-Oh! World Championship 2008

Expand your Winning Deck

Input these passwords from the Shop Menu, but remember that these codes will only work for cards that are already in your deck! If you're not sure which cards you already have, go to the Duelist Menu and choose Card List.

Cheat	*Code*
7	67048711
4-Starred Ladybug of Doom	83994646
7 Colored Fish	23771716
7 Completed	86198326
A Cat of Ill Omen	24140059
"A" Cell Breeding Device	34541863
"A" Cell Incubator	64163367
"A" Cell Scatter Burst	73262676
A Deal with Dark Ruler	06850209
A Feather of the Phoenix	49140998
A Feint Plan	68170903
A Hero Emerges	21597117
A Legendary Ocean	00295517
A Man with Wdjat	51351302
A Rival Appears!	05728014
A Wingbeat of Giant Dragon	28596933
Abare Ushioni	89718302
Absolute End	27744077
Absorbing Kid from the Sky	49771608
Abyss Soldier	18318842
Abyssal Designator	89801755
Accumulated Fortune	98444741
Acid Rain	21323861
Acid Trap Hole	41356845
Acrobat Monkey	47372349
Adhesion Trap Hole	62325062
Adhesive Explosive	53828396
Advanced Ritual Art	46052429
Aegis of Gaia	47060347
After the Struggle	25345186
Agido	16135253
Airknight Parshath	18036057
Aitsu	48202661
Alien Gray	62437709
Alien Hunter	62315111
Alien Hypno	38468214
Alien Infiltrator	76573247
Alien Mars	99532708
Alien Mother	24104865
Alien Psychic	58012107
Alien Shocktrooper	97127906
Alien Skull	25920413
Alien Telepath	91070115
Alien Warrior	98719226
Alkana Knight Joker	06150044
Alligator's Sword	64428736
Alligator's Sword Dragon	03366982
Allure Queen Level 3	87257460
Allure Queen Level 5	23756165
Allure Queen Level 7	50140163
Alpha the Magnet Warrior	99785935
Altar for Tribute	21070956
Amazoness Archer	91869203
Amazoness Archers	67987611
Amazoness Blowpipper	73574678
Amazoness Chain Master	29654737
Amazoness Paladin	47480070
Amazoness Swordswoman	94004268
Amazoness Tiger	10979723
Amoeba	95174353
Amphibian Beast	67371383
Amphibious Bugroth	64342551
Amplifier	00303660

(continued)

Yu-Gi-Oh! World Championship 2008 (cont.)

Cheat	Code
Amulet of Ambition	05183693
An Owl of Luck	23927567
An Unfortunate Report	19763315
Ancient Elf	93221206
Ancient City - Rainbow Ruins	34487429
Ancient Gear	31557782
Ancient Gear Beast	10509340
Ancient Gear Cannon	80045583
Ancient Gear Castle	92001300
Ancient Gear Drill	67829249
Ancient Gear Engineer	01953925
Ancient Gear Explosive	04446672
Ancient Gear Fist	40830387
Ancient Gear Gadjiltron Chimera	86321248
Ancient Gear Gadjiltron Dragon	50933533
Ancient Gear Golem	83104731
Ancient Gear Knight	39303359
Ancient Gear Soldier	56094445
Ancient Gear Tank	37457534
Ancient Gear Workshop	59811955
Ancient Lamp	54912977
Ancient Lizard Warrior	43230671
Ancient Rules	10667321
Ancient Telescope	17092736
Andro Sphinx	15013468
Angel 07	56784842
Ante	02204140
Anteatereatingant	13250922
Anti-Aircraft Flower	65064143
Anti-Fusion Device	72150572
Anti-Spell	53112492
Anti-Spell Fragrance	58921041
Apprentice Magician	09156135
Appropriate	48539234
Aqua Chorus	95132338
Aqua Dragon	86164529
Aqua Madoor	85639257
Aqua Spirit	40916023
Aquarian Alessa	22377815
Arcana Force Extra - The Light Ruler	05861892
Arcane Archer of the Forest	55001420
Archfiend General	48675364
Archfiend Marmot of Nefariousness	75889523
Archfiend of Gilfer	50287060

Cheat	Code
Archfiend's Oath	22796548
Archfiend's Roar	56246017
Archfiend Soldier	49881766
Archlord Zerato	18378582
Armaill	53153481
Armed Charger	90374791
Armed Dragon Level 10	59464593
Armed Dragon Level 3	00980973
Armed Dragon Level 5	46384672
Armed Dragon Level 7	73879377
Armed Ninja	09076207
Armed Samurai - Ben Kei	84430950
Armityle the Chaos Phantom	43378048
Armor Axe	07180418
Armor Break	79649195
Armored Glass	36868108
Armored Lizard	15480588
Armored Starfish	17535588
Armored Zombie	20277860
Array of Revealing Light	69296555
Arsenal Bug	42364374
Arsenal Robber	55348096
Arsenal Summoner	85489096
Assault on GHQ	62633180
Astral Barrier	37053871
Asura Priest	02134346
Aswan Apparition	88236094
A-Team: Trap Disposal Unit	13026402
Atomic Firefly	87340664
Attack and Receive	63689843
Attack Reflector Unit	91989718
Aussa the Earth Charmer	37970940
Autonomous Action Unit	71453557
Avatar of the Pot	99284890

(continued)

Cheat	Code
Axe Dragonute	84914462
Axe of Despair	40619825
Axe Raider	48305365
B. Skull Dragon	11901678
B.E.S. Covered Core	15317640
B.E.S. Crystal Core	22790789
B.E.S. Tetran	44954628
Baby Dragon	88819587
Babycerasarus	36042004
Back to Square One	47453433
Backfire	82705573
Backs to the Wall	32603633
Backup Soldier	36280194
Bad Reaction to Simochi	40633297
Bait Doll	07165085
Ballista of Rampart Smashing	00242146
Banisher of the Light	6152825
Banisher of the Radiance	94853057
Banner of Courage	10012614
Bark of Dark Ruler	41925941
Baron of the Fiend Sword	86325596
Barrel Behind the Door	78783370
Barrel Dragon	81480460
Barrier Statue of the Abyss	84478195
Barrier Statue of the Drought	19740112
Barrier Statue of the Heavens	46145256
Barrier Statue of the Inferno	47961808
Barrier Statue of the Stormwinds	73356503
Barrier Statue of the Torrent	10963799
Basic Insect	89091579

Cheat	Code
Battery Charger	61181383
Batteryman AA	63142001
Batteryman C	19733961
Batteryman D	55401221
Battle Footballer	48094997
Battle Ox	05053103
Battle Steer	18246479
Battle-Scarred	94463200
Battle Warrior	55550921
Bazoo The Soul-Eater	40133511
Beast Fangs	46009906
Beast Soul Swap	35149085
Beastking of the Swamps	99426834
Beastly Mirror Ritual	81933259
Beautiful Headhuntress	16899564
Beaver Warrior	32452818
Beckoning Light	16255442
Beelze Frog	49522489
Begone, Knave	20374520
Behemoth, the King of All Animals	22996376
Beiige, Vanguard of Dark World	33731070
Berserk Dragon	85605684
Berserk Gorilla	39168895
Beta the Magnet Warrior	39256679
Bickuribox	25655502
Big Bang Shot	61127349
Big Burn	95472621
Big Core	14148099
Big Evolution Pill	84808313
Big Eye	16768387
Big Insect	53606874
Big Koala	42129512
Big Shield Gardna	65240384
Big Wave Small Wave	51562916
Big-Tusked Mammoth	59380081
Bio-Mage	58696829
Birdface	45547649
Birthright	35539880
Black Horn of Heaven	50323155
Black Illusion Ritual	41426869
Black Luster Ritual	55761792
Black Luster Soldier	05405694
Black Luster Soldier- Envoy of Beginning	72989439
Black Magic Ritual	76792184
Black Pendant	65169794

(continued)

Yu-Gi-Oh! World Championship 2008 (cont.)

Cheat	Code
Black Petra	90654356
Black Stego	79409334
Black Tyranno	38670435
Blackland Fire Dragon	87564352
Blade Knight	39507162
Blade Rabbit	58268433
Blade Skater	97023549
Bladefly	28470714
Blast Held by a Tribute	89041555
Blast Magician	21051146
Blast Sphere	26302522
Blast with Chain	98239899
Blasting Fuse	99788587
Blaze Accelerator	69537999
Blazewing Butterfly	16984449
Blasting the Ruins	21466326
Blazing Inpachi	05464695
Blessings of the Nile	30653113
Blind Destruction	32015116
Block Attack	25880422
Blue Eyes Ultimate Dragon	23995346
Blue Eyes White Dragon	89631139
Blue Medicine	20871001
Blue-Eyes White Dragon (not SDK-001)	80906030
Book of Life	02204140
Book of Moon	14087893
Book of Secret Arts	91595718
Bottomless Shifting Sand	76532077
Bottomless Trap Hole	29401950
Bracchio-raidus	16507828
Brain Control	87910978
Breath of Light	20101223
Bright Castle	82878489
Broken Bamboo Sword	41587307
Burning Land	24294108

Cheat	Code
Burning Spear	18937875
Burst Breath	80163754
Burst Return	27191436
Burst Stream of Destruction	17655904
Buster Blader	78193831
Call of the Haunted	97077563
Call of the Mummy	04861205
Cannon Soldier	11384280
Card Destruction	72892473
Card of Safe Return	57953380
Card Trooper	85087012
Castle of Dark Illusions	00062121
Castle Walls	44209392
Catapult Turtle	95727991
Ceasefire	36468556
Celtic Guardian	90101050
Chain Destruction	01248895
Chain Energy	79323590
Chamberlain of the Six Samurai	44430454
Change of Heart	04031928
Chaos Emperor Dragon-Envoy of The End	82301904
Chimeratech Overdragon	64599569
Chorus of Sanctuary	81380218
Chosen One	21888494
Clay Charge	22479888
Cliff the Trap Remover	06967870
Clown Zombie	92667214
Cocoon of Evolution	40240595
Cold Wave	60682203
Collected Power	07565547
Compulsory Evacuation Device	94192409
Crass Clown	93889755
Crawling Dragon #2	38289717
Crawling Dragon	67494157
Creature Swap	31036355
Crimson Sunbird	46696593
Crush Card Virus	57728570
Crystal Beast Amber Mammoth	69937550
Crystal Beast Amethyst Cat	32933942
Crystal Beast Cobalt Eagle	21698716
Crystal Beast Emerald Tortoise	68215963
Crystal Beast Ruby Carbuncle	32710364

(continued)

Cheat	Code
Crystal Beast Sapphire Pegasus	07093411
Crystal Beast Topaz Tiger	95600067
Cunning of the Six Samurai	27178262
Curse of Anubis	66742250
Curse of Dragon	28279543
Curse of Fiend	12470447
Curse of Royal	02926176
Curse of the Masked Beast	94377247
Cyber Dragon	70095154
Cyber End Dragon	01546123
Cyber Harpie Lady	80316585
Cyber Raider	39978267
Cyber Shield	63224564
Cyberdark Dragon	40418351
Cyberdark Edge	77625948
Cyberdark Horn	41230939
Cyberdark Keel	03019642
Cyber-Tech Alligator	48766543
Cyclone Laser	05494820
D.D. Assailant	70074904
D.D. Survivor	48092532
D.D. Warrior	37043180
Damage Condenser	28378427
Dancing Fairy	90925163
Dark Artist	72520073
Dark Avatar	21208154
Dark Balter the Terrible	80071763
Dark Blade	11321183
Dark Chimera	32344688
Dark Coffin	01804528
Dark Core	70231910
Dark Energy	04614116
Dark Eraser	57793869
Dark Jeroid	90980792
Dark Magic Curtain	99789342
Dark Magician Girl	38033121
Dark Magician of Chaos	40737112
Dark Magician	40609080
Dark Rabbit	99261403
Dark Ruler Vandalgyon	24857466
Dark Sage	92377303
Dark Scorpion Burglars	40933924
Dark Scorpion Combination	20858318
Dark Spirit of the Silent	93599951
Dark World Dealings	74117290
Darkfire Dragon	17881964
Darkness Approaches	80168720
Dark-Piercing Light	45895206

Cheat	Code
Deal of Phantom	69122763
De-Fusion	95286165
Delinquent Duo	44763025
Delta Attacker	39719977
Demise, King of Armageddon 2	7242666
Desert Sunlight	93747864
Despair from the Dark	71200730
De-Spell	19159413
Destiny Board	94212438
Destiny Draw	45809008
Destiny Hero Disk Commander	56570271
Destiny Hero Dreadmaster	40591390
Destiny Hero Malicious	09411399
Destruction Punch	05616412
Dian Keto the Cure Master	84257639
Dimensionhole	22959079
DNA Surgery	74701381
Don Zaloog	76922029
Dora of Fate	67464807
Dragon Capture Jar	50045299
Dragon Treasure	01435851
Dragon Zombie	66672569
Dragoness the Wicked Knight	70681994
Dragonic Attack	32437102
Dragon's Gunfire	55991637
Dragon's Rage	54178050
Dream Clown	13215230
Drill Bug	88733579
Driving Snow	00473469
Dunames Dark Witch	12493482
Dungeon Worm	51228280
Dust Barrier	31476755

(continued)

Yu-Gi-Oh! World Championship 2008 (cont.)

Cheat	*Code*
Dust Tornado	60082869
Earth Chant	59820352
Eatgaboon	42578427
Ectoplasmer	97342942
Ekibyo Drakmord	69954399
Electro-Whip	37820550
Elegant Egotist	90219263
Elemental Absorber	94253609
Elemental Dragon	30314994
Elemental Hero Avian	21844576
Elemental Hero Bladedge	59793705
Elemental Hero Burstinatrix	58932615
Elemental Hero Bubbleman	79979666
Elemental Hero Clayman	84327329
Elemental Hero Dark Neos	28677304
Elemental Hero Flame Wingman	35809262
Elemental Hero Grand Neos	48996596
Elemental Hero Neos	89943723
Elemental Hero Ocean	371195861
Elemental Hero Rampart Blaster	47737087
Elemental Hero Sparkman	20721928
Elemental Hero Stratos	40044918
Elemental Hero Thunder Giant	61204971
Elemental Mistress Doriado	99414168
Elf's Light	39897277
Embodiment of Apophis	28649820
Enchanting Fitting Room	30531525
Enemy Controller	98045062
Enishi, Shien's Chancellor	38280762
Eradicating Aerosol	94716515
Eternal Draught	56606928
Eternal Rest	95051344
Exarion Universe	63749102
Exile of the Wicked	26725158
Exiled Force	74131780
Exodia the Forbidden One	33396948
Exodius the Ultimate Forbidden One	13893596
Exxod, Master of the Guard	55737443
Fairy Box	21598948
Fairy Meteor Crush	97687912
Fairy's Hand Mirror	17653779
Feather Shot	19394153
Feather Wind	71060915
Feral Imp	41392891
Fiend Kraken	77456781

Cheat	*Code*
Final Destiny	18591904
Final Flame	73134081
Fire Princess	64752646
Fissure	66788016
Flame Cerebrus	60862676
Flame Manipulator	34460851
Flame Swordsman	45231177
Flying Kamakiri #1	84834865
Follow Wind	98252586
Foolish Burial	81439173
Forced Requisition	74923978
Forest	87430998
Fusion Gate	24094653
Fusion Sage	26902560
Gaia Power	56594520
Gaia the Dragon Champion	66889139
Gaia the Fierce Knight	06368038
Gamble	37313786
Garoozis	14977074
Gate Guardian	25833572
Gearfried the Iron Knight	00423705
Gear Golem the Moving Fortress	30190809
Gemini Elf	69140098
Germ Infection	24668830
Giant Flea	41762634
Giant Soldier of Stone	13039848
Giant Trunade	42703248
Gift of the Mystical Elf	98299011
Gigantes	47606319
Gilford the Lightning	36354007
Goblin Elite Attack Force	80306040
Goblin Fan	04149689
Goblin's Secret Remedy	11868825
Goddess of Whim	67959180

(continued)

Cheat	Code
Goddess with the Third Eye	53493204
Gokibore	15367030
Gorgon's Eye	52648457
Gorz the Emissary of Darkness	44330098
Graceful Charity	79571449
Graceful Dice	74137509
Grandmaster of the Six Samurai	83039729
Grappler	02906250
Gravedigger Ghoul	82542267
Gravekeeper's Assailant	25262697
Gravekeeper's Servant	16762927
Gravekeeper's Spear Soldier	63695531
Graverobber's Retribution	33737664
Gravity Axe - Grarl	32022366
Gravity Bind	85722772
Great Moth	14141448
Great Shogun Shien	63176202
Great White	13429800
Green Gadget	41172955
Griffore	53829412
Ground Collapse	90502999
Guardian Sphinx	40659562
Gust Fan	55321970
Gust	73079365
Gyakutenno Megami	31122090
Hallowed Life Barrier	88789641
Hane-Hane	07089711
Harpie Lady	76812113
Harpie Lady 1	91932350
Harpie Lady 2	27927359
Harpie Lady 3	54415063
Harpie Lady Sisters	12206212
Harpie's Feather Duster	18144586

Cheat	Code
Harpie's Hunting Ground	75782277
Harpie's Pet Dragon	52040216
Heart of the Underdog	37562283
Heavy Storm	19613556
Helios The Primordial Sun	54493213
Helios Duo Megistus	54493213
Helios Tris Megistus	17286057
Helpoemer	76052811
Hercules Beetle	52584282
Hero Signal	22020907
Hero Spirit	81167171
Hinotama	46130346
Hitotsu-Me Giant	76184692
Horn Imp	69669405
Horn of Light	38552107
Horn of the Unicorn	64047146
Horus the Black Flame Dragon Level 4	75830094
Horus the Black Flame Dragon Level 6	11224103
Horus the Black Flame Dragon Level 8	48229808
House of Adhesive Tape	15083728
Human-Wave Tactics	30353551
Illusionist Faceless Mage	28546905
Imperial Order	61740673
Inferno Fire Blast	52684508
Inferno Reckless Summon	12247206
Infinite Cards	94163677
Infinite Dismissal	54109233
Injection Fairy Lily	79575620
Insect Armor with Laser Cannon	03492538
Insect Barrier	23615409
Insect Imitation	96965364
Insect Queen	91512835
Inspection	16227556
Interdimensional Matter Transporter	36261726
Invigoration	98374133
Invitation to a Dark Sleep	52675689
Jam Breeding Machine	21770260
Jam Defender	21558682
Jar of Greed	83968380
Jellyfish	14851496
Jinzo #7	77585513
Jirai Gumo	15401633
Judge Man	30113682

(continued)

Yu-Gi-Oh! World Championship 2008 (cont.)

Cheat	*Code*
Judgement of Anubis	55256016
Just Desserts	24068492
Kairyu-Shin	76634149
Kazejin	62340868
Killer Needle	88979991
King of Yamimakai	69455834
Kishido Spirit	60519422
Kojikocy	01184620
Koumori Dragon	67724379
Krokodilus	76512652
Kunai with Chain	37390589
Kuriboh	40640057
La Jinn the Mystical Genie of the Lamp	97590747
Labyrinth of Nightmare	66526672
Labyrinth Tank	99551425
Labyrinth Wall	67284908
Larvae Moth	87756343
Laser Cannon Armor	77007920
Last Day of Witch	90330453
Last Will	85602018
Launcher Spider	87322377
Lava Battleguard	20394040
Lava Golem	00102380
Left Arm of the Forbidden One	07902349
Left Leg of the Forbidden One	44519536
Legendary Sword	61854111
Light Laser	11471117
Light and Darkness Dragon	47297616
Light of Intervention	62867251
Lightning Blade	55226821
Lightning Vortex	69162969
Limiter Removal	23171610
Lord of D.	17985575
Luminous Spark	81777047
Luster Dragon #2	17658803
Luster Dragon (1900/1600)	11091375
Machine Conversion Factory	25769732
Machine King	25769732
Mage Power	46700124
Magic Cylinder	62279055
Magic Drain	59344077
Magic Jammer	77414722
Magic Thorn	53119267
Magical Hats	81210420
Magical Scientist	34206604
Magic-Arm Shield	96008713

Cheat	*Code*
Magician of Faith	31560081
Magician's Circle	00050755
Maha Vailo	93013676
Majestic Mech - Goryu	95701283
Major Riot	09074847
Makyura the Destructor	21593977
Malevolent Nuzzler	99597615
Malfunction	06137095
Mammoth Graveyard	40374923
Man-Eater Bug	54652250
Manju of the Ten Thousand Hands	95492061
Masaki the Legendary Swordsman	44287299
Mask of Brutality	82432018
Mask of Darkness	28933734
Mask of Dispel	20765952
Mask of Restrict	29549364
Mask of the Accursed	56948373
Mask of Weakness	57882509
Masked Dragon	39191307
Masked Sorcerer	10189126
Megamorph	22046459
Mesmeric Control	48642904
Messenger of Peace	44656491
Metal Detector	75646520
Metal Guardian	68339286
Metalmorph	68540058
Metalzoa	50705071
Metamorphosis	46411259
Meteor Black Dragon	90660762
Meteor Dragon	64271667
Meteor of Destruction	33767325
Meteorain	01918087
Michizure	37580756

(continued)

Cheat	Code
Millennium Shield	32012841
Milus Radiant	07489323
Mind Control	37520316
Minor Goblin Official	01918087
Mirror Force	44095762
Moai Interceptor Cannons	45159319
Monster Recovery	93108433
Monster Reincarnation	74848038
Monster Tamer	97612389
Mooyan Curry	58074572
Morphing Jar	33508719
Mother Grizzly	57839750
Mountain	50913601
Mucus Yolk	70307656
Muka Muka	46657337
Multiplication of Ants	22493811
Multiply	40703222
Mushroom Man	14181608
Mustering of the Dark Scorpions	68191243
Mysterious Puppeteer	54098121
Mystic Horseman	68516705
Mystic Plasma Zone	18161786
Mystic Probe	49251811
Mystical Elf	15025844
Mystical Moon	36607978
Mystical Space Typhoon	05318639
Mystik Wok	80161395
Necroface	28297833
Necro Gardna	04906301
Negate Attack	14315573
Neo-Spacian Air Hummingbird	54959865
Neo-Spacian Aqua Dolphin	17955766
Neo-Spacian Flame Scarab	89621922

Cheat	Code
Neo-Spacian Glow Moss	17732278
Neo-Spacian Grand Mole	80344569
Nightmare's Steelcage	58775978
Obnoxious Celtic Guard	52077741
Ocean Dragon Lord Neo-Daedalus	10485110
Offerings to the Doomed	19230407
Ojama Black	79335209
Ojama Green	12482652
Ojama King	90140980
Ojama Trio	29843091
Ojama Yellow	42941100
Ookazi	19523799
Ordeal of a Traveler	39537362
Order to Charge	78986941
Order to Smash	39019325
Pandemonium	94585852
Panther Warrior	42035044
Paralyzing Potion	50152549
Parrot Dragon	62762898
Pendulum Machine	24433920
Penguin Knight	36039163
Penguin Soldier	93920745
Perfect Machine King	18891691
Perfectly Ultimate Great Moth	48579379
Petit Dragon	75356564
Petit Moth	58192742
Pikeru's Circle of Enchantment	74270067
Pineapple Blast	90669991
Polymerization	24094653
Pot of Greed	55144522
Premature Burial	70828912
Prevent Rat	00549481
Princess of Tsurugi	51371017
Princess Pikeru	75917088
Prohibition	43711255
Pumpking the King of Ghosts	29155212
Punished Eagle	74703140
Pyramid Energy	76754619
Pyramid Turtle	77044671
Rabid Horseman	94905343
Raigeki	12580477
Raimei	56260110
Rain of Mercy	66719324
Rainbow Dragon	79856792

(continued)

Yu-Gi-Oh! World Championship 2008 (cont.)

Cheat	Code
Raise Body Heat	51267887
Raiza the Storm Monarch	73125233
Rare Fish	80516007
Raregold Armor	07625614
Raviel, Lord of Phantasms	69890967
Reaper of the Cards	33066139
Reasoning	58577036
Reckless Greed	37576645
Red Gadget	86445415
Red Medicine	38199696
Red-Eyes B. Chick	36262024
Red-Eyes B. Dragon	74677422
Red-Eyes Black Metal Dragon	64335804
Red-Eyes Darkness Dragon	96561011
Reign-Beaux, Overlord of Dark World	99458769
Reinforcement of the Army	32807846
Reinforcements	17814387
Relinquished	64631466
Reload	22589918
Remove Trap	51482758
Respect Play	08951260
Restructer Revolution	99518961
Return from the Different Dimension	27174286
Reverse Trap	77622396
Right Arm of the Forbidden One	70903634
Right Leg of the Forbidden One	08124921
Ring of Destruction	83555666
Ring of Magnetism	20436034
Riryoku Field	70344351
Robbin' Goblin	88279736
Rock Ogre Grotto #1	68846917
Rogue Doll	91939608
Rope of Life	93382620
Royal Decree	51452091
Royal Magic Library	70791313
Rude Kaiser	26378150
Ruin, Queen of Oblivion	46427957
Rush Recklessly	70046172
Ryu Kokki	57281778
Ryu-Kishin Powered	24611934
Ryu-Kishin	15303296
Ryu-Ran	02964201
Sage's Stone	13604200
Saggi the Dark Clown	66602787
Sakuretsu Armor	56120475
Salamandra	32268901
Sanga of the Thunder	25955164
Sangan	26202165
Sasuke Samurai	16222645
Sasuke Samurai #2	11760174
Sasuke Samurai #3	77379481
Sasuke Samurai #4	64538655
Satellite Cannon	50400231
Scapegoat	73915051
Servant of Catabolism	02792265
Seven Tools of the Bandit	03819470
Shadow Ghoul	30778711
Shadow of Eyes	58621589
Share the Pain	56830749
Shield & Sword	52097679
Shift	59560625
Shining Angel	95956346
Shooting Star Bow - Ceal	95638658
Shrink	55713623
Silent Magician Level 4	73665146
Silent Magician Level 8	72443568
Silver Bow and Arrow	01557499
Silver Fang	90357090
Simorgh Bird of Divinity	14989021
Sinister Serpent	08131171
Skill Drain	82732705
Skilled Dark Magician	73752131
Skull Dice	00126218
Skull Invitation	98139712
Skull Lair	06733059
Skyscraper	63035430
Slate Warrior	78636495
Snake Fang	00596051
Snatch Steal	45986603

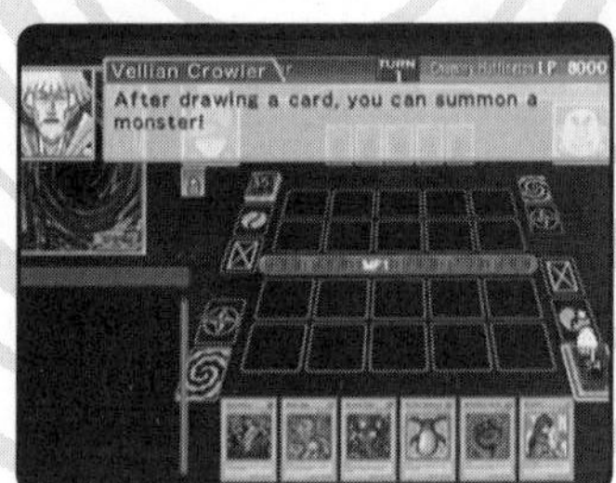

(continued)

Cheat	Code
Sogen	86318356
Solemn Judgment	41420027
Solemn Wishes	35346968
Soul of the Pure	47852924
Soul Release	05758500
Soul Resurrection	92924317
Spark Blaster	97362768
Sparks	76103675
Spear Dragon	31553716
Special Hurricane	42598242
Spell Shield Type-8	38275183
Spellbinding Circle	18807108
Spiral Spear Strike	49328340
Spirit Barrier	53239672
Spirit of the Six Samurai	65685470
Spirit's Invitation	92394653
Spirit Message "A"	94772232
Spirit Message "I"	31893528
Spirit Message "L"	30170981
Spirit Message "N"	67287532
Spirit Reaper	23205979
Spiritualism	15866454
Spring of Rebirth	94425169
Stamping Destruction	81385346
Statue of the Wicked	65810489
Steel Scorpion	13599884
Steel Shell	02370081
Stim-Pack	83225447
Stop Defense	63102017
Suijin	98434877
Summoned Skull	70781052
Super Conductor Tyranno	85520851
Super Rejuvenation	27770341
Swamp Battleguard	40453765
Swift Gaia the Fierce Knight	16589042
Sword Arm of Dragon	13069066
Sword of Dark Destruction	37120512
Sword of the Deep-Seated	98495314
Sword of the Soul-Eater	05372656
Swords of Revealing Light	72302403
Swordstalker	50005633
System Down	18895832
Tailor of the Fickle	43641473
The Cheerful Coffin	41142615
The Dark Door	30606547
The Dragon's Bead	92408984
The Emperor's Holiday	68400115
The Forceful Sentry	42829885
The Grave of the Enkindling	84136000

Cheat	Code
The Inexperienced Spy	81820689
The Law of the Normal	66926224
The Little Swordsman of Aile	25109950
The Masked Beast	49064413
The Reliable Guardian	16430187
The Sanctuary in the Sky	56433456
The Shallow Grave	43434803
The Six Samurai Irou	27782503
The Six Samurai Kamon	90397988
The Six Samurai Nisashi	31209181
The Six Samurai Yaichi	64398890
The Six Samurai Yariza	69025477
The Six Samurai Zanji	95519486
The Snake Hair	29491031
The Wicked Avatar	21208154
The Wicked Dreadroot	62180201
The Wicked Eraser	57793869
The Wicked Worm Beast	06285791
Thousand Dragon	41462083
Thousand Energy	05703682
Thousand-Eyes Restrict	63519819
Thunder of Ruler	91781589
Tiger Axe	40907090
Time Machine	80987696
Time Wizard	71625222
Toll	82003859
Toon Alligator	59383041
Toon Summoned Skull	91842653
Torike	80813021
Tragedy	35686187
Trap Dustshoot	64697231
Trap Hole	04206964
Trap Jammer	19252988
Trap Master	46461247

(continued)

Cheat	*Code*
Tremendous Fire	46918794
Triangle Ecstasy Spark	12181376
Tribute Doll	02903036
Tribute to the Doomed	79759861
Tutan Mask	03149764
Twin Swords of Flashing Light - Tryce	21900719
Two-Headed King Rex	94119974
Two-Pronged Attack	83887306
Tyhone	72842870
Type Zero Magic Crusher	21237481
Tyrant Dragon	94568601
UFOroid	07602840
UFO Turtle	60806437
Ultimate Offering	80604091
Ultimate Tyranno	15894048
Umi	22702055
Umiiruka	82999629
Upstart Goblin	70368879
Uraby	01784619
Uria, Lord of Searing Flames	06007213
V-Tiger Jet	51638941
Vampire Genesis	22056710
Vampire Lord	53839837
Vanity's Ruler	72634965
Vengeful Bog Spirit	95220856
Versago the Destroyer	50289460
Vile Germs	39774685
Violet Crystal	15052462
Vorse Raider	14898066
VW-Tiger Catapult	58859575
VWXYZ-Dragon Catapult Cannon	84243274
W-Wing Catapult	96300057
Waboku	12607053
Wall of Illusion	13945283
Wall of Revealing Light	17078030

Cheat	*Code*
Wall Shadow	63162310
Warrior Elimination	90873992
Wasteland	23424603
Water Dragon	85066822
Wave Motion Cannon	18992735
White Magical Hat	15160365
Windstorm of Etaqua	59744639
Winged Dragon Guardian of Fortress #1	87796900
Winged Kuriboh	57116033
Witch of the Black Forest	78010363
Wolf	49417509
World Supression	12253117
X-Head Cannon	62651957
XY-Dragon Cannon	02111707
XZ-Tank Cannon	99724761
Yami	59197169
Y-Dragon Head	65622692
Yellow Gadget	13834120
Yellow Luster Shield	04542651
YZ-Tank Dragon	251194460
Z-Metal Tank	645000000
Zanki	30090452
Zera the Mant	69123138
Z-Metal Tank	64500000
Zoa	24311372
Zombie Warrior	31339260

Ace Combat Advance

Unlock All Missions and Aircraft
To unlock all missions and aircraft, including the F-A Stealth Fighter, enter QF9B9F59 on the code screen. Not only will you have access to all 12 missions, but you'll already be credited with an S rank for each one.

Barbie as the Princess and the Pauper

Unlock the Arcade Stage
If you want to practice or play against all of the bosses in the game, just enter this code at the Password screen: Princess Anneliese, Serafina, Erika, Wolfie

Explore the Other Game Stages
You can also explore other areas by entering these codes at the Password screen:

Level	***Password***
Level 1-2	Preminger, Wolfie, Erika, Serafina
Level 1-3	Wolfie, Preminger, Serafina, Preminger
Level 1-4	Preminger, Wolfie, Serafina, Wolfie
Level 1 Boss	Serafina, Wolfie, Eriak, Preminger
Level 2-1	Princess Anneliese, Preminger, Wolfie, Erika
Level 2-2	Preminger, Princess Anneliese, Wolfie, Erika
Level 2-3	Preminger, Serafina, Premigner, Erika
Level 2-4	Serafina, Erika, Preminger, Wolfie
Level 2 Boss	Preminger, Erika, Searfina, Wolfie
Level 3-1	Wolfie, Preminger, Wolfie, Erika
Level 3-2	Serafina, Preminger, Erika, Serafina
Level 3-3	Erika, Wolfie, Serafina, Princess Anneliese
Level 3-4	Erika, Serafina, Erika, Preminger
Level 3 Boss	Preminger, Serafina, Princess Anneliese, Serafina
Level 4-1	Wolfie, Serafina, Preminger, Serafina
Level 4-2	Preminger, Serafina, Princess Anneliese, Preminger
Level 4-3	Wolfie, Serafina, Erika, Serafina
Level 4-4	Serafina, Preminger, Wolfie, Preminger
Level 4 Boss	Erika, Serafina, Princess Anneliese, Wolfie
The Final Boss	Erika, Princess Anneliese, Princess Anneliese, Man

Wii Xbox 360 Xbox GC PS3 PS2 DS GBA PSP

Batman Begins

Super Speed
Using this code will make Batman walk and run much faster than normal. Pause your game and press Right, Right, Right, Left, Left, Left, Up, Down. If you enter the code correctly, you'll hear a voice say, "What the—The Batman!"

It's a Bird! It's a Plane! It's—Batman?
After using this code, you'll think Batman has been taking flying lessons from his pal, the Man of Steel. Pause your game and press L, R, L, R, Up, Up, Down, Down to increase Batman's jumping ability to superhuman levels. If you enter the code correctly, you'll hear a voice say, "What the—The Batman!"

Invincibility
To make Batman invincible to most attacks and environmental hazards (like fire and steam), pause your game and press Up, Up, Down, Down, Left, Right, Left, Right. If you enter the code correctly, you'll hear a voice say, "What the—The Batman!"

Remove Help Graphics from the Screen
To remove the bat-shaped health meter and other help graphics from the screen, pause the game and press Up, Down, Up, Down, Up, Down, L, R. If you enter the code correctly, you'll hear a voice say, "What the—The Batman!"

Batman: Rise of Sin Tzu

Invincibility
With enemies like the Scarecrow and Bane, even Batman could use an extra edge in combat once in a while. To make Batman impervious to almost all harm, go to the Continue option and enter "_NDTH_" as your password. Be sure to highlight OK and press A, or the code won't work. Now start a new game or enter another password to continue your game.

(continued)

Unlock (Almost) All Levels
Go to the Continue option and enter "_FLYMF" as your password. When the game begins, you'll start on the level select map with the cursor on The Showdown. However, if you start this level, instead of fighting Sin Tzu, you'll see the ending cinematic and then the credits. You can, however, go backward and select earlier levels.

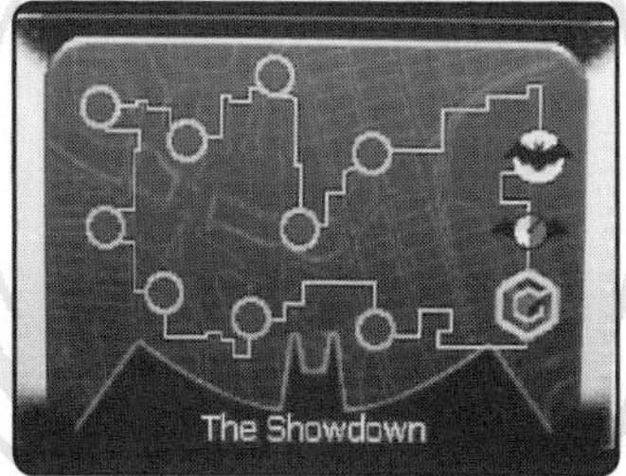

The Showdown with Sin Tzu
To head to the ultimate battle with Sin Tzu, go to the Continue option and enter "4V252V" as your password. Even if you use the Invincibility code, you'll still be in for a battle royal!

Insider Tip
The Invincibility code armors the Dark Knight against all basic combat damage, and even the fiery attacks of Sin Tzu. However, it won't protect him against falls from great heights. It can also make the final battle against Sin Tzu less stable than normal. If Sin Tzu's recharge animation seems to be repeating in a loop, back away from him a few steps, and he'll eventually start attacking again or move on to the next stage of the battle.

Wii | Xbox 360 | Xbox | GC | PS3 | PS2 | DS | GBA | PSP

Cars Mater-National Championship

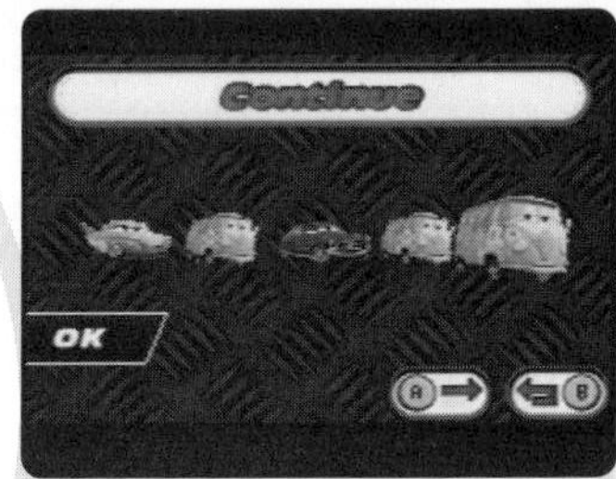

Open Expert Mode and All Tracks!
Cars Mater-National Championship for Game Boy Advance might seem easy until you take to the track in Expert Mode! From the Main Menu, choose Continue and enter the following Cars characters as your password:

Flo, Fillmore, Doc, Fillmore, Sarge

You'll also be able to choose unlocked cars for most races, but remember that some Cars characters are not available for racing in certain challenges.

Danny Phantom: The Ultimate Enemy

Unlockable Mini-Games
To unlock the BK Promotions mini-games, go to the Options menu, then to the Passwords screen, and enter one of the following passwords. If you enter a password correctly, you'll exit the Passwords screen and be taken to the BK Promotions screen, where you can begin the unlocked mini-game.

Mini-game	*Password*
Levitating	JAZZ
Sam's X-Ray Ecto Detector	SEEK
Dash's Haunted Locker	DASH
Hidin' Ghost Seek	ECTO

Easy and Hard Difficulty
The game usually features only one difficulty level: Normal. To unlock the Easy and Hard modes, go to the Options menu, then to the Passwords screen, and enter the password VLAD. The new modes will appear on the Mode Select screen.

Hidden Ghost Arena Mini-Game
To play the hidden Ghost Arena mini-game, go to the Options menu, then to the Passwords screen, and enter the password RUSH. You'll be able to play as either the young Danny Phantom or the grown up Dan Phantom, challenging each of the game's bosses in turn.

Insider Tip
The Hidden Ghost Arena mini-game does not appear on the BK Promotions screen, and you must enter the password each time you wish to play.

Donkey Kong Country

50 Extra Lives
Go to the Select Save Slot menu and move Donkey Kong's head down to Erase but don't press the A Button! Instead, hold SELECT and press the following buttons in this order: B, A, R, R, A, L

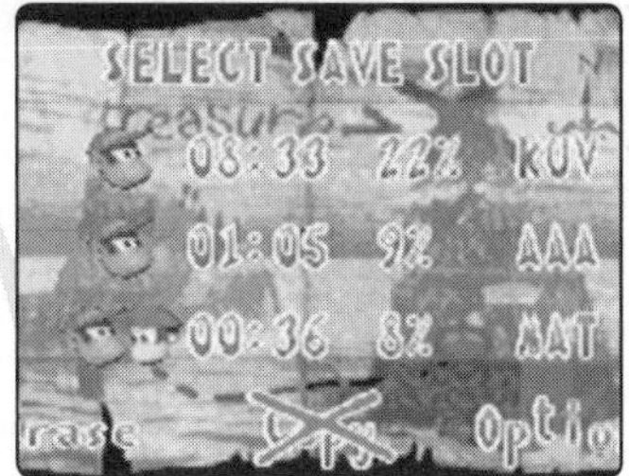

You can now choose any game file (new or old) and begin that game with 50 additional lives.

Donkey Kong Country 2: Diddy's Kong Quest

Extra Lives, Coins, and More
At the File Select screen, choose the Options menu and then select codes to enter the following codes:

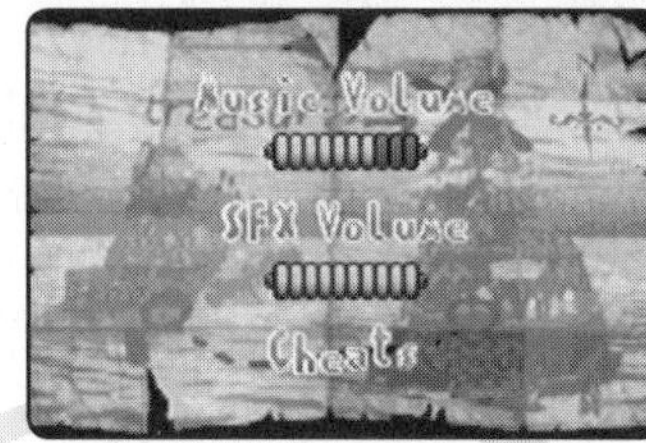

Cheat	*Code*
Begin with 15 lives	HELPME
Begin with 55 lives	WEAKLING
Eliminate all DK and halfway barrels in the game	ROCKARD
Eliminate all DK barrels, keep the halfway barrels	WELLARD
Start out with 10 coins	RICHEMAN
Start out with 50 coins	WELLRICH
Unlock all levels	FREEDOM

Dragon Ball GT: Transformation

Invincibility, One-Hit Defeats, and More

You won't need your Super Seiyan powers to defeat your foes if you have these handy codes. Enter any of the following codes during normal gameplay, not while the game is paused.

Cheat	*Code*
Invincibility	Up, Down, Left, Right, Up, Down, L, R, A, B
Max Stats	Down, Down, Down, Up, Up, Up, Right, Right, Right, Up, Down, Right, Up, B
One-Hit Defeats	Up, Down, Down, Up, Left, Right, Right, Left, L, R, R, L, B
Refill Energy	Down, Up, Right, Right, Right, Left, Right, Left, B
Refill Health	Down, Up, Left, Left, Up, Right, Down, B
Temporary Infinite Energy	Up, Down, Up, Down, Left, Left, Right, Right, Up, B
Temporary Super Speed	Right, Up, Down, Right, Up, Down, Right, Up, B
Temporary Super Strength	Right, Up, Right, Right, Up, Right, Up, Left, Left, B

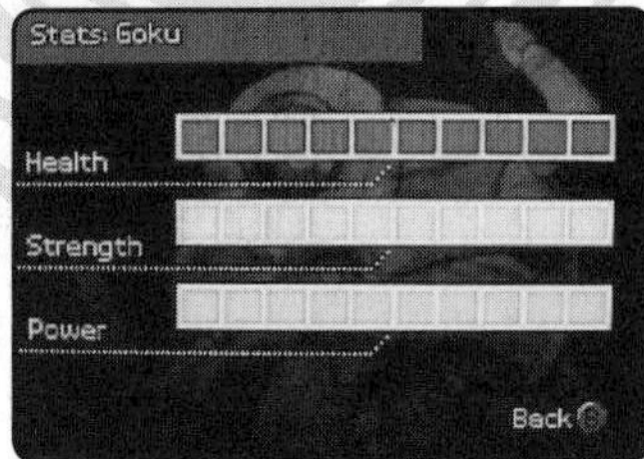

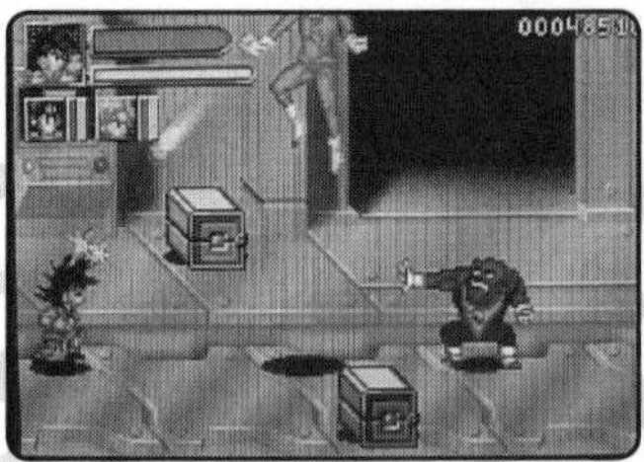

The Incredibles

Update Mr. Incredible's Costume

To make sure that Mr. Incredible always wears his red costume, enter FG6Y as your password. Even in the stages set in the past, Mr. Incredible will appear in his updated duds.

Infinite Lives

We know that comic characters never really die, but to make absolutely sure that Mr. Incredible will always live to fight another day, enter 69DD as your password. Instead of three lives, your life counter will show the symbol for infinity, and you'll never run out.

(continued)

Invincibility

Normally even Mr. Incredible has his limits, but if you enter 96KR as your password, not only will you be invincible, but you'll have infinite energy for special moves and all your attacks will be powered-up.

Stage Select

To unlock the stage select cheat, first enter ZYQ8 as your password. If you enter the password correctly, you'll return to the Main menu. Press L or R to select a stage (watch the new stage counter on the bottom of the screen), highlight New Game, and press A to begin your game.

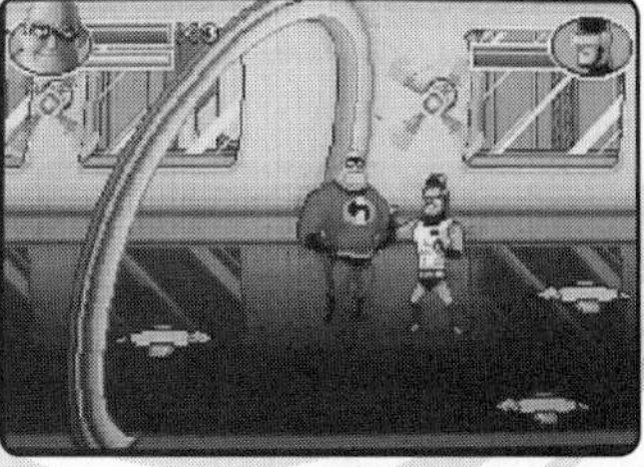

Wii | Xbox 360 | Xbox | GC | PS3 | PS2 | DS | GBA | PSP

Justice League Heroes: The Flash

Unlockable Extras

Enter the codes on the Title screen quickly but firmly. Timing is crucial, so it may take several tries before you're successful.

Cheat	*Code*
Big Flash	Hold B and press Left, Up, Right, Down, Left, Up, Right, Down, Select
Little Flash	Hold B and press Down, Down, Down, Left, Up, Up, Up, Right, Select
Big Enemies and Destructible Objects	Hold B and press Up, Up, Down, Down, Left, Right, Left, Right, Select
Small Enemies and Destructible Objects	Hold B and press Down, Down, Up, Up, Right, Left, Right, Left, Select
Nine Lives	Hold B and press Up, Down, Up, Up, Down, Down, Up, Down, Select
Five Justice Icons	Hold B and press Up, Down, Left, Right, Right, Left, Down, Up, Select

Insider Tips

When entering the codes, make sure the words Press Start are flashing on the screen. If the game mode selector is on the screen, the codes won't work.

You can enter multiple codes, but you need to release the B button in between each code.

LEGO Star Wars II: The Original Trilogy

Fast-Forward to the Best Scenes in the Game!

Want to see the Death Star explode over and over again? Enter these codes at the bar inside the Cantina, then press the A Button.

View Mos Eisely Spaceport scene	82434
View Obi-Wan's House scene	40214
View Mos Eisley Cantina scene	13197
View Alderaan explosion scene	27000
View Trash Compactor scene	11911
View Death Star Hangar scene	80500
View Death Star Explosion scene	52577
View Wampa Cave scene	42352
View Millennium Falcon scene	89910
View Dark Cave scene	50250
View Carbonite Chamber scene	08433
View Sensor Balcony scene	61806
View Yoda's Hut scene	06881
View Ewok Village scene	31299
View Death Star 2 Explosion Scene	52583

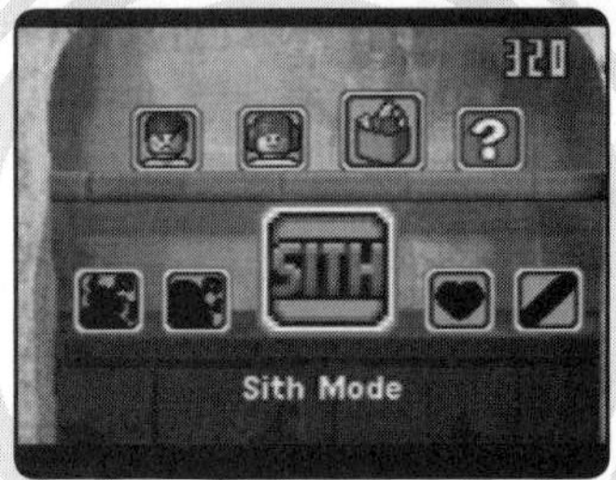

View Emperor's Lair	20876
View Death Star Subsector 1 Scene	51999
View final scene in game	01138
Unlock Sith Mode	11340
Unlock Dancing Girl	70546
Unlock Jedi Spirit	75046
Unlock Bubble Blaster	80873

(continued)

LEGO Star Wars II: The Original Trilogy (cont.)

Codes for Cool Stuff in the Extras Menu
Enter these codes at the bar inside the Cantina, then press the A Button:

Unlock Sith Mode	11340
Unlock Dancing Girl	70546
Unlock Jedi Spirit	75046
Unlock Bubble Blaster	80873

Power Rangers Dino Thunder

Powerful Passwords
If Mesogog and his minions have you on the ropes, power up with these passwords to get back on top.

Stage (Normal Difficulty)	*Password*
Puzzle 1	BG5
Blue Ranger 1	QVN
Megazord 1	LZP
Yellow Ranger 1	BXN
Megazord 2	G03
Red Ranger 2	QX2
Puzzle 2	L03
Yellow Ranger	2G66
Blue Ranger 2	L66
Megazord 3	L27
Yellow Ranger 3	G8Q
Puzzle 3	G4R

Stage (Normal Difficulty)	*Password*
Blue Ranger 3	288
Megazord 4	249
Red Ranger 3	XV8
Megazord 5	0ZT
Yellow Ranger 4	8VS
Puzzle 4	4ZT
Red Ranger 4	YX6
Blue Ranger 4	9XQ
Megazord 6	50R
Red Ranger 5	166
Megazord 7	127

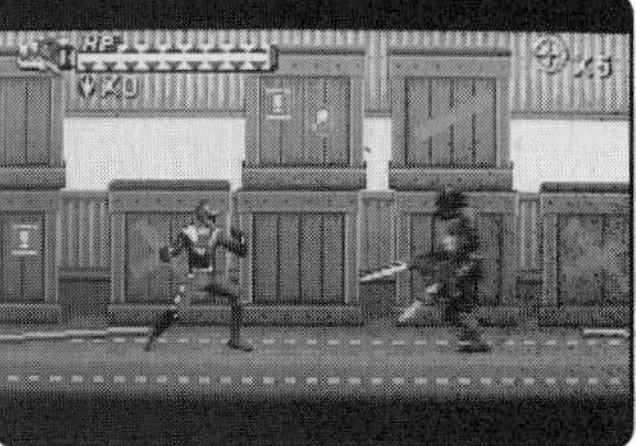

(continued)

Power Rangers Dino Thunder (cont.)

Stage (Hard Difficulty)	*Password*
Puzzle 1	GHC
Blue Ranger 1	LWB
Megazord 1	Q!Y
Yellow Ranger 1	GYX
Megazord 2	B1Y
Red Ranger 2	LYX
Puzzle 2	Q1F
Yellow Ranger 2	B70
Blue Ranger 2	Q7J
Megazord 3	Q3K
Yellow Ranger 3	B9J
Puzzle 3	B5K

Stage (Hard Difficulty)	*Password*
Blue Ranger 3	69G
Megazord 4	65H
Red Ranger 3	0WG
Megazord 5	X!H
Yellow Ranger 4	4WG
Puzzle 4	8!1
Red Ranger 4	1YJ
Blue Ranger 4	5YJ
Megazord 6	91!
Red Ranger 5	Y70
Megazord 7	Y31

Ratatouille

Invincibility, Stage Select, and More
While you can pause your game and earn a password, the following codes give you powers that you won't find in a typical game.

Cheat	*Code*
Invincibility	X4V!3RJ
Open all snapshots	3R1CQRR
Stage Select	H3L!X3!
Unlock all Cooking Games	JV4ND1Z

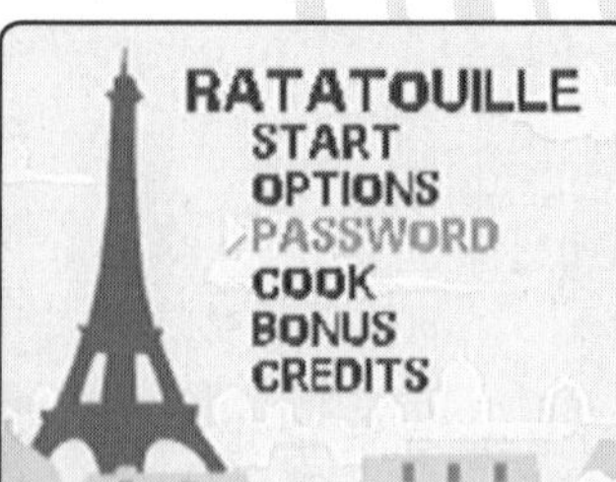

Insider tip
Enter multiple codes at the Password menu so you can be invincible and skip ahead to new levels! After entering the Stage Select code, press the L or R button to scroll through your choices at each game chapter screen.

Shining Soul II

Unlockable Extras

Using a specific name can boost your character's stats or award you a special item at the beginning of the game. Keep in mind that you can't access the Item menu (to equip Items) until after you're given the quest to find Princess Camille.

Cheat	Code
Dexterity +5	Yoshi
Intelligence +5, Resist Lightning +30	Dengeki
Strength +5	Ninky
Vitality +5	Taicho
Resist Dark +30	Montaka
Resist Fire +30	Iyoku
Resist Ice +30	Mizupin
Resist Poison +30	Hachi
Atlus Ring	Vjum
Dream Hat	Nindri
Power Gloves	VJxSS

Insider Tip

Match up a name with a character type that is already strong in the boosted area; for example, using the name Ninky for the Brawler brings his Strength from an already hard-hitting 16 to a formidable 21. As for the bonus items, highlight them in the Item list to see which stats they affect.

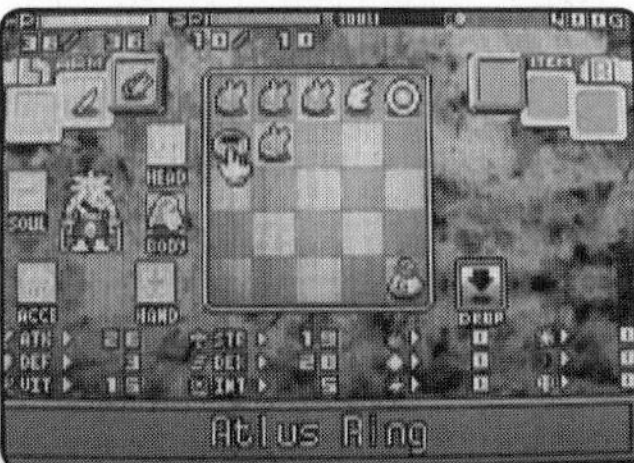

Star Wars: Flight of the Falcon

Cheat Unlock Code

Before using the passwords below, you must first enter this cheat unlock code or the cheat passwords won't work. Begin a game and then pause it. While paused, hold L and R and press Up, Right, A, Start, A, Down, A, Start, and Start. The game will resume. Now return to the Main menu to use any of the following cheat passwords.

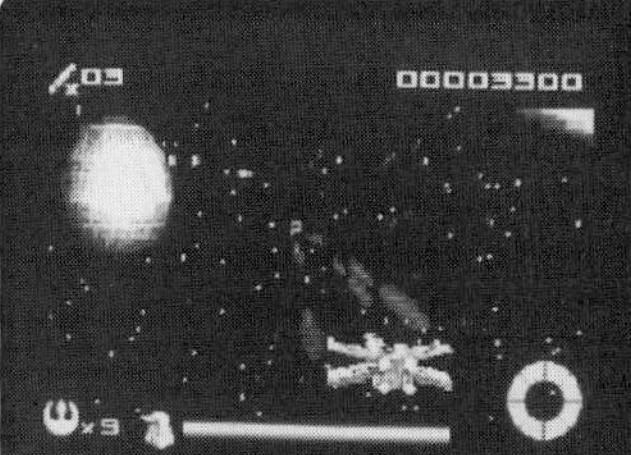

Unlimited Torpedoes and Rapid-Fire Blasters

To equip the Falcon with unlimited torpedoes, enter BLOB on the Password screen before you begin your game or enter your level password. If you'd like to throw in rapid-fire blasters for good measure (just hold down the A button to fire continuously), enter GOGO on the Password screen.

(continued)

Unlimited Shields and Unlimited Lives

To ensure that you never run out of shield power, enter SPVD on the Password screen before you begin your game or enter your level password. If you'd like to have unlimited lives instead, enter M0NG on the Password screen.

Why use unlimited lives instead of unlimited shields? With unlimited lives, you retain at least some of the challenge in the game. You'll still have to avoid being damaged or destroyed, and if you lose a ship, you'll have to start the current stage over again.

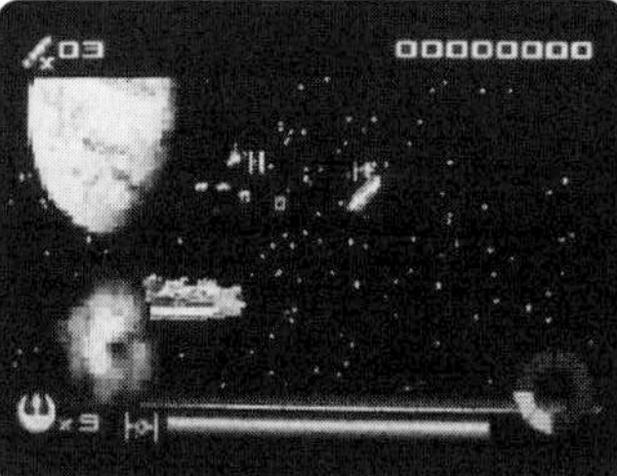

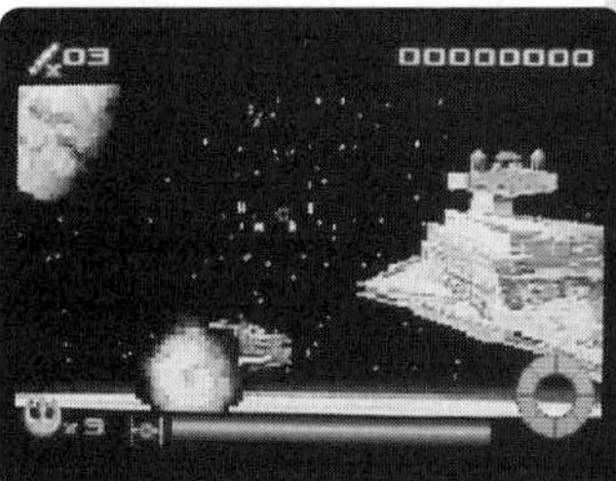

Mission Select and Bonus Game

To enable the Stage Select cheat, enter FVNK on the Password screen and then begin a new game. Only Episode IV will appear on the Episode Select screen. Go to the Mission Briefing screen and press Right or Left to select any mission from any episode. To unlock the side-scrolling bonus game, enter RRV2 on the Password screen, and then begin a new game. On the Episode Select screen, press Right or Left until you find the bonus game. Note that the bonus game password does not require you to enter the cheat unlock code first.

ATV Offroad Fury: Blazin' Trails

Player Profile Passwords

To enter the Blazin' Trails cheats, choose Options from the Main Menu and then select Player Profile. Select the Enter Cheat option and enter the codes below. Pay close attention to the unusual spelling as well as the upper and lowercase letters:

Unlock all bike parts	TRICK IT OUT
Unlock all ATVs except G-Ride and Fury bike	TO LAZY
Unlock all exhausts	SMOG TEST
Unlock all events (enter a zero as the "O")	N0Game
Unlock Ravage Talon ATVs	+THREE
Unlock rims	Dubs
Unlock all music videos	Billboards
Earn 1500 credits	$moneybags$
Unlock all rider gear	Duds
Unlock everything except the Fury bike	All Access

Insider Tip:
Our favorite code remains the All Access pick because you can grab the Sand Storm ATV, pair it with ITP Holeshot XC tires and destroy the competition!

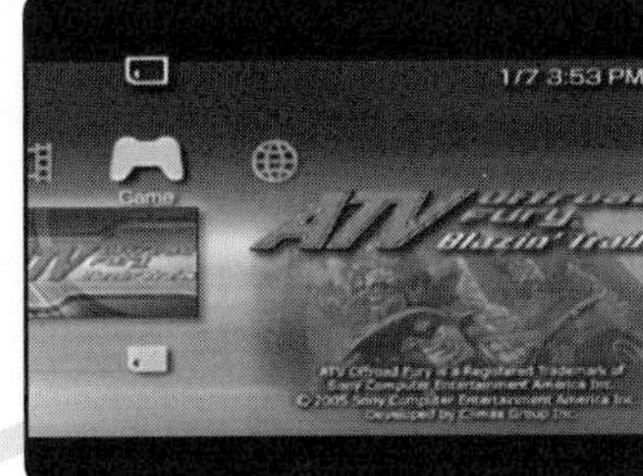

Cars

Unlockable Bonus Speedway (Reversed)

Enter this code at the Main menu to race the Bonus Speedway in reverse:

Hold L while pressing X, Square, Triangle, X, Triangle, and then Square.

Go to Custom Race mode and you should see the Bonus Speedway (Reversed).

Crazy Taxi Fare Wars

Tough Fares
If you think you know your way around town, try entering these codes. If you need help, your passenger will tell you which way to go!

Crazy Taxi Mode	
Eliminate directional arrows	Press and hold R and START while choosing your driver.
Eliminate green destination indicator	Press and hold L and START while choosing your driver.
Eliminate arrows and destination indicator	Press and hold L, R, and START while choosing your driver.

Crazy Taxi 2 Mode	
Eliminate directional arrows	Press and hold START while choosing a driver.
Eliminate green destination indicator	Press and hold Triangle while choosing a driver.
Eliminate arrows and destination indicator	Press and hold Triangle and START while choosing a driver.

Exit

Jump Ahead in the Game
Before you can enter these advanced situation codes, you'll need to finish all training stages in Situation 1. If you haven't completed the training stages, you'll hear a busy signal when you enter the codes, and you won't be able to access these advanced situations on the Stage Select screen. The following codes must be entered in order. For example, if you want to jump ahead to Situation 9, enter the Situation 8 code first. If you want to jump ahead to Situation 10, enter the Situation 9 code first.

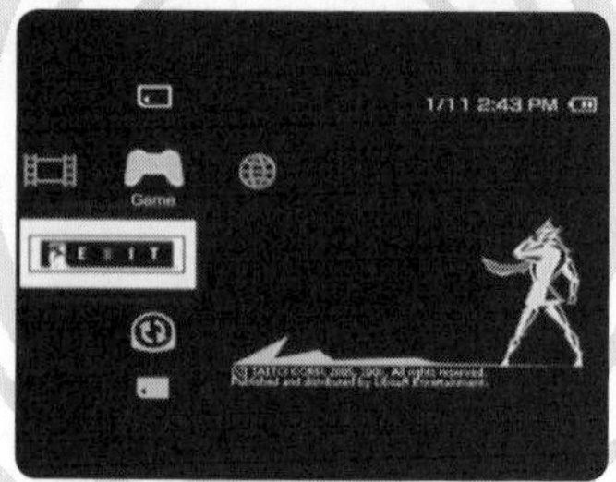

Situation 8	L Button, R Button, Left, Right, Square, Circle, X, Triangle
Situation 9	Triangle, Down, Circle, Left, X, Up, Square, Right
Situation 10	Right, Down, Up, Left, Circle, X, R Button, L Button

More Great Codes for the Great One
To unlock all the alternate uniforms, extra players, game play features and game modes, choose Gretzky Challenge from the Main Menu and then select the Unlockables Menu. Now press START to access the Unlockables Code Entry screen and enter these codes:

Eliminate Skater Fatigue	CAFFEINATED
Perfect Slapshots	SLAP THAT PUCK
Unlock Perfect Aim Mode	THREAD THE NEEDLE
Unlock All Unlockable Features in the Game	SHOENLOC
Unlock All Vintage Uniforms	OLD N BUSTED
Unlock Big Boards Checking Feature	ALL ABOARD
Unlock RoboEnforcer Model-44 Player	ROBO CHECKS
Earn One Gretzky Point	CANADIAN DOLLAR
Unlock Montreal Canadians 1910 Uniforms	THE HABS
Unlock Montreal Canadians 1924 Uniforms	LE HABITANT
Unlock Detroit Red Wings 1927 Uniforms	BEEP BEEP
Unlock Chicago Blackhawks 1939 Uniforms	CAPONE
Unlock Boston Bruins 1928 Uniforms	WICKED HAAAAAHD
Unlock Ottawa Senators 1929 Uniforms	THE SENANATOR
Unlock Toronto Maple Leafs 1930 Uniforms	NORTH OF THE BORDER
Unlock Pittsburgh Penguins 1967 Away Uniforms	POPPIN TALK
Unlock Minnesota North Stars 1970 Uniforms	TWIN STARS
Unlock Kansas City Scouts 1975 Uniforms	YOU LITTLE DEVIL
Unlock New York Rangers 1976 Away Uniforms	NEW YORK NEW YORK
Unlock Calgary Flames 1977 Away Uniforms	FLAME ON
Unlock Colorado Rockies 1977 Uniforms	DEVIL MADE ME DO IT
Unlock Vancouver Canucks 1977 Home Uniforms	GREAT WHITE NORTH
Unlock Washington Capitals 1977 Home Uniforms	CONGRESSIONAL WISDOM
Unlock Washington Capitals 1977 Away Uniforms	PORK BARREL
Unlock New York Islanders 1978 Away Uniforms	ORDWAY MADE ME DO IT
Unlock Philadelphia Flyers 1967 Away Uniforms	CHEESESTEAK
Unlock Edmonton Oilers 1979 Away Uniforms	A SCARY SIGHT TO THE HOME CROWD
Unlock Edmonton Oilers 1979 Home Uniforms	THREADS OF CHAMPS
Unlock St. Louis Blues 1979 Away Uniforms	A BLUE NOTE
Unlock St. Louis Blues 1979 Home Uniforms	MARDI GRAS
Unlock Quebec Nordiques 1980 Uniforms	FRENCH FOR CANADIAN
Unlock Edmonton Oilers 1983 Away Uniforms	ALL HAIL WAYNE
Unlock Pittsburgh Penguins 1988 Away Uniforms	STEEL TOWN
Unlock Los Angeles Kings 1989 Away Uniforms	KING GRETZKY
Unlock Los Angeles Kings 1989 Home Uniforms	KING WAYNE
Unlock Los Angeles Kings 1967 Away Uniform	VOLLEY DOLLY
Unlock Winnipeg Jets 1990 Away Uniforms	PORTAGE AND MAIN
Unlock Winnipeg Jets 1990 Home Uniforms	MIDDLE OF CANADA
Unlock San Jose Sharks 1993 Away Uniforms	SHARK BAIT
Unlock St. Louis Blues 1995 Away Uniforms	VINTAGE BLUES
Unlock New York Rangers 1999 Home Uniforms	UPPER WEST SIDE
Unlock New York Rangers 1999 Away Uniforms	SOHO
Unlock Alternate Anaheim Mighty Ducks Uniforms	FLYING VEE
Unlock Alternate Atlanta Thrashers Uniforms	THRASHED TO THE MAX

(continued)

Gretzky NHL (cont.)

Unlock Alternate Boston Bruins Uniforms	NOMAR STILL RULES
Unlock Alternate Buffalo Sabres Uniforms	IN THE SNOW BELT
Unlock Alternate Calgary Flames Uniforms	THREE ALARM BLAZE
Unlock Alternate Chicago Blackhawks Uniforms	WINDY CITY
Unlock Alternate Colorado Avalanche Uniforms	SNOW DRIFTS
Unlock Alternate Columbus Blue Jackets Uniforms	BLUE SHOES
Unlock Alternate Dallas Stars Uniforms	HOCKEY IN TEXAS
Unlock Alternate Edmonton Oilers Uniforms	PUMPIN OIL
Unlock Alternate Florida Panthers Uniforms	SOUTH BEACH
Unlock Alternate Los Angeles Kings Uniforms	IT IS GOOD TO BE THE KING
Unlock Alternate Minnesota Wild Uniforms	COLD AS HECK
Unlock Alternate Nashville Predators Uniforms	ALIEN VS NASHVILLE
Unlock Alternate New York Islanders Uniforms	LAWNG ISLAND
Unlock Alternate New York Rangers Uniforms	GREAT WHITE WAY
Unlock Alternate Ottawa Senators Uniforms	MAJORITY RULE
Unlock Alternate Philadelphia Flyers Uniforms	FANATICAL
Unlock Alternate San Jose Sharks Uniforms	GET A BIGGER BOAT
Unlock Alternate Toronto Maple Leafs Uniforms	HEY TERRANCE
Unlock Alternate Vancouver Canucks Uniforms	WEST COAST EH
Unlock 1979 Wayne Gretzky	UNSTOPPABLE GREATNESS
Unlock 1987 Wayne Gretzky	GLORY DAZE
Unlock 1994 Wayne Gretzky	WEST COAST WAYNE
Unlock 1999 Wayne Gretzky	A LEGEND ON ICE
Unlock "Hazy Shades of Blue!!!" message	BLUE HAZE
Unlock "Marshmallow Fluff!!!" message	PEANUTBUTTER AND FLUFF

Hot Shots Golf Open Tee

Everyone Plays, with All Goodies and Rankings

If you invite everyone out to play on all the courses with all the times, you'd better have your rank maxed out! Use this code to unlock everything in the game with all the goodies and rankings. Go to the Create Data menu and enter 5TNEPO as your player name. You can verify that you did it right by checking Data and Status at the Main menu.

LEGO Star Wars II: The Original Trilogy

Unlockable Characters and Ships

To unlock characters and ships for use in Free Play (replay) mode, go to the bar in the Cantina, select the Enter Codes option, and type in the following codes. If you enter a code correctly, you'll see a message telling you what you've unlocked, and you can then buy it in the Characters menu, as long as you have enough credits. Remember that you must complete a stage at least once to enable Free Play for that stage, and that ships are available in certain stages only.

Cheat	Code
Beach Trooper	UCK868
Ben Kenobi's Ghost	BEN917
Bespin Guard	VHY832
Bib Fortuna	WTY721
Boba Fett	HLP221
Death Star Trooper	BNC332
Ewok	TTT289
Gamorean Guard	YZF999
Gonk Droid	NFX582
Grand Moff Tarkin	SMG219
Greedo	NAH118
Han Solo (with hood)	YWM840
IG-88	NXL973
Imperial Guard	MMM111
Imperial Officer	BBV889
Imperial Shuttle Pilot	VAP664

Cheat	Code
Imperial Spy	CVT125
Jawa	JAW499
Lobot	UUB319
Palace Guard	SGE549
Rebel Pilot	CYG336
Rebel Trooper (Hoth)	EKU849
Sandtrooper	YDV451
Skiff Guard	GBU888
Snowtrooper	NYU989
Stormtrooper	PTR345
The Emperor	HHY382
TIE Fighter	HDY739
TIE Fighter Pilot	NNZ316
TIE Interceptor	QYA828
Tusken Raider	PEJ821
Ugnaught	UGN694

Madden NFL 07

Tricky High Score

Play perfectly long enough in the End to End mini game and you'll open up some extra tunes and other hidden items in Madden 07, but did you know that there's a simple trick to scoring fast? As you run toward the opposing player, pause the game and note which way the player is attempting to tackle. Now put your fingers on the key to dodge the player, and hit it as soon as you un-pause the game. Shoot for some combos and you'll earn the high score without playing into overtime.

Midnight Club 3 DUB Edition

Road Trip!

San Diego has a good tuner scene, but if you're tired being trounced on the same mean streets, you can use a cheat code to open Atlanta and Detroit. Choose Options on the Main menu and then enter the Cheat menu. Now input the following code as one word all in lowercase letters: roadtrip

(continued)

Midnight Club 3 DUB Edition (cont.)

Rubber Bumpers?

Tired of driving in the red? The surging crimson damage gauge around your speedometer can be a nuisance, especially while taking down tough rivals at rush hour. Luckily there's a code that disables your damage meter. Choose Options on the Main menu and then enter the Cheat menu. Now input the following code as one word all in lowercase letters: ontheroad

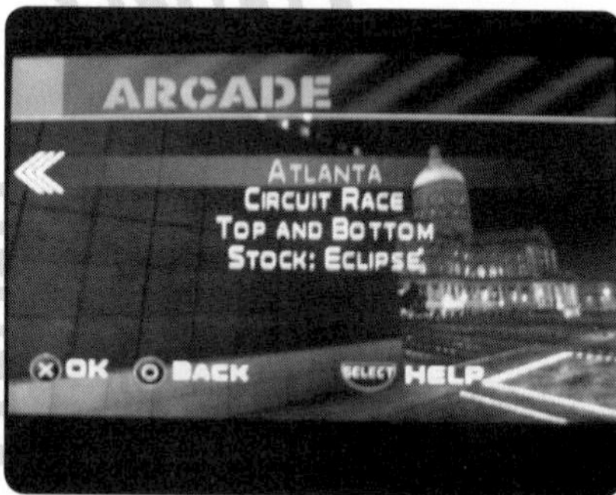

> **Insider Tip**
> You can combine these two codes and explore all the areas in Midnight Club 3 DUB Edition without worrying about a fender-bender.

MLB 07: The Show

Unlock the Silver and Gold Era Teams

Add legendary pros to your team lineup by entering the following code on the direction buttons at the game's Main menu screen: Left, Up, Right, Down, Down, Left, Up, Down

Big Heads and a Big Baseball (and Back Again)

To give all of the players big heads and enlarge the baseball, pause the game (tap START) while your player is pitching or batting and enter the following on the direction buttons: Left, Right, Up, Up, Left, Up, Up, Left

To change the size of the ball back to normal, pause the game again (press START) and enter this code on the direction buttons: Left, Up, Down, Right, Left, Left, Up, Down

MX vs. ATV Unleashed

Unlock Cash, Bikes, and Gear!

Are you broke as a joke or too lazy to grind for gear? Here's your racing solution! To enter these codes, choose Options from the Main Menu and then select Cheat Codes.

Activate Pro physics	IAMTOOGOOD
Earn a million store points	BROKEASAJOKE
Open all freestyle tracks	HUCKIT
Unlock all 500cc bikes	BIGBORE
Unlock all 50cc bikes	MINIMOTO
Unlock all ATVS	COUCHES
Unlock all bikes	BRAPP
Unlock all gear	WARDROBE
Unlock all riders	WANNABE
Unlock all Supercross tracks	GOINSIDE
Unlock all vehicles in the game	LEADFOOT
Unlock everything in the game	TOOLAZY

NBA Ballers Rebound

Slammin' on the Secret Codes

From the Main Menu, select Inside Stuff to access the Phrase-ology Menu. Before you can access the Phrase-ology menu, you'll need to create a Gamer Profile on your PSP memory card. Use the word combinations in the Phrase-ology Menu to spell out the following codes, and press the Square Button to finish:

Unlock Allen Iverson's recording studio	THE ANSWER
Unlock Alonzo Mourning's alternate gear	ZO
Unlock ballers and cinema movies	NBA BALLERS TRUE PLAYA
Unlock Ben Gordon's yacht as a crib	NICE YACHT
Unlock Chris Webber's alternate gear	24 SECONDS
Unlock Clyde Drexler's alternate gear	CLYDE THE GLIDE
Unlock Dikembe Mutumbo's alternate gear	IN THE PAINT
Unlock Emanuel Ginobili's alternate gear	MANU
Unlock Jerry Stackhouse's alternate gear	STOP DROP AND ROLL
Unlock Julius Irving's alternate gear	ONE ON ONE
Unlock Karl Malone's Devonshire Estate	ICE HOUSE
Unlock Kevin McHale's alternate gear	HOLLA BACK
Unlock Kobe Bryant's Italian Estate	EURO CRIB
Unlock Lebron James's alternate gear	KING JAMES

(continued)

NBA Ballers Rebound (cont.)

Unlock Magic Johnson's alternate gear	LAKER LEGENDS
Unlock Nene Hilario's alternate gear	RAGS TO RICHES
Unlock Pete Maravich's alternate gear	PISTOL PETE
Unlock Rasheed Wallace's alternate gear	BRING DOWN THE HOUSE
Unlock Richard Hamilton's alternate gear	RIP
Unlock Stephon Marbury's alternate gear	PLATINUM PLAYA
Unlock Steve Francis's alternate gear	RISING STAR
Unlock Tim Duncan's alternate gear	MAKE IT TAKE IT
Unlock Wilt Chamberlain's alternate gear	WILT THE STILT
Unlock Yao Ming's Childhood Grade School	PREP SCHOOL

Insider Tip:
Once you have these stupid-fresh codes entered, save everything to your Gamer Profile and you're good to go whenever you start another game!

NFL Street 2 Unleashed

Big Codes for Big Plays
From the Main Menu, select Options and enter these codes at the NFL Street 2 Unleashed Cheat & Codes Menu:

Activate Unlimited Turbo	NozBoost
Activate Max Catch ability	MagnetHands
Force other team to fumble in Fumble Mode	GreasedPig
Unlock AFC East All-Stars team	EAASFSCT
Unlock AFC North All-Stars team	NAOFRCTH
Unlock AFC South All-Stars team	SAOFUCTH
Unlock AFC West All-Stars team	WAEFSCT
Unlock EA Field	EAField
Activate Gargantuan Players mode	BIGSmash
Unlock NFC East All-Stars team	NNOFRCTH
Unlock NFC North All-Stars team	NNAS66784
Unlock NFC South All-Stars team	SNOFUCTH
Unlock NFC West All-Stars team	ENASFSCT
Activate No Fumble mode	GlueHands
Unlock Team Reebok	Reebok

Insider Tip:
Pay close attention to the UPPERCASE and lowercase letters while entering the codes in NFL Street 2 Unleashed. Use the R Button to toggle between the two. Also, some codes will only work in Quick Game modes, but you can use the All-Star Teams and Team Reebok codes in other games. And finally—don't forget to save your game after you enter these codes! Once you have the codes entered, they'll be saved to the player profile on your PSP Memory Card and you'll never have to enter all letters and numbers again!

Ratatouille

Unlock All Mini-Games, Recipes, and More
These codes work best if you enter them and "Resume" a game instead of loading a file or starting a new game. At the Main menu choose Options and then Extras. Now choose Cheats and enter the following codes:

Cheat	***Code***
Earn maximum cheese	saycheese
Make foes tough to defeat	deepfryer
Unlocks all mini games in all modes	mattelme
Unlocks all multiplayer mode races	raceison
Unlock all recipes	anyonecancook
Unlocks all videos	gusteauvid
Unlocks very easy game play mode	pieceocake

You'll usually hear a musical tone if you enter the code right.

Star Trek: Tactical Assault

Instant Armada
Jump rank and choose any ship for Skirmish mode with this easy unlock code. Choose Skirmish on the Main menu and wait for the screen to load, then press: Up, Down, Left, Right, Select, Start, Square

If you enter the code correctly you should hear the sound of a photon torpedo. You can also use these unlocked ships in Multiplayer mode.

Infinite Crew Upgrades
If a Starfleet commander is only as good as his crew, using this code leaves you with no excuse for failure. Load or start your campaign game, then choose Crew Upgrades and wait for the crew member descriptions to appear. Now enter: Up, Down, Left, Right Select, Start, Select

You'll add five crew upgrade points to your score. Need more? Keep entering the code and you'll increase your total by another five points.

(continued)

Star Trek: Tactical Assault (cont.)

Unlock New Missions
To skip ahead and explore new missions, enter the following code on the Main menu: Up, Down, Left, Right, Select, Start, Start

You'll hear the sound of a photon torpedo being fired if you correctly enter the code. Now enter the Campaign menu and choose Next Mission. Press the R button on the Mission Briefing screen to scroll ahead to new missions.

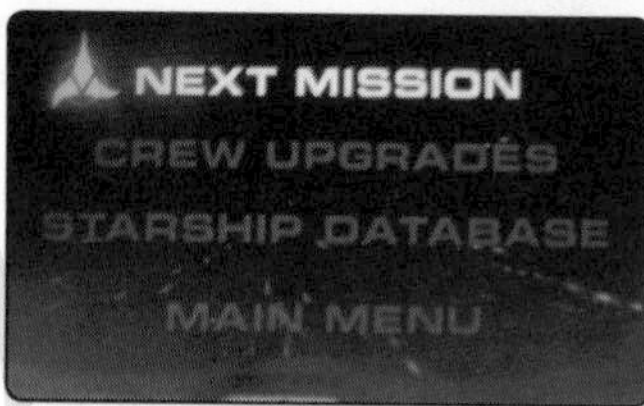

Unlock Your Inner Klingon
Normally you would have to start out as a Starfleet lackey in Star Trek: Tactical Assault, but you can beam off the Federation ships and join the ranks of the Klingon campaign by entering this code on the main menu: Up, Down, Left, Right, Select, Start, Triangle

Thrillville: Off the Rails

In-Game Cheats
These Thrillville: Off the Rails codes for PSP are easy to input because they are identical until you push the last button. You must enter these codes while the game is in progress.

Earn an additional $50,000 - Square, Circle, Triangle, Square, Circle, Triangle, X Button
Add an extra 500 Thrill Points to your game - Circle, Square, Triangle, Circle, Square, Triangle, Square
Unlock all mini-games - Square, Circle, Triangle, Square, Circle, Triangle, Right D-Pad
Unlock all missions - Square, Circle, Triangle, Square, Circle, Triangle, Square
Unlock all parks - Square, Circle, Triangle, Square, Circle, Triangle, Square
Unlock all rides - Square, Circle, Triangle, Square, Circle, Triangle, Triangle

Insider Tip:
You can keep entering Money and Thrill Point codes until you have everything you need to build an incredible park!

Tiger Woods PGA TOUR 07

Save It Up
Are there codes for Tiger Woods 07? No, but the game does have a save feature that allows you to quit and save your game after every fantastic shot and hole at or under par.

If you ever wonder how your buddies opened all the good gear and improved their golf skills so quickly, this is what they did. This save cheat works on almost any game that allows you to save and exit before tough challenges. Some gamers consider this option better than any secret code!

Virtua Tennis World Tour

Extra Aces for Your Game!
Entering codes for Virtua Tennis World Tour can be a bit tricky. Remember to hold the L Button while quickly entering the following codes at the Main Menu (not the title screen). If you enter these codes correctly, you'll hear a musical tone.

Unlock all tennis courts - Up, Down, Left, Right, Square, Square, Square

Unlock the King and Queen courts - Up, Down, Up, Down, Square, Triangle, Square

Start a tour with $1,000,000 - Up, Down, Left, Down, Triangle, Triangle, Triangle

Earn $2,000 every week in World Tour - Up, Down, Right, Down, Triangle, Square, Triangle

Unlock all racquets and clothing - Right, Left, Right, Right, Up, Up, Up

Play in old-fashioned Sepia tone mode - Up, Down, Left, Right Left, Left, Left

All games are rated E for Everyone.

Video Game Secrets is produced by becker&mayer!, Bellevue, Washington
www.beckermayer.com

If you have questions or comments about this product, please visit www.beckermayer.com/customerservice.html and click on the Customer Service Request Form.

Edited by Betsy Pringle and Mia Mar
Designed by Andrew Hess
Design Production by Mia Mar
Production by Blake Mitchum
Project Managed by Betsy Pringle and Lisa Douglass
Special thanks to Paul Shinoda, Wynn Rankin, Kent Carmical, Nathan Cavanaugh, Zena Chew, Sara DeBell, Matthew Munson, Megan Munson, Annika Shinoda, Denise Shinoda, and Kira Shinoda

Scholastic Inc.
New York, NY
www.scholastic.com

08054
Printed in the United States of America

ISBN-10: 1-60380-028-X
ISBN-13: 978-1-60380-028-0
10 9 8 7 6 5 4 3 2